THE OFFICIAL GUIDE TO GMAT

Prepared for the Graduate Management Admission Council
by Educational Testing Service

Inquiries concerning this publication should be directed to GMAT Program Direction Office,
Educational Testing Service, Princeton, New Jersey 08541.

This publication was produced under the direction of the Publications Committee of the Graduate Management Admission Council. The members of the committee for 1981–82 are listed below.

Robert F. Krampf, Chairman
Kent State University

Anne S. Davis
Georgia Institute of Technology

Charles F. Maguire
The Pennsylvania State University

The committee gratefully acknowledges test development staff at Educational Testing Service who prepared the explanatory material for the *Guide*.

Contents

Graduate Management Admission Council

The Graduate Management Admission Council is both a service organization and a professional organization. As a service organization, the council provides information to schools and students by which both can make more reasoned choices in the admissions process. The council's service functions fulfill two objectives. The first is to improve the selection process for graduate management education by

■ developing and administering appropriate testing instruments,

■ informing schools and students as to the appropriate use of such instruments and other materials related to the selection process,

■ serving as a medium of information exchange between students and schools.

The council's second objective as a service organization is to disseminate information to various publics concerned with graduate management education.

As a professional organization the council serves as a forum for interchange among those who share a common interest in education for management.

The council, consisting of representatives of 64 graduate schools of management, sponsors the Graduate Management Admission Test. Educational Testing Service consults with the council on matters of general policy, develops test material, administers the test, and conducts research projects aimed at improving the test.

BOARD OF TRUSTEES

Mary Corbitt Clark, Chairman
Northwestern University

Henry W. Woudenberg, Vice-Chairman
Kent State University

C. David Billings
University of Alabama at Huntsville

Joyce E. Cornell
Columbia University

Ellen Ruben
University of California, Los Angeles

Richard D. Teach
Georgia Institute of Technology

Robert B. Turrill
University of Southern California

MEMBER SCHOOLS

Boston University
School of Management

Bowling Green State University
College of Business Administration

Carnegie-Mellon University
Graduate School of Industrial Administration

College of William and Mary
School of Business Administration

Columbia University
Graduate School of Business

Cornell University
Graduate School of Business and Public Administration

Dartmouth College
Amos Tuck School of Business Administration

Duke University
Fuqua School of Business

East Carolina University
School of Business

Emory University
Graduate School of Business Administration

Florida State University
College of Business

Georgia Institute of Technology
College of Management

Georgia State University
College of Business Administration, Graduate Division

Harvard University
Graduate School of Business Administration

Indiana University (Bloomington)
Graduate School of Business

Kent State University
Graduate School of Management

Massachusetts Institute of Technology
Sloan School of Management

Michigan State University
Graduate School of Business Administration

New York University
Graduate School of Business Administration

Northeastern University
Graduate School of Business Administration

Northwestern University
J. L. Kellogg Graduate School of Management

The Ohio State University
College of Administrative Science

The Pennsylvania State University
Graduate Programs in Business Administration

Purdue University
Krannert Graduate School of Management

Rutgers University
Graduate School of Management

San Francisco State University
School of Business

Seton Hall University
W. Paul Stillman School of Business

Stanford University
Graduate School of Business

State University of New York at Buffalo
School of Management

Syracuse University
School of Management—M.B.A. Program

Texas Christian University
M. J. Neeley School of Business

Tulane University
School of Business

University of Arizona
College of Business and Public Administration

University of California, Berkeley
Graduate School of Business Administration

University of California, Los Angeles
Graduate School of Management

University of Chicago
Graduate School of Business

University of Cincinnati
College of Business Administration

University of Connecticut (Storrs)
School of Business Administration

University of Denver
Graduate School of Business and Public Management

University of Georgia
Graduate School of Business Administration

University of Hawaii at Manoa
College of Business Administration

University of Illinois at Chicago
College of Business Administration

University of Maryland
College of Business and Management

The University of Michigan
Graduate School of Business Administration

University of Missouri—St. Louis
School of Business Administration

The University of North Carolina at Chapel Hill
Graduate School of Business Administration

University of Notre Dame
College of Business Administration

University of Pittsburgh
Graduate School of Business

University of Rhode Island
College of Business Administration

The University of Rochester
The Graduate School of Management

University of South Carolina
College of Business Administration

University of South Florida
College of Business Administration

University of Southern California
Graduate School of Business Administration

The University of Tennessee, Knoxville
College of Business Administration

The University of Tulsa
College of Business Administration

University of Utah
Graduate School of Business

University of Virginia
The Colgate Darden Graduate School of Business
   Administration

University of Washington
Graduate School of Business Administration

University of Wisconsin—Milwaukee
School of Business Administration

Vanderbilt University
Owen Graduate School of Management

Virginia Polytechnic Institute and State University
College of Business

Washington State University
College of Business and Economics

Washington University (St. Louis)
Graduate School of Business Administration

The Wharton School (University of Pennsylvania)
Graduate Division

Introduction

The Official Guide to GMAT has been designed and written by the staff of Educational Testing Service, which prepares the Graduate Management Admission Test used by many graduate schools of business and management as one criterion in considering applications for admission to their graduate programs. This book is intended to be a comprehensive guide to the kinds of verbal and mathematical questions likely to appear in the GMAT. All questions used to illustrate the various types of questions are taken from three actual editions of the GMAT administered prior to June 1982.

The GMAT is not a test of knowledge in specific subjects— for example, it does not test knowledge specifically or uniquely acquired in accounting or economics courses. Rather, it is a test of certain skills and abilities that have been found to contribute to success in graduate programs in business and management. For this reason, it is important to familiarize yourself with the general types of questions likely to be found in all editions of the GMAT and the reasoning skills and problem-solving strategies that these types of questions demand. This book illustrates each type of question that appears in the GMAT and explains in detail some of the most effective strategies for mastering each type of question.

The most efficient and productive way to use this book is to read first through Chapter I, which provides an overview of the test. Each type of question is briefly described, the directions are given, one or two examples are presented, and the skills each question type measures are outlined. You should pay particular attention to the directions for each question type. This is especially important for the Data Sufficiency and Analysis of Situations questions, which have lengthy and complex directions.

Chapters III-VII provide detailed illustrations and explanations of individual question types. After you read Chapter I, you will find the most advantageous way to use the book is to choose a chapter on a particular question type, read carefully the introductory material, and then do the sample tests in that chapter. As you take the sample tests, follow the directions and time specifications given. When you complete a set of sample tests, use the answer keys that follow them to check your responses. Then review each sample test carefully, spending as much time as is necessary to familiarize yourself with the range of questions or problems presented in the sample tests.

Note that certain answers in the sample test answer keys are marked with asterisks. These are the answers to questions used as illustrative examples in the explanatory material that follows the answer keys.

In Chapter III, Problem Solving, and Chapter IV, Data Sufficiency, answers with asterisks are also followed by page numbers. These indicate the pages containing complete explanations of the solutions for the problems. At the end of each explanation in these two chapters you will find a reference to the appropriate section(s) of Chapter II, Math Review.

You may find it useful to read through all of Chapter II before working through Chapters III and IV, or you may wish to use Chapter II as a reference, noting the suggested sections at the end of each explanation in Chapters III and IV as you go along. However, since Chapter II is intended to provide you with a comprehensive review of the basic mathematical concepts used in the quantitative sections of the GMAT, you may find it valuable to read through the chapter as a whole.

The introductory material, sample tests, and answer keys to the sample tests in Chapter V, Reading Comprehension, and Chapter VI, Analysis of Situations, should be approached in the way suggested above. In these chapters, as in Chapters III and IV, certain answers in the sample test answer keys are preceded by asterisks. These are the answers to questions used as detailed illustrations in the explanatory material. No page references are given because of the intended purpose of the explanatory material. In these chapters, the explanatory material is designed to give you a complete view of the question type. The explanatory material should be read as a whole, because many questions not marked by asterisks are mentioned as additional examples of questions also representative of the given question type. The explanatory materials for Reading Comprehension and Analysis of Situations have been written as thorough explanations of the reasoning and problem-solving challenges each question type presents. Demonstrating strategies for successfully meeting these challenges, regardless of the particular content of the questions or problems that appear in a specific edition of the GMAT, is the objective of these explanations. Consequently, flipping from a particular question to a particular explanation will be counterproductive.

All Writing Ability questions appearing in editions of the GMAT from June 1982 forward will be in the Sentence Correction format. Chapter VII, however, presents the kinds of problems covered in this section of the GMAT in two formats: Usage and Sentence Correction. Both kinds of questions focus on the grammatical and syntactical skills measured by the Writing Ability section of the GMAT; both will be helpful in preparing you to deal with Writing Ability questions. The explanatory material in this chapter is organized by the type of grammatical or syntactical problem a question may present, and these problems are explained in detail.

After you complete the review and practice built in to each chapter you should turn to the complete GMAT reprinted in Chapter VIII. It will be most helpful in preparing yourself to take the GMAT if you regard the test in Chapter VIII as a facsimile of the test you will take for scoring. Time yourself on each section, and follow directions exactly as given.

Following the GMAT reprinted in Chapter VIII are an answer key and information about scoring and score interpretation, as well as guidelines for the use of GMAT scores.

I Description of the Graduate Management Admission Test

The Graduate Management Admission Test is designed to help graduate schools assess the qualifications of applicants for advanced study in business and management. The test can be used by both schools and students in evaluating verbal and mathematical skills as well as general knowledge and preparation for graduate study. Note, however, that GMAT scores should be considered as only one of several indicators of ability.

FORMAT

The current GMAT consists entirely of multiple-choice questions, which are divided among eight separately timed sections; the total testing time is about four hours. Each question offers five choices from which the examinee is to select the best answer.

Every form of the test contains two sections of trial questions that are needed for pretesting and equating purposes. These questions, however, are not identified, and you should do your best on all questions. The answers to trial questions are not counted in your test score.

Both the Graduate Management Admission Council and Educational Testing Service are aware of the limits of the multiple-choice format, particularly in measuring an applicant's ability to formulate general concepts or to develop detailed supportive or opposing arguments. However, in a national testing program designed for a wide variety of people with different backgrounds, the use of a large number of short, multiple-choice questions has proved to be an effective and reliable way of providing a fair and valid evaluation.

CONTENT

It is important to recognize that the GMAT evaluates skills and abilities that develop over relatively long periods of time. Although the sections are basically verbal or mathematical, the complete test provides one method of measuring overall ability. The GMAT does not test specific knowledge obtained in college course work, and it does not seek to measure achievements in any specific areas of study.

The Graduate Management Admission Council recognizes that questions arise concerning techniques for taking standardized examinations such as the GMAT, and it is hoped that the descriptions, sample tests, and explanations given here, along with the full-length sample test, will give you a practical familiarity with both the concepts and techniques required by GMAT questions.

The material on the following pages provides a general description and brief discussion of the objectives and techniques for each question type and applies to editions of the GMAT appearing in June 1982 and thereafter. The descriptions of the types of GMAT questions in this section may differ slightly from particular examples of GMAT items appearing in later chapters because the examples have been taken from GMAT editions used prior to 1982.

Following this general description of the GMAT are a math review designed to help you review basic mathematical skills useful in the Problem Solving and Data Sufficiency sections of the GMAT and five chapters, one for each question type, that present sample tests with answer keys and detailed explanations of the specific question type and of selected questions and answers from the sample tests. (The sample tests are made up of questions that have appeared in the actual GMAT.) Methods of determining the best answer to a particular kind of question as well as explanations of the different kinds of questions appearing in any one section are also presented in these chapters. The general level of difficulty for each question discussed is given to provide you with a guide to how past candidates have performed. Chapter VIII contains a full-length GMAT. It is followed by an answer key and scoring information, which explains how GMAT scores are calculated and how they are interpreted.

PROBLEM SOLVING QUESTIONS

This section of the GMAT is designed to test (1) basic mathematical skills, (2) understanding of elementary mathematical concepts, and (3) the ability to reason quantitatively and to solve quantitative problems. Although some problems in the test are in a mathematical setting, the major emphasis is on solving problems based on "real life" situations.

WHAT IS MEASURED

Problem Solving questions test your ability to understand verbal descriptions of situations and to solve problems using arithmetic, elementary algebra, or commonly known concepts of geometry.

The directions for Problem Solving questions read as follows:

Directions: In this section solve each problem, using any available space on the page for scratchwork. Then indicate the *best* answer in the appropriate space on the answer sheet.

Note: Figures which accompany problems in this test are intended to provide information useful in solving the problems. They are drawn as accurately as possible EXCEPT when it is stated in a specific problem that its figure is not drawn to scale. All figures lie in a plane unless otherwise indicated. All numbers used are real numbers.

DATA SUFFICIENCY QUESTIONS

Each of the problems in the Data Sufficiency section of the GMAT consists of a question, often accompanied by some initial information, and two statements, labeled (1) and (2), containing additional information. You must decide whether sufficient information to answer the question is given by either (1) or (2) individually or—if not—by both combined.

These are the directions that you will find for the Data Sufficiency section of the GMAT. Read them carefully.

Directions: Each of the data sufficiency problems below consists of a question and two statements, labeled (1) and (2), in which certain data are given. You have to decide whether the data given in the statements are sufficient for answering the question. Using the data given in the statements plus your knowledge of mathematics and everyday facts (such as the number of days in July or the meaning of counterclockwise), you are to blacken space

A if statement (1) ALONE is sufficient, but statement (2) alone is not sufficient to answer the question asked;

B if statement (2) ALONE is sufficient, but statement (1) alone is not sufficient to answer the question asked;

C if BOTH statements (1) and (2) TOGETHER are sufficient to answer the question asked, but NEITHER statement ALONE is sufficient;

D if EACH statement ALONE is sufficient to answer the question asked;

E if statements (1) and (2) TOGETHER are NOT sufficient to answer the question asked, and additional data specific to the problem are needed.

Note: A figure in a data sufficiency problem will conform to the information given in the question, but will not necessarily conform to the additional information given in statements (1) and (2). All figures lie in a plane unless otherwise indicated.

Example:

In $\triangle PQR$, what is the value of x?

(1) PQ = PR
(2) y = 40

Explanation: According to statement (1), PQ = PR; therefore, $\triangle PQR$ is isosceles and y = z. Since $x + y + z = 180$, $x + 2y = 180$. Since statement (1) does not give a value for y, you cannot answer the question using statement (1) by itself. According to statement (2), y = 40; therefore, $x + z = 140$. Since statement (2) does not give a value for z, you cannot answer the question using statement (2) by itself. Using both statements together you can find y and z; therefore you can find x, and the answer to the problem is C.

All numbers used are real numbers.

WHAT IS MEASURED

Data Sufficiency questions are designed to measure your ability to analyze a quantitative problem, to recognize which information is relevant, and to determine at what point there is sufficient information to solve the problem.

READING COMPREHENSION QUESTIONS

The Reading Comprehension section is made up of several reading passages about which you will be asked interpretive,

applicative, and inferential questions. The passages are approximately 500 words long, and they discuss topics from the social sciences, the physical and biological sciences, and the humanities. Because each section includes at least one passage from each of the three areas you will probably be generally familiar with some of the material; however, neither the passages nor the questions assume detailed knowledge of the topics discussed.

WHAT IS MEASURED

Reading Comprehension questions measure your ability to understand, analyze, and apply information and concepts presented in written form. All questions are to be answered on the basis of what is stated or implied in the reading material, and no specific knowledge of the material is required. Reading Comprehension, therefore, evaluates your ability to

- understand words and statements in the reading passages (Questions of this type are not vocabulary questions. These questions test your understanding of and ability to use specialized terms as well as your understanding of the English language. You may also find that questions of this type ask about the overall meaning of a passage);

- understand the logical relationships between significant points and concepts in the reading passages (For example, such questions may ask you to determine the strong and weak points of an argument or to evaluate the importance of arguments and ideas in a passage);

- draw inferences from facts and statements in the reading passages (The inference questions will ask you to consider factual statements or information and, on the basis of that information, reach a general conclusion);

- make simple arithmetical calculations using the data in the reading passages (These simple calculations may involve the interpretation of numerical data or the use of simple arithmetic to reach conclusions about material in a passage).

The directions for Reading Comprehension questions read as follows:

Directions: Each passage in this group is followed by questions based on its content. After reading a passage, choose the best answer to each question and blacken the corresponding space on the answer sheet. Answer all questions following a passage on the basis of what is *stated* or *implied* in that passage.

ANALYSIS OF SITUATIONS QUESTIONS

The Analysis of Situations section of the GMAT asks you to classify on the basis of relative importance the facts and conditions that make up a management or business situation. Each section contains at least one passage describing a decision-making process that is occasioned by the need to solve a problem. The passage discusses the nature of the problem, gives the facts and conditions related to the situation, and suggests possible solutions to the problem.

In each passage a decision must be made: which of the possible alternatives will best solve the problem? Generally, no decision is reached in the passage, but the possible alternatives are fully examined, and the facts and conditions that affect the outcome are evaluated from different points of view. Given this information, you must classify the facts and conditions as objectives, factors, assumptions, or unimportant issues. You must also decide how important each of the factors is in making the decision. If a factor is of primary importance, it is a major factor. If a factor is only of secondary importance, it is a minor factor. If an aspect of the decision-making situation is insignificant as a factor, it is an unimportant issue.

WHAT IS MEASURED

The Analysis of Situations section is one measure of your ability to analyze and evaluate the major aspects of a business or management situation. It tests your perception of the financial, material, and legal aspects of a problem in terms of their importance with respect to each other and with respect to making a decision.

This section does not presuppose either practical or academic knowledge of specific business terms and practices. Although many of the passages are based on business or management situations, the problems can be solved using only common sense and logical reasoning.

The directions for Analysis of Situations questions read as follows:

Directions: The passage in this section is followed by questions that require you to classify certain of the facts presented in the passage on the basis of their importance, as illustrated in the following example:

SAMPLE PASSAGE

Fred North, a prospering hardware dealer in Hillidale, Connecticut, felt that he needed more store space to accommodate a new line of farm equipment and repair parts that he intended to carry. A number of New York City commuters had recently purchased tracts of land in the environs of Hillidale and there had taken up farming on a small scale. Mr. North, foreseeing a potential increase in farming in that area, wanted to expand his business to cater to this market. North felt that the most feasible and appealing recourse open to him would be to purchase the adjoining store property owned by Mike Johnson, who used the premises for his small grocery store. Johnson's business had been on the decline for over a year since the advent of a large supermarket in the town. North felt that Johnson would be willing to sell the property at reasonable terms, and this was important since North, after the purchase of the new merchandise, would have little capital available to invest in the expansion of his store.

The following questions consist of items related to the passage above. Consider each item separately in terms of the passage and on the answer sheet blacken space

A if the item is a *Major Objective* in making the decision; that is, one of the outcomes or results sought by the decision-maker;

B if the item is a *Major Factor* in making the decision; that is, a consideration, explicitly mentioned in the passage, that is basic in determining the decision;

C if the item is a *Minor Factor* in making the decision; that is, a secondary consideration that affects the criteria tangentially, relating to a Major Factor rather than to an Objective;

D if the item is a *Major Assumption* in making the decision; that is, a supposition or projection made by the decision-maker before weighing the variables;

E if the item is an *Unimportant Issue* in making the decision; that is, a factor that is insignificant or not immediately relevant to the situation.

SAMPLE QUESTIONS

1. Increase in farming in the Hillidale area ⓐ ⓑ ⓒ ● ⓔ

2. Acquisition of property for expanding store ● ⓑ ⓒ ⓓ ⓔ

3. Cost of Johnson's property ⓐ ● ⓒ ⓓ ⓔ

4. State of Johnson's grocery business ⓐ ⓑ ● ⓓ ⓔ

5. Quality of the farm equipment North intends to sell ⓐ ⓑ ⓒ ⓓ ●

The correct designation for number 1 is (D), a *Major Assumption,* since North bases his whole expansion project on his supposition that the new commuter-farmers in the Hillidale area are indicative of a trend in that direction. Number 2 is (A), a *Major Objective,* inasmuch as North's immediate purpose is to obtain room for expansion. (B), a *Major Factor,* is the correct answer for number 3 because North's present lack of capital renders cost a vital consideration. The best classification of number 4 is (C), a *Minor Factor,* because the depreciating value of Johnson's business influences his willingness to sell and also the price he will demand for his property; thus, this factor pertains to 3, the cost of Johnson's property, and is an indirect consideration in the case. Number 5, finally, is (E), an *Unimportant Issue,* for the quality of North's goods has no relevance to the situation at hand, i.e., the desire for room to expand his business.

WRITING ABILITY QUESTIONS

Writing Ability questions in editions of the GMAT appearing in June 1982 and thereafter use the Sentence Correction format only; they ask you which of the five choices best expresses an idea or relationship. The questions will require you to be familiar with the stylistic conventions and grammatical rules of standard written English and to demonstrate your ability to improve incorrect or ineffective expressions.

WHAT IS MEASURED

Sentence Correction questions test two broad aspects of language proficiency:

1. *Correct expression.* A correct sentence is grammatically and structurally sound. It conforms to all the rules of standard

written English (for example: noun-verb agreement, noun-pronoun agreement, pronoun consistency, pronoun case, and verb tense sequence). Further, a correct sentence will not have dangling, misplaced, or improperly formed modifiers, will not have unidiomatic or inconsistent expressions, and will not have faults in parallel construction.

2. *Effective expression.* An effective sentence expresses an idea or relationship clearly and concisely as well as grammatically. This does not mean that the choice with the fewest and simplest words is necessarily the best answer. It means that there are no superfluous words or needlessly complicated expressions in the best choice.

In addition, an effective sentence uses proper diction. (Diction refers to the standard dictionary meaning of words and the appropriateness of words in context.) In evaluating the diction of a sentence, you must be able to recognize whether the words are well chosen, accurate, and suitable for the context. You must also be able to tell whether the words fail, because of inaccuracy or inappropriateness, to convey a clear and accurate idea.

The directions for Sentence Correction questions read as follows:

Directions: In each of the following sentences, some part of the sentence or the entire sentence is underlined. Beneath each sentence you will find five ways of phrasing the underlined part. The first of these repeats the original; the other four are different. If you think the original is better than any of the alternatives, choose answer A; otherwise choose one of the others. Select the best version and blacken the corresponding space on your answer sheet. This is a test of correctness and effectiveness of expression. In choosing answers, follow the requirements of standard written English; that is, pay attention to grammar, choice of words, and sentence construction. Choose the answer that produces the most effective sentence—clear and exact, without awkwardness or ambiguity. Do not make a choice that changes the meaning of the original sentence.

Examples:

A thunderclap is a complex acoustic signal <u>as a result of</u> rapid expansion of heated air in the path of a lightning flash.

(A) as a result of
(B) caused as a result of
(C) resulting because of the
(D) resulting from the
(E) that results because there is

In choice A, *is a . . . signal as a result of* is incorrect. It is the thunderclap that results from the expansion; its being a signal is irrelevant. In choice B, it is superfluous to use both *caused* and *result,* and it is also superfluous to use both *result* and *because* in choices C and E. In choice C, *because of* is not the correct preposition to use after *resulting; from* is correct and is used in the best answer, D.

<u>Ever since the Civil War, the status of women was</u> a live social issue in this country.

(A) Ever since the Civil War, the status of women was
(B) Since the Civil War, women's status was
(C) Ever since the Civil War, the status of women has been
(D) Even at the time of the Civil War, the status of women has been
(E) From the times of the Civil War, the status of women has been

In choice A, the verb following *women* should be *has been,* not *was,* because *ever since* denotes a period of time continuing from the past into the present. For the same reason, *was* is inappropriately used with *since* in choice B. In choice D, *even at* changes the meaning of the original sentence substantially and does not fit with *has been; was* is correct with *even at.* In choice E, *times* is incorrect; the standard phrase is *from the time of.* C is the best answer.

GENERAL TEST-TAKING SUGGESTIONS

1. Although the GMAT stresses accuracy more than speed, it is important to use the allotted time wisely. You will be able to do so if you are familiar with the mechanics of the test and the kinds of materials, questions, and directions in the test. Therefore, become familiar with the formats and requirements of each section of the test.

2. After you become generally familiar with all question types, use the individual chapters on each question type in this book (Chapters III-VII), which include sample tests and detailed explanations, to prepare yourself for the actual GMAT in Chapter VIII. When taking the test, try to follow all the requirements specified in the directions and keep within the time limits. While this test is useful for familiarization, it cannot be used to predict your performance on the actual test.

3. Read all test directions carefully. Since many answer sheets give indications that the examinees do not follow directions, this suggestion is particularly important. The directions explain exactly what each section requires in order to answer each question type. If you read hastily, you may miss important instructions and seriously jeopardize your scores.

4. Answer as many questions as possible, but avoid random guessing. Your GMAT scores will be based on the number of questions you answer correctly minus a fraction of the number you answer incorrectly. Therefore, it is unlikely that mere guessing will improve your scores significantly, and it does take time. However, if you have some knowledge of a question and can eliminate at least one of the answer choices as wrong, your chance of getting the best answer is improved, and it will be to your advantage to answer the question. If you know nothing at all about a particular question, it is probably better to skip it. The number of omitted questions will not be subtracted.

5. Take a watch to the examination and be sure to note the time limits for each section. Since each question has the same weight, it is not wise to spend too much time on one question if that causes you to neglect other questions.

6. Make every effort to pace yourself. Work steadily and as rapidly as possible without being careless.

7. A wise practice is to answer the questions you are sure of first. Then, if time permits, go back and attempt the more difficult questions.

8. Read each question carefully and thoroughly. Before answering a question, determine exactly what is being asked. Never skim a question or the possible answers. Skimming may cause you to miss important information or nuances in the question.

9. Do not become upset if you cannot answer a question. A person can do very well without answering every question or finishing every section. No one is expected to get a perfect score.

10. When you take the test, you will mark your answers on a separate answer sheet. As you go through the test, be sure that the number of each answer on the answer sheet matches the corresponding question number in the test book. Your answer sheet may contain space for more answers or questions than there are in the test book. Do not be concerned, but be careful. Indicate each of your answers with a dark mark that completely fills the response position on the answer sheet. Light or partial marks may not be properly read by the scoring machine. Indicate only one response to each question, and erase all unintended marks completely.

GMAT: TEST SPECIFICATIONS

All editions of the GMAT are constructed to measure the same skills and meet the same specifications. Thus, each section of the test is constructed according to the same specifications for every edition of the GMAT. These specifications include definite requirements for the number of questions, the points tested by each question, the kinds of questions, and the difficulty of each question.

Because the various editions of the test inevitably differ somewhat in difficulty, they are made equivalent to each other by statistical methods. This equating process makes it possible to assure that all reported scores of a given value denote approximately the same level of ability regardless of the edition being used or of the particular group taking the test at a given time.

TEST DEVELOPMENT PROCESS

Educational Testing Service professional staff responsible for developing the verbal measures of the GMAT have backgrounds and advanced degrees in the humanities or in measurement. Those responsible for the quantitative portion have advanced degrees in mathematics or related fields.

Standardized procedures have been developed to guide the test-generation process, to assure high-quality test material, to avoid idiosyncratic questions, and to encourage development of test material that is widely appropriate.

An important part of the development of test material is the review process. Each question, as well as any stimulus material on which questions are based, must be reviewed by several independent critics. In appropriate cases, questions are also reviewed by experts outside ETS who can bring fresh perspectives to bear on the questions in terms of actual content or in terms of test sensitivity to minority and women's concerns.

After the questions have been reviewed and revised as appropriate, they are assembled into clusters suitable for trial during actual administrations of the GMAT. In this manner, new questions are tried out under standard testing conditions, by representative samples of GMAT examinees. Questions being tried out do not affect examinees' scores but are themselves evaluated: they are analyzed statistically for usefulness and weaknesses. The questions that perform satisfactorily become part of a pool of questions from which future editions of the GMAT can be assembled; those that do not are rewritten to correct the flaws and tried out again—or discarded.

In preparing those sections of the GMAT that will contribute to the scoring process, the test assembler uses only questions that have been successfully tried out. The test assembler considers not only each question's characteristics but also the relationship of the question to the entire group of questions with respect to the test specifications discussed above. When the test has been assembled, it is reviewed by a second test specialist and by the test development coordinator for the GMAT. After satisfactory resolution of any points raised in these reviews, the test goes to a test editor. The test editor's review is likely to result in further suggestions for change, and the test assembler must decide how these suggested changes will be handled. If a suggested change yields an editorial improvement, without jeopardizing content integrity, the change is adopted; otherwise, new wording is sought that will meet the dual concerns of content integrity and editorial style. The review process is continued at each stage of test assembly and copy preparation, down to careful scrutiny of the final proof immediately prior to printing.

All reviewers except the editor and proofreader must attempt to answer each question without the help of the answer key. Thus, each reviewer "takes the test," uninfluenced by knowledge of what the question writer or test assembler believed each answer should be. The answer key is certified as official only after at least three reviewers have agreed independently on the correct answer for each question.

The extensive, careful procedure described here has been developed over the years to assure that every question in any new edition of the GMAT is appropriate and useful and that the combination of questions that make up the new edition is satisfactory. Nevertheless, the appraisal is not complete until after the new edition has been administered during a national test administration and subjected to a rigorous process of item analysis to see whether each question yields the expected results. This further appraisal sometimes reveals that a question is not satisfactory after all; it may prove to be ambiguous, or require information beyond the scope of the test, or be otherwise unsuitable. Answers to such questions are not used in computing scores.

Math Review

Although this chapter provides a review of some of the mathematical concepts of arithmetic, algebra, and geometry, it is not intended to be a textbook. You should use this chapter to familiarize yourself with the kinds of topics that are tested in the GMAT. You may wish to consult an arithmetic, algebra, or geometry book for a more detailed discussion of some of the topics.

The topics that are covered in Section A, arithmetic, include:

1. Properties of integers
2. Fractions
3. Decimals
4. Real numbers
5. Positive and negative numbers
6. Ratio and proportion
7. Percents
8. Equivalent forms of a number
9. Powers and roots of numbers
10. Mean
11. Median
12. Mode

The content of Section B, algebra, does not extend beyond what is covered in a first-year high school course. The topics included are:

1. Simplifying algebraic expressions
2. Equations
3. Solving linear equations with one unknown
4. Solving two linear equations with two unknowns
5. Solving factorable quadratic equations
6. Exponents
7. Absolute value
8. Inequalities

Section C, geometry, is limited primarily to measurement and intuitive geometry or spatial visualization. Knowledge of theorems and the ability to construct proofs, skills that are usually developed in a formal geometry course, are not tested. The topics included in this section are:

1. Lines
2. Intersecting lines and angles
3. Perpendicular lines
4. Parallel lines
5. Polygons (convex)
6. Triangles
7. Quadrilaterals
8. Circles
9. Solids
10. Rectangular solids
11. Cylinders
12. Pyramids
13. Coordinate geometry

Section D, word problems, presents examples of and solutions to the following types of word problems:

1. Rate
2. Work
3. Mixture
4. Interest
5. Discount
6. Profit
7. Sets
8. Geometry

A. ARITHMETIC

1. INTEGERS

An *integer* is any number in the set $\{\ldots -3, -2, -1, 0, 1, 2, 3, \ldots\}$. If N and P are integers and if N is the product of P and another integer, then P is a *divisor (factor)* of N, and N is said to be a *multiple* of P. For example, 7 is a divisor or factor of 28 since 28 is the product of 7 and another integer, 4, and 28 is said to be a multiple of 7. If P is a divisor of N, then N is also said to be *divisible* by P. For example, 42 is divisible by 7 since $42 = 6 \cdot 7$.

Any integer that is divisible by 2 is an *even integer;* the set of even integers is $\{\ldots -4, -2, 0, 2, 4, 6, 8, \ldots\}$. Integers that are not divisible by 2 are *odd integers,* i.e., $\{\ldots -3, -1, 1, 3, 5, \ldots\}$.

If at least one factor of a product of integers is even, then the product is even; otherwise the product is odd. If two integers are both even or both odd, then their sum and their difference are even. Otherwise, their sum and their difference are odd.

A *prime* number is an integer that has exactly two different positive divisors, 1 and itself. For example, 2, 3, 5, 7, 11, and 13 are prime numbers, but 15 is not, since 15 has four different positive divisors, 1, 3, 5, and 15. The number 1 is not a prime number, since it has only one positive divisor.

The numbers -2, -1, 0, 1, 2, 3, 4, 5 are *consecutive integers.* Consecutive integers can be represented by

$$n, n + 1, n + 2, n + 3, \ldots,$$

where n is an integer. The numbers 0, 2, 4, 6, 8 are *consecutive even integers,* and 1, 3, 5, 7, 9 are *consecutive odd integers.* Consecutive even integers can be represented by $2n$, $2n + 2$, $2n + 4, \ldots$, and consecutive odd integers can be represented by $2n + 1$, $2n + 3$, $2n + 5, \ldots$.

Properties of the integer 1. If n is any number, then $1 \cdot n = n$ and for any number $n \neq 0$, $n \cdot \dfrac{1}{n} = 1$. The number 1 can be expressed in many ways, e.g., $\dfrac{n}{n} = 1$ for any number

$n \neq 0$. Multiplying or dividing an expression by 1, in any form, does not change the value of that expression.

Properties of the integer zero. The integer zero is nonpositive and non-negative. If n is any number, then $n + 0 = n$ and $n \cdot 0 = 0$. Division by zero is not defined.

2. FRACTIONS

In a fraction $\frac{n}{d}$, n is the *numerator* and d is the *denominator*. The denominator of a fraction can never be zero, because division by zero is not defined.

Two fractions are said to be *equivalent* if they represent the same number. For example, $\frac{4}{8}$, $\frac{3}{6}$, and $\frac{1}{2}$ are equivalent since all three represent the number $\frac{1}{2}$.

Addition and subtraction of fractions. To add or subtract two fractions with a common denominator, simply perform the required operations with the numerators, leaving the common denominator the same. For example, $\frac{3}{5} + \frac{4}{5} = \frac{3+4}{5} = \frac{7}{5}$, and $\frac{5}{7} - \frac{2}{7} = \frac{5-2}{7} = \frac{3}{7}$. If two fractions do not have a common denominator, a common denominator should be found before the fractions are added or subtracted. For example, to add $\frac{3}{5}$ and $\frac{4}{7}$, express them as equivalent fractions with the same denominator by multiplying the numerator and denominator of the first fraction by 7 and the numerator and denominator of the second fraction by 5, obtaining $\frac{21}{35}$ and $\frac{20}{35}$, respectively;

$$\frac{21}{35} + \frac{20}{35} = \frac{41}{35}.$$

Also,

$$\frac{2}{3} + \frac{1}{6} = \frac{2}{3} \cdot \frac{2}{2} + \frac{1}{6} = \frac{4}{6} + \frac{1}{6} = \frac{5}{6}.$$

Multiplication and division of fractions. To multiply two fractions, simply multiply the two numerators and multiply the two denominators. For example, $\frac{2}{3} \times \frac{4}{7} = \frac{2 \times 4}{3 \times 7} = \frac{8}{21}$. To divide by a fraction, invert the divisor (i.e., find its *reciprocal*) and multiply. For example, $\frac{2}{3} \div \frac{4}{7} = \frac{2}{3} \times \frac{7}{4} = \frac{14}{12} = \frac{7}{6}$.

In the problem above, the reciprocal of $\frac{4}{7}$ is $\frac{7}{4}$. In general, the reciprocal of a fraction $\frac{n}{d}$ is $\frac{d}{n}$, where n and d are not zero.

Mixed numbers. A number that consists of a whole number and a fraction, e.g., $7\frac{2}{3}$, is a mixed number. $7\frac{2}{3}$ means $7 + \frac{2}{3}$.

To change a mixed number into a fraction, multiply the whole number by the denominator of the fraction and add this number to the numerator of the fraction; then put the result over the denominator of the fraction. For example,

$$7\frac{2}{3} = 7 + \frac{2}{3} = \frac{3}{3}(7) + \frac{2}{3} = \frac{(3 \cdot 7) + 2}{3} = \frac{23}{3}.$$

When the numerator of a fraction is greater than or equal to its denominator, the fraction is called an improper fraction. $\frac{23}{3}$ is an improper fraction.

3. DECIMALS

Decimal notation is another way of expressing numbers. The position of the period or *decimal point* determines the place value of the digits. For example, the digits in the number 7,654.321 have the following place values:

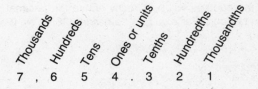

Some examples of decimals follow.

$$0.321 = \frac{3}{10} + \frac{2}{100} + \frac{1}{1,000} = \frac{321}{1,000}$$

$$0.0321 = \frac{0}{10} + \frac{3}{100} + \frac{2}{1,000} + \frac{1}{10,000} = \frac{321}{10,000}$$

$$1.56 = 1 + \frac{5}{10} + \frac{6}{100} = \frac{156}{100}$$

Sometimes decimals are expressed as the product of a number with only one digit to the left of the decimal point and a power of 10. For example, 231 may be written as 2.31×10^2 and 0.0231 may be written as 2.31×10^{-2}. The exponent on the 10 indicates the number of places that the decimal point is to be moved in the number that is to be multiplied by a power of 10 to obtain the product. The decimal point is moved to the right if the exponent is positive and to the left if the exponent is negative. For example, 20.13×10^3 is equal to 20,130 and 1.91×10^{-4} is equal to 0.000191.

Addition and subtraction of decimals. To add or subtract two decimals, the decimal points of both numbers should be lined up. If one of the numbers has fewer digits to the right of the decimal point than the other, zeros may be added to the right of the last digit. For example, to add 17.6512 and 653.27, set up the numbers in a column and add:

$$
\begin{array}{r}
17.6512 \\
+ 653.2700 \\
\hline
670.9212
\end{array}
$$

Likewise, 653.27 minus 17.6512 =

$$
\begin{array}{r}
653.2700 \\
- 17.6512 \\
\hline
635.6188
\end{array}
$$

Multiplication of decimals. To multiply decimals, multiply the numbers as if they were whole numbers and then insert the decimal point in the product so that the number of digits to the right of the decimal point is equal to the sum of the numbers of digits to the right of the decimal points in the numbers being multiplied. For example:

$$
\begin{array}{r}
2.09 \quad \text{(2 digits to the right)} \\
\times \ 1.3 \quad \text{(1 digit to the right)} \\
\hline
627 \\
209 \ \ \\
\hline
2.717 \quad \text{(2 + 1 = 3 digits to the right)}
\end{array}
$$

Division of decimals. To divide a number (the dividend) by a decimal (the divisor), move the decimal point of the divisor to the right until the divisor is a whole number. Then move the decimal point of the dividend the same number of places to the right, and divide as you would by a whole number. The decimal point in the quotient will be directly above the decimal point in the new dividend. For example, to divide 698.12 by 12.4:

$$12.4\overline{)698.12}$$

will be replaced by

$$124\overline{)6981.2}$$

and the division would proceed as follows:

$$
\begin{array}{r}
56.3 \\
124\overline{)6981.2} \\
620\ \ \ \\
\hline
781\ \ \\
744\ \ \\
\hline
372 \\
372 \\
\hline
\end{array}
$$

4. REAL NUMBERS

All *real* numbers correspond to points on the number line and all points on the number line correspond to real numbers. All real numbers except zero are either positive or negative.

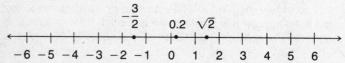

On a number line, numbers corresponding to points to the left of zero are negative and numbers corresponding to points to the right of zero are positive. For any two numbers on the number line, the number to the left is less than the number to the right; for example, $-4 < -3$, $\frac{1}{2} < \frac{3}{4}$, and $0.05 < 0.12$.

To say that the number n is between 1 and 4 on the number line means that $n > 1$ and $n < 4$; i.e., $1 < n < 4$.

The distance between a number and zero on the number line is called the *absolute value* (magnitude) of the number. Thus 3 and -3 have the same absolute value, 3, since they are both three units from zero. The absolute value of 3 is denoted $|3|$. Examples of absolute values of numbers are

$$|-5| = |5| = 5, \ \left|-\frac{7}{2}\right| = \frac{7}{2}, \text{ and } |0| = 0.$$

Note that the absolute value of any nonzero number is positive.

5. POSITIVE AND NEGATIVE NUMBERS

Addition and subtraction. To add two numbers that have the same sign, add the absolute values of the numbers and insert the common signs. For example,

$$(-7) + (-9) = -16$$

because

$$(-7) + (-9) = -(|-7| + |-9|) = -(7 + 9) = -16.$$

To add two numbers with different signs, find the positive difference between their absolute values and insert the sign of the number with the greater absolute value. For example,

$$(-13) + 19 = 6$$

because

$$(-13) + 19 = +(|19| - |-13|) = +(19 - 13) = 6.$$

Similarly,

$$-16 + 8 = -8$$

because

$$-16 + 8 = -(|-16| - |8|) = -(16 - 8) = -8.$$

To find the difference between two numbers, express the difference as a sum and add as indicated above. For example:

$$(-7) - (5) = -7 + (-5) = -12$$
$$6 - (-4) = 6 + [-(-4)] = 6 + 4 = 10$$
$$-54 - (-23) = -54 + [-(-23)] = -54 + 23$$
$$= -(54 - 23) = -31$$

(Note that for any number n, $-(-n) = n$.)

Multiplication and division. To multiply or divide two numbers with the same sign, multiply or divide their absolute values; i.e., the product and quotient are positive. For example:

$$(-13)(-3) = (13)(3) = 39$$
$$(-14) \div (-2) = 14 \div 2 = 7$$

To multiply or divide two numbers with different signs, multiply or divide their absolute values and insert a negative sign; i.e., the product and quotient are negative. For example:

$$(13)(-3) = -(13)(3) = -39$$
$$(-14) \div 2 = -(14 \div 2) = -7$$
$$(-1)(-2)(-3) = (-1)(2)(3) = -6$$

Some properties of real numbers that are used frequently follow. If x, y, and z are real numbers, then

(1) $x + y = y + x$ and $xy = yx$. For example, $17 \cdot 5 = 5 \cdot 17 = 85$.

(2) $(x + y) + z = x + (y + z)$ and $(x \cdot y)z = x(y \cdot z)$. For example, $(5 \cdot \sqrt{3})(\sqrt{3}) = 5(\sqrt{3} \cdot \sqrt{3}) = 5 \cdot 3 = 15$.

(3) $x(y + z) = xy + xz$. For example, $718(36) + 718(64) = 718(36 + 64) = 718(100) = 71,800$.

6. RATIO AND PROPORTION

The *ratio* of the number a to the number b (b ≠ 0) is $\frac{a}{b}$.

A ratio may be expressed or represented in several ways. For example, the ratio of the number 2 to the number 3 can be written 2 to 3, 2:3, and $\frac{2}{3}$. The order of the terms of a ratio is important. For example, the ratio of the number of months with exactly 30 days to the number with exactly 31 days is $\frac{4}{7}$, not $\frac{7}{4}$.

A *proportion* is a statement that two ratios are equal; for example, $\frac{2}{3} = \frac{8}{12}$ is a proportion. One way to solve a proportion involving an unknown is to cross multiply, obtaining a new equality. For example, to solve for n in the proportion $\frac{2}{3} = \frac{n}{12}$, cross multiply $\frac{2}{3} \diagdown\!\!\!\!\diagup \frac{n}{12}$, obtaining 24 = 3n; dividing both sides by 3, n = 8.

7. PERCENTS

Percent means per hundred or number out of 100. A percent can be represented as a fraction with a denominator of 100. For example, $37\% = \frac{37}{100} = 0.37$.

To find a certain percent of a number, multiply the number by the percent expressed as a decimal or fraction. For example,

$$20\% \text{ of } 90 = 0.20 \times 90 = 18$$

or

$$20\% \text{ of } 90 = \frac{20}{100} \times 90 = \frac{1}{5} \times 90 = 18.$$

Percents greater than 100. Percents greater than 100 are represented by numbers greater than 1. For example:

$$300\% = \frac{300}{100} = 3$$

$$250\% \text{ of } 80 = 2.5 \times 80 = 200$$

Percents less than 1. 0.5% means $\frac{1}{2}$ of 1 percent. For example, 0.5% of 10 is equal to $0.005 \times 10 = 0.05$.

Percent change. Often a problem will ask for the percent increase from one number to another number. For example, "If the price of an item increases from \$24 to \$30, what is the percent increase in price?" To find the percent increase, first find the amount of the increase; then divide this increase by the original amount, and express this quotient as a percent. In the example above, the percent increase would be found in the following way: the amount of the increase is (30 − 24) = 6. Therefore, the percent increase is $\frac{6}{24} = 25\%$.

Likewise, to find the percent decrease (e.g., the price of an item is reduced from \$30 to \$24), first find the amount of the decrease; then divide this decrease by the original amount, and express this quotient as a percent. In the example above, the amount of the decrease is (30 − 24) = 6. Therefore, the percent decrease is $\frac{6}{30} = 20\%$.

Note that the percent increase from 24 to 30 is not the same as the percent decrease from 30 to 24.

8. EQUIVALENT FORMS OF A NUMBER

In solving a particular problem, it may be helpful to convert the given form of a number to a more convenient form.

To convert a fraction to a decimal, divide the numerator by the denominator, e.g., $\frac{3}{4} = 0.75$.

To convert a number to a percent, multiply by 100. For example, 0.75 = 75%.

The decimal 0.625 means $\frac{625}{1,000}$ (see page 15). This fraction may be simplified by dividing the numerator and denominator by common factors. For example:

$$\frac{625}{1,000} = \frac{5 \cdot 5 \cdot 5 \cdot 5}{2 \cdot 2 \cdot 2 \cdot 5 \cdot 5 \cdot 5} = \frac{5}{8}$$

To convert a percent to a decimal, divide by 100; e.g.:

$$24\% = \frac{24}{100} = 0.24$$

In the following example, it is helpful to convert from one form of a number to another form.

Of the following, which is LEAST?

(A) 35%　(B) $\frac{9}{20}$　(C) 0.42　(D) $\frac{(0.9)(4)}{10}$　(E) $\frac{3}{13}$

These numbers can be compared more easily if they are all converted to decimals:

$$35\% = 0.35$$

$$\frac{9}{20} = 0.45$$

$$0.42 = 0.42$$

$$\frac{(0.9)(4)}{10} = 0.36$$

$$\frac{3}{13} = 0.231$$

Thus, $\frac{3}{13}$ is the least of the numbers.

9. POWERS AND ROOTS OF NUMBERS

When a number k is to be used n times as a factor in a product, it can be expressed as k^n, which means the nth power of k. For example, $2^2 = 2 \cdot 2 = 4$ and $2^3 = 2 \cdot 2 \cdot 2 = 8$ are powers of 2.

Squaring a number that is greater than 1, or raising it to a higher power, results in a larger number; squaring a number between 0 and 1 results in a smaller number. For example:

$$3^2 = 9 \qquad (9 > 3)$$
$$\left(\frac{1}{3}\right)^2 = \frac{1}{9} \qquad \left(\frac{1}{9} < \frac{1}{3}\right)$$
$$(0.1)^2 = 0.01 \qquad (0.01 < 0.1)$$

A *square root* of a non-negative number n is a number that when squared is equal to n. Every positive number n has two square roots, one positive and the other negative, but $\sqrt{n}$ denotes the positive number whose square is n. For example, $\sqrt{9}$ denotes 3. The two square roots of 9 are $\sqrt{9} = 3$ and $-\sqrt{9} = -3$.

10. MEAN

The *average* (*arithmetic mean*) of a set of n numbers is equal to the sum of the n numbers divided by n. For example, the average (arithmetic mean) of 9, 6, 5, and 12 is $\frac{9 + 6 + 5 + 12}{4} = 8$.

11. MEDIAN

When numbers are ordered from least to greatest or from greatest to least, the number in the middle is the *median*; i.e., there are equal numbers of values above and below the median. For example, the median of 4, 7, 3, 10, and 8 is 7, since, when ordered from least to greatest (3,4,7,8,10), 7 is the middle number. When there is an even number of values, the median is the average of the two middle values. For example, the median of 5,3,2,10,7, and 8 is $\frac{5 + 7}{2} = 6$.

12. MODE

The *mode* of a list of numbers is the number that occurs most frequently. For example, the mode of 1, 3, 6, 4, 3, and 5 is 3. The list of numbers 7, 6, 8, 12, and 9 does not have a mode. A list of numbers may have more than one mode. For example, the list of numbers 1,2,3,3,3,5,7,10,10,10,20 has two modes, 3 and 10.

B. ALGEBRA

In algebra, a letter such as x or n is used to represent an unknown quantity. For example, suppose Pam has 5 more pencils than Fred. If you let f represent the number of pencils that Fred has, then the number of pencils that Pam has is 5 + f. A combination of letters and mathematical operations, such as 5 + f, $\frac{3x^3}{2x - 5}$, and $19x^2 + 6x + 3$, is called an *algebraic expression*.

In the expression $9x - 6$, 9x and 6 are *terms* of the expression; 9 is called the *coefficient* of x.

1. SIMPLIFYING ALGEBRAIC EXPRESSIONS

Often when working with algebraic expressions, it is necessary to simplify them by factoring or combining *like* terms. For example, the expression $6x + 5x$ is equivalent to $(6 + 5)x$ or 11x. In the expression $9x - 3y$, 3 is a factor common to both terms: $9x - 3y = 3(3x - y)$. In the expression $5x^2 + 6y$, there are no like terms or common factors.

If there are common factors in the numerator and denominator of an expression, they can be divided out, provided that they are not equal to zero.

For example, if $x \neq 3$, $\frac{3xy - 9y}{x - 3}$ is equal to $\frac{3y(x - 3)}{x - 3}$. Since $\frac{x - 3}{x - 3}$ is equal to 1, $\frac{3y(x - 3)}{x - 3} = 3y \cdot 1 = 3y$.

To multiply two algebraic expressions, each term of one expression is multiplied by each term of the other expression. For example:

$$(3x - 4)(9y + x) \text{ is equal to } 3x(9y + x) - 4(9y + x) =$$
$$(3x)(9y) + (3x)(x) + (-4)(9y) + (-4)(x) =$$
$$27xy + 3x^2 - 36y - 4x$$

An algebraic expression can be evaluated by substituting values of the unknowns in the expression. For example, if $x = 3$ and $y = -2$, $3xy - x^2 + y$ can be evaluated as

$$3(3)(-2) - (3)^2 + (-2) = -18 - 9 - 2 = -29.$$

2. EQUATIONS

A statement that two algebraic expressions are equal is an *equation*. Some examples of equations are

$$z = 3, 5x - 2 = 9,$$

and

$$3x + 1 = y - 2.$$

Two equations having the same solution(s) are equivalent. For example,

$$2 + x = 3$$

and

$$4 + 2x = 6$$

are equivalent equations, as are

$$3x - y = 6$$

and

$$6x = 2y + 12.$$

3. SOLVING LINEAR EQUATIONS WITH ONE UNKNOWN

To solve a linear equation (i.e., to find the value of the unknown that satisfies the equation) you need to isolate the unknown on one side of the equation. This can be done by performing the same mathematical operations on both sides of the equation. Remember that if the same number is added to or subtracted from both sides of the equation, this does not change the equality; likewise, multiplying or dividing both sides by the same non-zero number does not change the equality. For example, to solve the equation $\frac{5x - 6}{3} = 4$ for x, you can isolate x using the following steps:

$$\frac{5x - 6}{3} = 4$$

$$5x - 6 = 12 \quad \text{(multiplying by 3)}$$

$$5x = 12 + 6 = 18 \quad \text{(adding 6)}$$

$$x = \frac{18}{5} \quad \text{(dividing by 5)}$$

This value of x can be checked by substituting it in the original equation to determine whether it satisfies that equation. For example:

$$\frac{5\left(\frac{18}{5}\right) - 6}{3} = \frac{18 - 6}{3} = \frac{12}{3} = 4$$

Therefore, the value of x obtained above is the correct solution.

4. SOLVING TWO LINEAR EQUATIONS WITH TWO UNKNOWNS

If you have two equations that are not equivalent, you can find the values for the two unknowns that satisfy both equations. One way to solve for the two unknowns is to express one of the unknowns in terms of the other using one of the equations, and then substitute it into the remaining equation to obtain an equation with one unknown. This equation can be solved and the value substituted in the other equation to find the value of the other unknown. For example, the following two equations can be solved for x and y.

$$(1) \ 3x + 2y = 11$$
$$(2) \ x - y = 2$$

In equation (2), $x = 2 + y$. Substitute that value in equation (1):

$$3(2 + y) + 2y = 11$$
$$6 + 3y + 2y = 11$$
$$6 + 5y = 11$$
$$5y = 5$$
$$y = 1$$

If $y = 1$, then $x = 2 + 1 = 3$.

Another way to solve for x and y is to solve the two equations simultaneously. The purpose is to eliminate one of the unknowns. This can be done by making the coefficients of one of the unknowns the same (disregarding the sign) in both equations and either adding the equations or subtracting one equation from the other. For example, to solve the equations below simultaneously

$$(1) \ 6x + 5y = 29$$
$$(2) \ 4x - 3y = -6$$

multiply equation (1) by 3 and equation (2) by 5 to get

$$18x + 15y = 87$$
$$20x - 15y = -30$$

By adding the two equations you can eliminate y and get $38x = 57$ or $x = \frac{3}{2}$. Then substitute $\frac{3}{2}$ for x in one of the equations to find $y = 4$. These answers can be checked by substituting both values into both of the original equations.

5. SOLVING FACTORABLE QUADRATIC EQUATIONS

An equation that can be put in the standard form

$$ax^2 + bx + c = 0,$$

where a, b, and c are real numbers and $a \neq 0$, is a *quadratic* equation. For example,

$$x^2 + 6x + 5 = 0,$$
$$x^2 - 2x = 0,$$
$$\text{and} \quad x^2 - 4 = 5$$

are quadratic equations. Some quadratic equations can be solved by factoring. For example:

$$(1) \ x^2 + 6x + 5 = 0$$
$$(x + 5)(x + 1) = 0$$
$$x + 5 = 0 \text{ or } x + 1 = 0$$
$$x = -5 \text{ or } x = -1$$

$$(2) \ x^2 - 2x = 0$$
$$x(x - 2) = 0$$
$$x = 0 \text{ or } x = 2$$

$$(3) \ 3x^2 - 3 = 8x$$
$$3x^2 - 8x - 3 = 0$$
$$(3x + 1)(x - 3) = 0$$
$$3x + 1 = 0 \text{ or } x - 3 = 0$$
$$x = -\frac{1}{3} \text{ or } x = 3$$

In general, first put the quadratic equation into the standard form $ax^2 + bx + c = 0$, then factor the left-hand side of the equation; i.e., find two linear expressions whose product is the given quadratic expression. Since the product of the factors is equal to zero, at least one of the factors must be equal to zero. The values found by setting the factors equal to zero are called the *roots* of the equation. These roots can be checked by substituting them into the original equation to determine whether they satisfy the equation.

A quadratic equation has at most two real roots and may have just one or even none. For example, the equation $x^2 - 6x + 9 = 0$ can be expressed as $(x - 3)^2 = 0$ or $(x - 3)(x - 3) = 0$; thus the only root is $x = 3$.

An expression in the form $a^2 - b^2$ is equal to

$$(a - b)(a + b).$$

For example, if

$$9x^2 - 25 = 0,$$

then

$$(3x - 5)(3x + 5) = 0;$$

$$x = \frac{5}{3} \text{ and } x = -\frac{5}{3}.$$

6. EXPONENTS

A positive integer exponent on a number indicates the number of times that number is to be a factor in the product. For example, x^5 means $x \cdot x \cdot x \cdot x \cdot x$; i.e., x is a factor in the product 5 times.

Some rules about exponents are:

Let r, s, x, and y be positive integers.

(1) $(x^r)(x^s) = x^{(r+s)}$; for example, $2^2 \cdot 2^3 = (2 \cdot 2)(2 \cdot 2 \cdot 2) = 2^5 = 32$.

(2) $(x^r)(y^r) = (xy)^r$; for example, $3^3 \cdot 4^3 = 12^3 = 1,728$.

(3) $\left(\dfrac{x}{y}\right)^r = \dfrac{x^r}{y^r}$; for example, $\left(\dfrac{2}{3}\right)^3 = \dfrac{2^3}{3^3} = \dfrac{8}{27}.$

(4) $\dfrac{x^r}{x^s} = x^{r-s}$; for example, $\dfrac{4^5}{4^2} = \dfrac{4 \cdot 4 \cdot 4 \cdot 4 \cdot 4}{4 \cdot 4} = 4^3 = 64.$

(5) $x^{\frac{r}{s}} = \left(x^{\frac{1}{s}}\right)^r = \left(x^r\right)^{\frac{1}{s}} = \sqrt[s]{x^r}$; for example, $x^{\frac{1}{2}} = \sqrt{x}$ and $9^{\frac{1}{2}} = \sqrt{9} = 3.$

(6) $x^{-r} = \dfrac{1}{x^r}$; for example, $3^{-2} = \dfrac{1}{3^2} = \dfrac{1}{9}.$

(7) $x^0 = 1$; for example, $6^0 = 1$. 0^0 is undefined.

The rules above also apply when the numbers are not integers.

7. ABSOLUTE VALUE

The absolute value of x, denoted $|x|$, is defined to be x if $x \geqq 0$ and $-x$ if $x < 0$. Note that $\sqrt{x^2}$ denotes the non-negative square root of x^2, that is, $\sqrt{x^2} = |x|$.

8. INEQUALITIES

A statement that indicates that two expressions are not equal is an *inequality.* The symbols of inequality are:

$\neq$ not equal to

$>$ greater than

$\geqq$ greater than or equal to

$<$ less than

$\leqq$ less than or equal to

Some examples of inequalities are $5x - 3 < 9$, $6x \geqq y$, and $\dfrac{1}{2} < \dfrac{3}{4}$. Solving an inequality is similar to solving an equation; the unknown is isolated on one side of the inequality. Like an equation, the same number can be added to or subtracted from both sides of the inequality or both sides of an inequality can be multiplied or divided by a positive number without changing the truth of the inequality. However, multiplying or dividing an inequality by a negative number reverses the direction of the inequality. For example, $6 > 2$, but $(-1)(6) < (-1)(2)$.

To solve the inequality $3x - 2 > 5$ for x, isolate x by using the following steps:

$$3x - 2 > 5$$
$$3x > 5 + 2$$
$$3x > 7$$
$$x > \frac{7}{3}$$

To solve the inequality $\dfrac{5x - 1}{-2} < 3$ for x, isolate x by using the following steps:

$$\frac{5x - 1}{-2} < 3$$
$$5x - 1 > -6$$
$$5x > -5$$
$$x > -1$$

C. GEOMETRY

1. LINES

A *line* contains infinitely many points and extends indefinitely. The word "line" refers to a straight line.

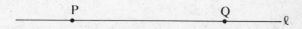

The line above can be referred to as line PQ or line ℓ. The part of the line from P to Q is called a *line segment.* P and Q are the *endpoints* of the segment. The notation PQ is used to denote both the segment and the length of the segment. The intention of the notation can be determined from the context.

2. INTERSECTING LINES AND ANGLES

If two lines intersect, the opposite angles are vertical angles and have the same measure. In the figure

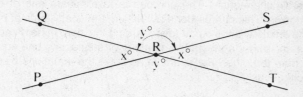

$\angle$PRQ and $\angle$SRT are vertical angles and $\angle$QRS and $\angle$PRT are vertical angles.

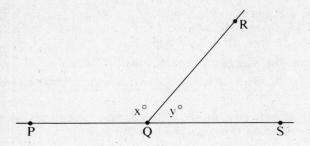

In the figure above, PQS is a straight line, or straight angle, and $x + y = 180$. $\angle PQR$ and $\angle RQS$ are adjacent angles since they share a common side.

An angle that has a measure of 90° is a *right* angle.

3. PERPENDICULAR LINES

If two lines intersect at right angles, the lines are *perpendicular.* For example:

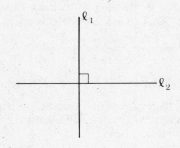

ℓ_1 and ℓ_2 are perpendicular, or $\ell_1 \perp \ell_2$. A right angle symbol in an angle of intersection indicates that the lines are perpendicular.

4. PARALLEL LINES

If two lines that are in the same plane do not intersect, the two lines are *parallel.* In the figure

lines ℓ_1 and ℓ_2 are parallel, or $\ell_1 \parallel \ell_2$. If two parallel lines are intersected by a third line, as shown below, the following angle relationships are true.

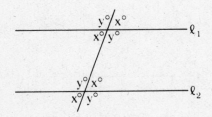

5. POLYGONS (CONVEX)

A closed plane figure formed by three or more line segments is a *polygon.* Each of the segments of a polygon is called a *side.* Each side of a polygon intersects exactly two other sides at the endpoints. The points of intersection of the sides are *vertices.* The term "polygon" will be used to mean the convex polygon; i.e., a polygon in which each interior angle has a measure of less than 180°.

The following figures are polygons:

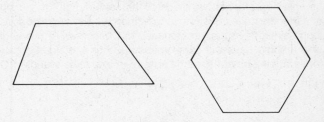

Note that "polygon" will not be used to refer to figures such as the following since $x > 180$.

Other figures that are not polygons are:

A polygon with three sides is a *triangle;* with four sides, a *quadrilateral;* with five sides, a *pentagon;* and with six sides, a *hexagon.*

The sum of the angle measures of a triangle is 180°. In general, the sum of the angle measures of a polygon with n sides is equal to $(n - 2)180°$. For example, a pentagon has $3(180) = 540$ degrees.

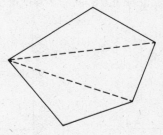

Note that a pentagon can be partitioned into three triangles and therefore the sum of the angle measures can be found by adding the sum of the angle measures of three triangles.

The *perimeter* of a polygon is the sum of the lengths of its sides.

The commonly used phrase "area of a polygon (or any other plane figure)" will be used to mean the area of the region enclosed by that figure.

6. TRIANGLES

An *equilateral* triangle has all sides of equal length. All angles of an equilateral triangle have equal measure. An *isosceles* triangle has at least two sides of the same length. If two sides of a triangle have the same length, then the two angles opposite those sides have the same measure. Conversely, if two angles of a triangle have the same measure, then the sides opposite those angles have the same length. In isosceles triangle PQR,

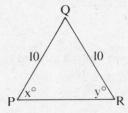

x = y since PQ = QR.

A triangle that has a right angle is a *right* triangle. In a right triangle, the side opposite the right angle is the *hypotenuse,* and the other two sides are the *legs.* An important theorem concerning right triangles is the *Pythagorean theorem,* which states: In a right triangle, the square of the length of the hypotenuse is equal to the sum of the squares of the lengths of the legs.

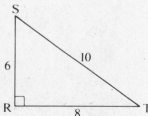

In right $\triangle RST$, $(RS)^2 + (RT)^2 = (ST)^2$. For example, if RS = 6 and RT = 8, then ST = 10, since $6^2 + 8^2 = 36 + 64 = 100 = (ST)^2$ and $ST = \sqrt{100}$. Any triangle in which the lengths of the sides are in the ratio 3:4:5 is a right triangle. In general, if a, b, and c are the lengths of the sides of a triangle and $a^2 + b^2 = c^2$, then the triangle is a right triangle.

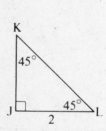
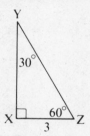

In 45°−45°−90° triangles, the lengths of the sides are in the ratio 1:1:$\sqrt{2}$. For example, in $\triangle JKL$, if JL = 2, then

JK = 2, and KL = $2\sqrt{2}$. In 30°−60°−90° triangles, the lengths of the sides are in the ratio 1:$\sqrt{3}$:2. For example, in $\triangle XYZ$, if XZ = 3, then XY = $3\sqrt{3}$, and YZ = 6.

Area. The area of a triangle is equal to:

$$\frac{\text{(the length of the altitude)} \times \text{(the length of the base)}}{2}$$

The *altitude* of a triangle is the segment drawn from a vertex perpendicular to its opposite side, the *base.*

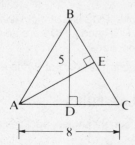

In $\triangle ABC$, BD is the altitude to base AC and AE is the altitude to base BC. The area of $\triangle ABC$ is equal to

$$\frac{BD \times AC}{2} = \frac{5 \cdot 8}{2} = 20.$$

The area is also equal to $\frac{AE \times BC}{2}$. If $\triangle ABC$ above is isosceles and AB = BC, then altitude BD bisects the base, i.e., AD = DC = 4. Similarly, any altitude of an equilateral triangle bisects the side to which it is drawn.

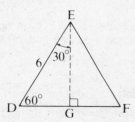

In equilateral triangle DEF, if DE = 6, then DG = 3, and EG = $3\sqrt{3}$. The area of $\triangle DEF$ is equal to $\frac{3\sqrt{3} \cdot 6}{2} = 9\sqrt{3}$.

7. QUADRILATERALS

A polygon with four sides is a *quadrilateral*. A quadrilateral in which both pairs of opposite sides are parallel is a *parallelogram*. The opposite sides of a parallelogram also have equal length.

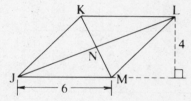

In parallelogram JKLM, JK ∥ LM and JK = LM; KL ∥ JM and KL = JM.

The diagonals of a parallelogram bisect each other (i.e., KN = NM and JN = NL).

The area of a parallelogram is equal to

(the length of the altitude) × (the length of the base).

The area of JKLM is equal to 4 × 6 = 24.

A parallelogram with right angles is a *rectangle,* and a rectangle with all sides of equal length is a *square.*

The perimeter of WXYZ = 2(3) + 2(7) = 20 and the area of WXYZ is equal to 3 · 7 = 21. The diagonals of a rectangle are equal; therefore WY = XZ = $\sqrt{9 + 49}$ = $\sqrt{58}$.

Note that a quadrilateral can have two right angles and not be a rectangle. For example, the figures

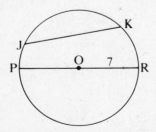

are not rectangles. But, if it is known that a quadrilateral has at least three right angles, then it must be a rectangle.

8. CIRCLES

A *circle* is a set of points in a plane that are all located the same distance from a fixed point (the *center* of the circle).

A *chord* of a circle is a line segment that has its endpoints on the circle. A chord that passes through the center of the circle is a *diameter* of the circle. A *radius* of a circle is a segment from the center of the circle to a point on the circle. The words "diameter" and "radius" are also used to refer to the length of these segments.

The *circumference* of a circle is the distance around the circle. If r is the radius of the circle, then the circumference is equal to 2πr, where π is approximately $\frac{22}{7}$ or 3.14. The *area* of a circle is equal to πr².

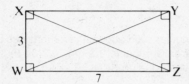

In the circle above, O is the center of the circle and JK and PR are chords. PR is a diameter and OR is a radius. If

OR = 7, then the circumference of the circle is 2π(7) = 14π and the area of the circle is π(7)² = 49π.

The number of degrees of arc in a circle (or the number of degrees in a complete revolution) is 360.

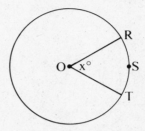

In the circle with center O above, if x = 60, then arc RST is $\frac{60}{360}$ of the circumference of the circle.

A line that has exactly one point in common with the circle is said to be *tangent* to the circle, and that common point is called the *point of tangency.* A radius or diameter with an endpoint at the point of tangency is perpendicular to the tangent line.

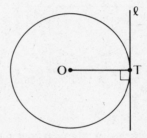

The line ℓ above is tangent to the circle and radius OT is perpendicular to ℓ.

Two different circles that have the same center, as shown below, are *concentric* circles.

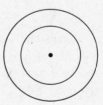

If each vertex of a polygon lies on a circle, then the polygon is *inscribed* in the circle and the circle is *circumscribed* about the polygon. If each side of a polygon is tangent to a circle, then the polygon is *circumscribed* about the circle and the circle is *inscribed* in the polygon.

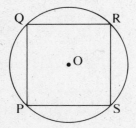 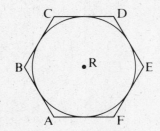

PQRS is inscribed in circle O and ABCDEF is circumscribed about circle R.

If a triangle is inscribed in a circle so that one of its sides is a diameter of the circle, then the triangle is a right triangle.

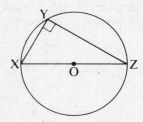

In the circle above, XZ is a diameter and $\angle XYZ = 90°$.

9. SOLIDS

The following are examples of three-dimensional figures called *solids*:

Rectangular Solid   Cylinder   Pyramid   Sphere   Cone

10. RECTANGULAR SOLIDS

The *rectangular solid* shown above is formed by six rectangular surfaces. Each rectangular surface is a *face*. Each solid or dotted line segment is an *edge*, and each point at which the edges meet is a *vertex*. A rectangular solid has six faces, twelve edges, and eight vertices. Opposite faces are parallel rectangles that have the same dimensions. A rectangular solid in which all edges are of equal length is a *cube*.

The *surface area* of a rectangular solid is equal to the sum of the areas of all the faces. The *volume* is equal to

(length) × (width) × (height) or (area of base) × (height).

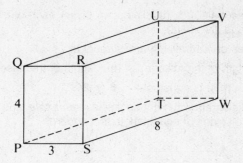

In the rectangular solid above, the dimensions are 3, 4, and 8. The surface area is equal to $2(3 \cdot 4) + 2(3 \cdot 8) + 2(4 \cdot 8) = 136$. The volume is equal to $3 \cdot 4 \cdot 8 = 96$.

11. CYLINDERS

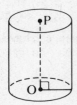

The figure above is a right circular *cylinder*. The two bases are circles of the same size with centers O and P, respectively, and altitude (height) OP is perpendicular to the bases. The surface area of a right circular cylinder with a base of radius r and height h is equal to $2(\pi r^2) + 2\pi rh$ (the sum of the areas of the two bases and the area of the curved surface).

The volume of a cylinder is equal to $\pi r^2 h$, i.e.:

(area of base) × (height).

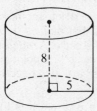

In the cylinder above, the surface area is equal to

$$2\pi (25) + 2\pi(5)(8) = 130\pi,$$

and the volume is equal to

$$25\pi(8) = 200\pi.$$

12. PYRAMIDS

Another solid with plane surfaces as faces is a *pyramid*. One of the faces (called the base) can be a polygon with any number of edges; the remaining faces are triangles. The figures below are pyramids. The shaded faces are the bases.

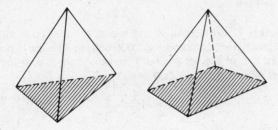

In the pyramid below, PQRS is a square, and the four triangles are the same size. V, the base of altitude TV, is the center of the square.

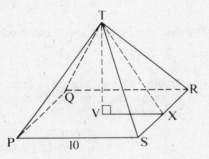

If the altitude TV = 12 and VX = $\frac{1}{2}$ PS = 5, then, by the Pythagorean theorem, TX = $\sqrt{5^2 + 12^2}$ = 13. If TX = 13, and SX = $\frac{1}{2}$ RS = 5, then TS = $\sqrt{13^2 + 5^2}$ = $\sqrt{194}$.

13. COORDINATE GEOMETRY

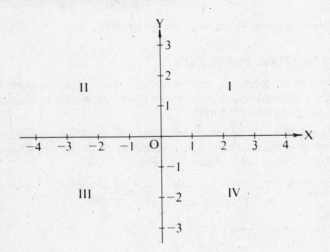

The figure above shows the rectangular *coordinate plane*. The horizontal line is called the *X-axis* and the perpendicular vertical line is called the *Y-axis*. The point at which these two axes intersect, designated O, is called the *origin*. The axes divide the plane into four quadrants, I, II, III, and IV, as shown.

Each point in the plane has an *x-coordinate* and a *y-coordinate*. A point is identified by an ordered pair (x,y) of numbers in which the x-coordinate is the first number and the y-coordinate is the second number.

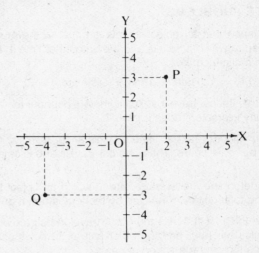

In the graph above, the (x,y) coordinates of point P are (2,3) since P is 2 units to the right on the X-axis and 3 units above on the Y-axis. Similarly, the (x,y) coordinates of point Q are (−4, −3). The origin O has coordinates (0,0).

One way to find the distance between two points in the coordinate plane is to use the Pythagorean theorem.

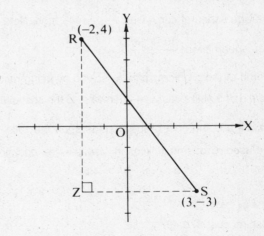

To find the distance between points R and S using the Pythagorean theorem, draw in the triangle as shown. Note that Z has (x,y) coordinates (−2, −3). RZ = 7 and ZS = 5. Therefore, the distance between R and S is equal to:

$$\sqrt{7^2 + 5^2} = \sqrt{74}.$$

D. WORD PROBLEMS

Many of the principles discussed in this chapter are used to solve word problems. The following discussion of word problems illustrates some of the techniques and concepts used in solving such problems.

1. RATE PROBLEMS

The distance that an object travels is equal to the product of the speed at which it travels and the amount of time it takes to travel that distance; i.e.,

$$\text{Rate} \times \text{Time} = \text{Distance}$$

Example 1: If a car travels at 70 kilometers per hour for 4 hours, how many kilometers does it travel?

Solution: Since rate × time = distance, simply multiply 70 km/hour × 4 hours. Thus, the car travels 280 kilometers in 4 hours.

To determine the average rate at which an object travels, divide the total distance traveled by the total amount of time.

Example 2: On a 400-mile trip car X traveled half the distance at 40 miles per hour and the other half at 50 miles per hour. What was the average speed of car X?

Solution: First it is necessary to determine the amount of traveling time. During the first 200 miles the car traveled at 40 mph; therefore, it took $\frac{200}{40} = 5$ hours to travel the first 200 miles. During the second 200 miles the car traveled at 50 mph; therefore, it took $\frac{200}{50} = 4$ hours to travel the second 200 miles. Thus, the average speed of car X was $\frac{400}{9} = 44\frac{4}{9}$ mph. Note that the average speed is *not* $\frac{40 + 50}{2} = 45$.

Some of the problems can be solved by using ratios.

Example 3: If 5 shirts cost $44, then what is the cost of 8 shirts?

Solution: If c is the cost of the 8 shirts, then the ratio $\frac{5}{44} = \frac{8}{c}$ may be used. Cross multiplication results in the equation

$$5c = 8 \cdot 44 = 352$$
$$c = \frac{352}{5} = 70.40$$

The 8 shirts cost $70.40.

2. WORK PROBLEMS

In a work problem, the rates at which certain persons or machines work alone are usually given and it is necessary to compute the rate at which they work together (or vice versa).

The basic formula for solving work problems is: $\frac{1}{r} + \frac{1}{s} = \frac{1}{h}$, where r and s are the number of hours it takes Rae and Sam, respectively, to complete a job when working alone and h is the number of hours it takes Rae and Sam to do the job when working together. The reasoning is that in 1 hour Rae does $\frac{1}{r}$ of the job, Sam does $\frac{1}{s}$ of the job, and Rae and Sam together do $\frac{1}{h}$ of the job.

Example 1: If machine X can produce 1,000 bolts in 4 hours and machine Y can produce 1,000 bolts in 5 hours, in how many hours can machines X and Y, working together at these constant rates, produce 1,000 bolts?

Solution: $\frac{1}{4} + \frac{1}{5} = \frac{1}{h}$

$$\frac{5}{20} + \frac{4}{20} = \frac{1}{h}$$
$$9h = 20$$
$$h = \frac{20}{9} = 2\frac{2}{9} \text{ hours}$$

Working together, machines X and Y can produce 1,000 bolts in $2\frac{2}{9}$ hours.

Example 2: If Art and Rita can do a job in 4 hours when working together at their respective rates and Art can do the job alone in 6 hours, in how many hours can Rita do the job alone?

Solution: $\frac{1}{6} + \frac{1}{R} = \frac{1}{4}$

$$\frac{6 + R}{6R} = \frac{1}{4}$$
$$6 + R = \frac{6R}{4}$$
$$24 + 4R = 6R$$
$$24 = 2R$$
$$12 = R$$

Working alone, Rita can do the job in 12 hours.

3. MIXTURE PROBLEMS

In mixture problems, substances with different characteristics are combined and it is necessary to determine the characteristics of the resulting mixture.

Example 1: If 6 pounds of nuts that cost $1.20 per pound are mixed with 2 pounds of nuts that cost $1.60 per pound, what is the cost per pound of the mixture?

Solution: The total value of the 8 pounds of nuts is

$$6(\$1.20) + 2(\$1.60) = \$10.40.$$

The price per pound is $\frac{\$10.40}{8} = \$1.30$.

Example 2: How many liters of a solution that is 15 percent salt must be added to 5 liters of a solution that is 8 percent salt so that the resulting solution is 10 percent salt?

Solution: For a solution to be 10% salt, the ratio of the number of liters of salt to the number of liters of solution must be $\frac{10}{100}$.
If n is the number of liters of 15% solution, then

$$\frac{\text{Amount of salt}}{\text{Total solution}} = \frac{(0.08)(5) + (0.15)n}{5 + n} = \frac{10}{100}$$

$$40 + 15n = 50 + 10n$$
$$5n = 10$$
$$n = 2 \text{ liters}$$

Two liters of 15% salt solution must be added to the 8% solution to obtain a 10% solution.

4. INTEREST PROBLEMS

Interest can be computed in two basic ways. With simple annual interest, the interest is computed on the principal only. If interest is compounded, then interest is computed on the principal as well as on any interest already earned.

Example 1: If $8,000 is invested at 6 percent simple annual interest, how much interest is earned after 3 months?

Solution: If the annual interest rate is 6%, then the interest for 1 year is 0.06(8,000) = $480. The interest earned in 3 months is $\frac{3}{12}$(480) = $120.

Example 2: If $10,000 is invested at 10 percent annual interest, compounded semiannually, what is the balance after 1 year?

Solution: The balance after the first 6 months would be 10,000 + (10,000)(0.05) = 10,500. The balance after one year would be 10,500 + (10,500)(0.05) = $11,025.

5. DISCOUNT

If a price is discounted by n percent, then the price becomes (100 − n) percent of the original price.

Example 1: A certain customer paid $24 for a dress. If this represented a 25 percent discount on the original price of the dress, what was the original price of the dress?

Solution: If p is the original price of the dress, then 0.75p is the discounted price and 0.75p = 24 or p = $32. The original price of the dress was $32.

Example 2: The price of an item is discounted by 20 percent and then this reduced price is discounted by an additional 30 percent. These two discounts are equal to an overall discount of what percent?

Solution: If p is the original price of the item, then 0.8p is the price after the first discount. The price after the second discount is (0.7)(0.8)p = 0.56p. This represents an overall discount of 44 percent (100 − 56).

6. PROFIT

Profit is equal to revenues minus expenses or selling price minus cost.

Example 1: A certain appliance costs a merchant $30. At what price should the merchant sell the appliance in order to make a gross profit of 50 percent of the cost of the appliance?

Solution: If s is the selling price of the appliance, then s − 30 = (0.5)(30) or s = $45. The merchant should sell the appliance for $45.

Note that in GMAT questions percent profit is calculated on the basis of cost unless otherwise specified in a particular question.

7. SETS

If S is the set of numbers 1, 2, 3, and 4, you can write S = {1,2,3,4}. Sets can also be represented by Venn diagrams. That is, the relationship among the members of sets can be represented by circles.

Example 1: Each of 25 people is enrolled in history, mathematics, or both. If 20 are enrolled in history and 18 are enrolled in mathematics, how many are enrolled in both history and mathematics?

Solution: Draw two intersecting circles to represent the number of people enrolled in history, mathematics, or both.

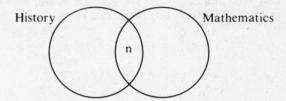

If n is the number of people enrolled in both, then 20 − n is the number enrolled in history only and 18 − n is the number enrolled in mathematics only.

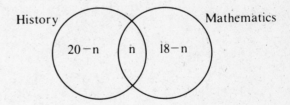

Since there is a total of 25 people, (20 − n) + n + (18 − n) = 25 or n = 13. Thirteen people are enrolled in both history and mathematics.

Example 2: In a certain production lot, 40 percent of the toys are red and the remaining toys are green. Half of the toys are small and half are large. If 10 percent of the toys are red and small and 40 toys are green and large, how many of the toys are red and large?

Solution: For this kind of problem, it is helpful to organize the information in a table:

	red	green	
small	10 %		50 %
large			50 %
	40 %	60 %	100 %

The numbers in the table are the percents given. The following percents can be computed on the basis of what is given:

	red	green	
small	10 %	40 %	50 %
large	30 %	20 %	50 %
	40 %	60 %	100 %

Since 20% of the toys (t) are green and large, 0.20t = 40 (40 toys are green and large) and t = 200. Therefore, 30% of the 200 toys or (0.3)(200) = 60 are red and large.

8. GEOMETRY PROBLEMS

The following is an example of a word problem involving geometry.

Example 1:

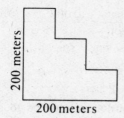

200 meters

200 meters

The figure above shows a piece of land. If all angles shown are right angles, what is the perimeter of the piece of land?

Solution: For reference, label the figure as

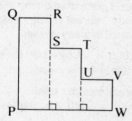

If all the angles are right angles, then QR + ST + UV = PW and RS + TU + VW = PQ. Hence, the perimeter of the land is 2PW + 2PQ = 2 × 200 + 2 × 200 = 800 meters.

Problem Solving

In these questions you are to solve each problem and select the best of the five answer choices given. The mathematics required to answer the questions does not extend beyond that assumed to be common to the mathematics background of all examinees.

The following pages include test-taking strategies, sample tests (with answer keys), and detailed explanations of selected problems from the sample tests. These explanations present possible problem-solving strategies for the examples. At the end of each explanation is a reference to the particular section(s) of Chapter II, Math Review, that you may find helpful in reviewing the mathematical concepts on which the problem is based. The sample problems are organized according to their content: arithmetic problems are first, followed by algebra and geometry problems.

TEST-TAKING STRATEGIES FOR PROBLEM SOLVING

1. Pacing yourself is very important. Take a watch with you and consult it from time to time. Work as carefully as possible, but do not spend valuable time checking answers or pondering over problems that you find difficult. Make a check mark in your test book next to the troublesome problems or those problems you feel you should double-check. When you have completed the section, go back and spend the remaining time on those difficult problems. Remember, each question has the same weight.

2. Space is available in the test book for scratchwork. Working a problem out in writing may help you avoid errors in solving the problem. If diagrams or figures are not presented, it may help if you draw your own.

3. Read each question carefully to determine what information is given and what is being asked. For word problems, take one step at a time, reading each sentence carefully and translating the information into equations.

4. Before attempting to answer a question, scan the answer choices; otherwise you may waste time putting answers in a form that is not given (for example, putting an answer in the form $\frac{\sqrt{2}}{2}$ when the options are given in the form $\frac{1}{\sqrt{2}}$ or finding the answer in decimal form, such as 0.25, when the choices are given in fractional form, such as $\frac{1}{4}$).

5. For questions that require approximations, scan the options to get some idea of the required closeness of approximation; otherwise, you may waste time on long computations where a short mental process would serve as well (for example, taking 48 percent of a number instead of half the number).

6. If you cannot solve a problem but you can eliminate some of the options as being unlikely, you should guess. If the options are equally plausible, you should not guess. Remember, a percentage of the wrong answers will be subtracted from the number of right answers to compensate for guessing, but the number of omitted questions will not be subtracted.

When you take the sample tests, use the answer spaces on the following page to mark your answers.

Answer Spaces for Sample Test I

1 Ⓐ Ⓑ Ⓒ Ⓓ Ⓔ	11 Ⓐ Ⓑ Ⓒ Ⓓ Ⓔ	21 Ⓐ Ⓑ Ⓒ Ⓓ Ⓔ
2 Ⓐ Ⓑ Ⓒ Ⓓ Ⓔ	12 Ⓐ Ⓑ Ⓒ Ⓓ Ⓔ	22 Ⓐ Ⓑ Ⓒ Ⓓ Ⓔ
3 Ⓐ Ⓑ Ⓒ Ⓓ Ⓔ	13 Ⓐ Ⓑ Ⓒ Ⓓ Ⓔ	23 Ⓐ Ⓑ Ⓒ Ⓓ Ⓔ
4 Ⓐ Ⓑ Ⓒ Ⓓ Ⓔ	14 Ⓐ Ⓑ Ⓒ Ⓓ Ⓔ	24 Ⓐ Ⓑ Ⓒ Ⓓ Ⓔ
5 Ⓐ Ⓑ Ⓒ Ⓓ Ⓔ	15 Ⓐ Ⓑ Ⓒ Ⓓ Ⓔ	25 Ⓐ Ⓑ Ⓒ Ⓓ Ⓔ
6 Ⓐ Ⓑ Ⓒ Ⓓ Ⓔ	16 Ⓐ Ⓑ Ⓒ Ⓓ Ⓔ	26 Ⓐ Ⓑ Ⓒ Ⓓ Ⓔ
7 Ⓐ Ⓑ Ⓒ Ⓓ Ⓔ	17 Ⓐ Ⓑ Ⓒ Ⓓ Ⓔ	27 Ⓐ Ⓑ Ⓒ Ⓓ Ⓔ
8 Ⓐ Ⓑ Ⓒ Ⓓ Ⓔ	18 Ⓐ Ⓑ Ⓒ Ⓓ Ⓔ	28 Ⓐ Ⓑ Ⓒ Ⓓ Ⓔ
9 Ⓐ Ⓑ Ⓒ Ⓓ Ⓔ	19 Ⓐ Ⓑ Ⓒ Ⓓ Ⓔ	29 Ⓐ Ⓑ Ⓒ Ⓓ Ⓔ
10 Ⓐ Ⓑ Ⓒ Ⓓ Ⓔ	20 Ⓐ Ⓑ Ⓒ Ⓓ Ⓔ	30 Ⓐ Ⓑ Ⓒ Ⓓ Ⓔ

Answer Spaces for Sample Test II

1 Ⓐ Ⓑ Ⓒ Ⓓ Ⓔ	11 Ⓐ Ⓑ Ⓒ Ⓓ Ⓔ	21 Ⓐ Ⓑ Ⓒ Ⓓ Ⓔ
2 Ⓐ Ⓑ Ⓒ Ⓓ Ⓔ	12 Ⓐ Ⓑ Ⓒ Ⓓ Ⓔ	22 Ⓐ Ⓑ Ⓒ Ⓓ Ⓔ
3 Ⓐ Ⓑ Ⓒ Ⓓ Ⓔ	13 Ⓐ Ⓑ Ⓒ Ⓓ Ⓔ	23 Ⓐ Ⓑ Ⓒ Ⓓ Ⓔ
4 Ⓐ Ⓑ Ⓒ Ⓓ Ⓔ	14 Ⓐ Ⓑ Ⓒ Ⓓ Ⓔ	24 Ⓐ Ⓑ Ⓒ Ⓓ Ⓔ
5 Ⓐ Ⓑ Ⓒ Ⓓ Ⓔ	15 Ⓐ Ⓑ Ⓒ Ⓓ Ⓔ	25 Ⓐ Ⓑ Ⓒ Ⓓ Ⓔ
6 Ⓐ Ⓑ Ⓒ Ⓓ Ⓔ	16 Ⓐ Ⓑ Ⓒ Ⓓ Ⓔ	26 Ⓐ Ⓑ Ⓒ Ⓓ Ⓔ
7 Ⓐ Ⓑ Ⓒ Ⓓ Ⓔ	17 Ⓐ Ⓑ Ⓒ Ⓓ Ⓔ	27 Ⓐ Ⓑ Ⓒ Ⓓ Ⓔ
8 Ⓐ Ⓑ Ⓒ Ⓓ Ⓔ	18 Ⓐ Ⓑ Ⓒ Ⓓ Ⓔ	28 Ⓐ Ⓑ Ⓒ Ⓓ Ⓔ
9 Ⓐ Ⓑ Ⓒ Ⓓ Ⓔ	19 Ⓐ Ⓑ Ⓒ Ⓓ Ⓔ	29 Ⓐ Ⓑ Ⓒ Ⓓ Ⓔ
10 Ⓐ Ⓑ Ⓒ Ⓓ Ⓔ	20 Ⓐ Ⓑ Ⓒ Ⓓ Ⓔ	30 Ⓐ Ⓑ Ⓒ Ⓓ Ⓔ

Answer Spaces for Sample Test III

1 Ⓐ Ⓑ Ⓒ Ⓓ Ⓔ	11 Ⓐ Ⓑ Ⓒ Ⓓ Ⓔ	21 Ⓐ Ⓑ Ⓒ Ⓓ Ⓔ
2 Ⓐ Ⓑ Ⓒ Ⓓ Ⓔ	12 Ⓐ Ⓑ Ⓒ Ⓓ Ⓔ	22 Ⓐ Ⓑ Ⓒ Ⓓ Ⓔ
3 Ⓐ Ⓑ Ⓒ Ⓓ Ⓔ	13 Ⓐ Ⓑ Ⓒ Ⓓ Ⓔ	23 Ⓐ Ⓑ Ⓒ Ⓓ Ⓔ
4 Ⓐ Ⓑ Ⓒ Ⓓ Ⓔ	14 Ⓐ Ⓑ Ⓒ Ⓓ Ⓔ	24 Ⓐ Ⓑ Ⓒ Ⓓ Ⓔ
5 Ⓐ Ⓑ Ⓒ Ⓓ Ⓔ	15 Ⓐ Ⓑ Ⓒ Ⓓ Ⓔ	25 Ⓐ Ⓑ Ⓒ Ⓓ Ⓔ
6 Ⓐ Ⓑ Ⓒ Ⓓ Ⓔ	16 Ⓐ Ⓑ Ⓒ Ⓓ Ⓔ	26 Ⓐ Ⓑ Ⓒ Ⓓ Ⓔ
7 Ⓐ Ⓑ Ⓒ Ⓓ Ⓔ	17 Ⓐ Ⓑ Ⓒ Ⓓ Ⓔ	27 Ⓐ Ⓑ Ⓒ Ⓓ Ⓔ
8 Ⓐ Ⓑ Ⓒ Ⓓ Ⓔ	18 Ⓐ Ⓑ Ⓒ Ⓓ Ⓔ	28 Ⓐ Ⓑ Ⓒ Ⓓ Ⓔ
9 Ⓐ Ⓑ Ⓒ Ⓓ Ⓔ	19 Ⓐ Ⓑ Ⓒ Ⓓ Ⓔ	29 Ⓐ Ⓑ Ⓒ Ⓓ Ⓔ
10 Ⓐ Ⓑ Ⓒ Ⓓ Ⓔ	20 Ⓐ Ⓑ Ⓒ Ⓓ Ⓔ	30 Ⓐ Ⓑ Ⓒ Ⓓ Ⓔ

PROBLEM SOLVING SAMPLE TEST I

Time—40 minutes

30 Questions

<u>Directions:</u> In this section solve each problem, using any available space on the page for scratchwork. Then indicate the <u>best</u> answer in the appropriate space on the answer sheet.

<u>Note:</u> Figures which accompany problems in this test are intended to provide information useful in solving the problems. They are drawn as accurately as possible EXCEPT when it is stated in a specific problem that its figure is not drawn to scale. All figures lie in a plane unless otherwise indicated.

All numbers used are real numbers.

I. 1. A television set costs $525 if the buyer pays cash. On an installment plan, the buyer pays 10 per cent down and $45 a month for 12 months. How much greater is the installment cost than the cash cost?

(A) $15.00   (B) $22.50   (C) $60.00

(D) $67.50   (E) $75.00

I. 2. How many 6-player teams can be formed from six 10-player teams, if no player is on more than one team?

(A) 6   (B) 8   (C) 10   (D) 11   (E) 12

I. 3. If $x + 3 = 6$, then $5(x - 3) =$

(A) −30   (B) −5   (C) 0   (D) 5   (E) 30

I. 4. Audrey went shopping with D dollars. She spent 20 per cent of her money on a blouse and 25 per cent of what was left on a pair of shoes. What per cent of the original D dollars did she spend?

(A) 25%   (B) 40%   (C) 45%

(D) 47%   (E) 50%

I. 5. For which of the following lengths of a side of an equilateral triangle would the perimeter be divisible by both 3 and 7 ?

(A) 3   (B) 4   (C) 5   (D) 6   (E) 7

I. 6. The value of a certain car depreciates in such a way that its value at the end of each year is $\frac{3}{4}$ of its value at the beginning of the same year. If the initial value of the car is $4,000, what is its value at the end of 3 years?

(A) $2,312.50   (B) $1,900.00   (C) $1,687.50

(D) $1,343.50   (E) $1,000.00

I. 7. A man drove 100 miles in 2 hours and 27 minutes. Of the following, which is the closest approximation to his average speed in miles per hour?

(A) 41   (B) 39   (C) 38   (D) 37   (E) 33

I. 8. The difference between which of the following pairs of numbers is equal to 4 times their product?

(A) 1, $\frac{1}{5}$ (B) 1, $\frac{1}{4}$ (C) 1, $\frac{3}{4}$

(D) 1, $\frac{4}{5}$ (E) 1, 4

g	h
6	1
3	2
2	3
$\frac{3}{2}$	4

I. 9. According to the table above, g =

(A) $\frac{h}{6}$ (B) $\frac{2h}{3}$ (C) $\frac{6}{h}$ (D) h + 5   (E) 6h

GO ON TO THE NEXT PAGE.

I. 10. In a firm with 200 employees, 25 per cent are women. If the firm has 20 people in the drafting department of whom 85 per cent are women, what per cent of the men employed by the firm are in the drafting department?

(A) 1.5%   (B) 2.0%   (C) 2.5%
(D) 3.0%   (E) 15.0%

$\frac{2}{3}$

I. 11. If the area of the triangle above is 1, then h =

(A) $\frac{1}{3}$ (B) $\frac{2}{3}$ (C) $\frac{4}{3}$ (D) $\frac{3}{2}$ (E) 3

I. 12. At the end of its first year of operation, a business firm had an income of $10,000 and expenses of $60,000. Each year thereafter the firm's income tripled and its expenses doubled. For which year in the firm's history did the firm first show no annual deficit?

(A) Third
(B) Fourth
(C) Fifth
(D) Sixth
(E) Seventh

Model	Capacity	Watts
A	10,000 BTU/hr	1,765
B	10,000 BTU/hr	870

I. 13. The table above shows the capacity and wattage for two models of air conditioners. If it costs $70 to operate model A for 1,000 hours and if the rate per kilowatt hour is the same for the two models, approximately how much will it cost to operate model B for the same length of time?

(A) $30   (B) $35   (C) $40   (D) $60   (E) $140

I. 14. If P and Q are two points in a region R of the plane, then P is said to be in an R-neighborhood of Q if a circle can be drawn with center Q so that P is inside that circle and the circle is entirely inside R. For which of the following regions R is P in an R-neighborhood of Q?

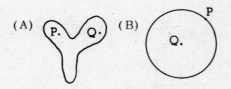

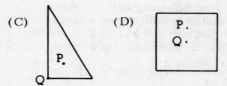

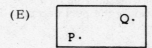

GO ON TO THE NEXT PAGE.

I. 15. If $P = \dfrac{S}{1 + nr}$ and P, S, n, and r are positive numbers, then in terms of P, S, and r what does n equal?

(A) $\dfrac{S - P}{Pr}$ (B) $\dfrac{S}{rP} - 1$ (C) $\dfrac{S - P}{r}$

(D) $\dfrac{S}{P} - r$ (E) $\dfrac{Pr}{S} - 1$

I. 16. Both the length and width of a certain rectangle are even numbers, and the length is three times the width. Each of the following could be the perimeter of such a rectangle EXCEPT

(A) 32   (B) 64   (C) 120   (D) 160   (E) 192

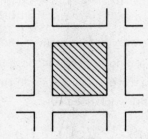

I. 17. The square plot of land represented by the shaded portion of the figure above has an area of 100 acres and is bounded by four roads. How many <u>square</u> lots, 1 acre in area and bordering on a road, can be made from this plot of land?

(A) 10   (B) 20   (C) 36   (D) 38   (E) 40

| 10 hectometers = 1 kilometer |
| 1 square hectometer = 1 hectare |
| 1 square kilometer = 0.386 square mile |

I. 18. According to the table above, how many square miles are there in 1 hectare?

(A) 386   (B) 38.6   (C) 3.86
(D) 0.0386   (E) 0.00386

I. 19. The average of the five numbers x, 417, 524, 630, and 950 is what per cent of the sum of the five numbers?

(A) 20%   (B) 22%   (C) 25%   (D) 30%

(E) It cannot be determined from the information given.

I. 20. If x is a real number such that $\dfrac{4}{3}x^4 = \dfrac{27}{4}$, then x is

(A) $\dfrac{9}{4}$ (B) $\dfrac{3}{2}$ (C) $\dfrac{9}{4}$ or $-\dfrac{9}{4}$

(D) $\sqrt{3}$ or $-\sqrt{3}$ (E) $\dfrac{3}{2}$ or $-\dfrac{3}{2}$

I. 21. A boy walking along a road at 3 kilometers per hour is overtaken by a truck traveling at 40 kilometers per hour. If the truck breaks down 1 kilometer beyond where it passes the boy, how many <u>minutes</u> after the breakdown does the boy reach the truck?

(A) $21\dfrac{1}{2}$ (B) 20   (C) $18\dfrac{34}{37}$

(D) $18\dfrac{26}{43}$ (E) $18\dfrac{1}{2}$

I. 22. On a certain assembly line, the rejection rate for Monday's production was 4 per cent, for Tuesday's 8 per cent, and for the two days combined 7 per cent. What was the ratio of Tuesday's production to Monday's production?

(A) $\dfrac{3}{1}$ (B) $\dfrac{2}{1}$ (C) $\dfrac{1}{1}$ (D) $\dfrac{1}{2}$ (E) $\dfrac{1}{3}$

GO ON TO THE NEXT PAGE.

I. 23. If x is the product of three consecutive positive integers, which of the following must be true?

    I. x is an integer multiple of 3.
    II. x is an integer multiple of 4.
    III. x is an integer multiple of 6.

(A) I only   (B) II only   (C) I and II only

(D) I and III only   (E) I, II, and III

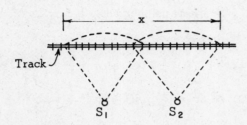

I. 24. In the figure above, two searchlights S_1 and S_2 are located 10,000 feet apart; each covers an area of radius 10,000 feet, and each is located 8,000 feet from the railroad track. To the nearest 1,000 feet, what is the total length x of track spanned by the searchlights?

(A) 24,000   (B) 22,000   (C) 20,000

(D) 16,000   (E) 12,000

I. 25. If $(x + 2)^2 = 9$ and $(y + 3)^2 = 25$, then the maximum value of $\frac{x}{y}$ is

(A) $\frac{5}{8}$ (B) 1   (C) 2   (D) $\frac{5}{2}$ (E) 5

I. 26. A number of tickets are divided evenly among n persons, $\frac{1}{6}$ of whom will not use them. If the total number of tickets were divided evenly among those who would use them, the increase in the share of each of these persons would be what fraction of his original share?

(A) $\frac{1}{6}$ (B) $\frac{1}{5}$ (C) $\frac{5}{6}$ (D) $\frac{6}{5}$ (E) $\frac{1}{5n}$

I. 27. In order to give his customers a 25 per cent discount on the price and still net a 25 per cent profit on the cost of an item, at what price should a merchant mark an item if it cost him $16.80 ?

(A) $21.00   (B) $21.90   (C) $25.20

(D) $26.25   (E) $28.00

I. 28. If P is a polygon with vertices on a circle of radius 1, which of the following must be true?

    I. The perimeter of P is less than 2π.
    II. The area of P is less than π.
    III. At least one side of P must be greater than 1.

(A) I only
(B) II only
(C) III only
(D) I and II only
(E) I, II, and III

I. 29. Typist Y can type a page in $\frac{2}{3}$ the time it takes X. Typist Z can do it in $\frac{3}{4}$ the time it takes Y. When all three are typing at the same time, what fraction of their total work does Y do?

(A) $\frac{8}{29}$ (B) $\frac{4}{13}$ (C) $\frac{1}{3}$ (D) $\frac{9}{23}$ (E) $\frac{1}{2}$

I. 30. What is the ratio of the area of a circle to the area of a right isosceles triangle inscribed in the circle?

(A) $\frac{3\pi}{2}$ (B) π (C) 2   (D) $\frac{\pi}{2}$ (E) 1

END OF SAMPLE TEST I

PROBLEM SOLVING SAMPLE TEST II

Time—40 minutes

30 Questions

<u>Directions:</u> In this section solve each problem, using any available space on the page for scratchwork. Then indicate the <u>best</u> answer in the appropriate space on the answer sheet.

Note: Figures which accompany problems in this test are intended to provide information useful in solving the problems. They are drawn as accurately as possible EXCEPT when it is stated in a specific problem that its figure is not drawn to scale. All figures lie in a plane unless otherwise indicated.

All numbers used are real numbers.

II. 1. A certain machine processes 6 photographs every 3 seconds. How many photographs can the machine process in 5 minutes?

(A) 120   (B) 150   (C) 200   (D) 600   (E) 1,800

II. 2. During a 1-cent sale Mr. Brown bought a comb for the usual price and a second comb for 1 cent. If he paid 30 cents for the 2 combs, the price of the second comb is what fraction of the price of the first comb?

(A) $\frac{1}{30}$ (B) $\frac{1}{29}$ (C) $\frac{1}{28}$ (D) $\frac{1}{15}$ (E) $\frac{1}{10}$

II. 3. If the rate of inflation for a particular year was 6 per cent, what was the rate of inflation for the month of October if it was twice the monthly average?

(A) 9%   (B) 6%   (C) 3%   (D) 1%   (E) 0.5%

II. 4. A certain type of concrete mixture is to be made of cement, sand, and gravel in a ratio $1:3:5$ by weight. What is the greatest number of kilograms of this mixture that can be made with 5 kilograms of cement?

(A) $13\frac{1}{3}$ (B) 15   (C) 25   (D) 40   (E) 45

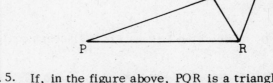

II. 5. If, in the figure above, PQR is a triangle, ∠P measures 20°, ∠PRS measures 60°, and ∠Q measures 50°, then what is the measure, in degrees, of ∠QRS ?

(A) 20   (B) 50   (C) 60   (D) 70   (E) 100

II. 6. The goods in a store were damaged by fire. The insurance company paid $18,750 for the loss, which was $\frac{2}{3}$ the amount for which the goods were insured. If the amount for which the goods were insured was $\frac{3}{4}$ the value of the inventory, what was the total value of the inventory?

(A) $9,375
(B) $16,667
(C) $18,750
(D) $21,094
(E) $37,500

GO ON TO THE NEXT PAGE.

II. 7. A beaker filled with liquid holds enough to exactly fill four size A test tubes or seven size B test tubes. If a size A test tube that is full is used to fill a size B test tube, what fraction of the liquid in the larger test tube will be left over?

(A) $\frac{3}{11}$ (B) $\frac{4}{11}$ (C) $\frac{3}{7}$ (D) $\frac{4}{7}$ (E) $\frac{7}{11}$

II. 8. In a group of 32 students, 20 are boys. If 22 of the students are seniors and if 3 girls in the group are not seniors, how many boys are seniors?

(A) 13   (B) 12   (C) 10   (D) 9

(E) It cannot be determined from the information given.

II. 9. If $x < 0$, which of the following is NOT necessarily true?

(A) $x^2 + x^3 < 0$ (B) $x^5 < x^2$ (C) $x^2 > 0$

(D) $\frac{1}{x} < 0$ (E) $\frac{1}{x^2} > 0$

II. 10. If 15 quarts of water evaporate from 60 quarts of a 3 per cent salt solution, what is the percentage of salt in the new solution?

(A) $3\frac{1}{2}\%$ (B) 4% (C) $4\frac{1}{2}\%$

(D) 5% (E) 6%

II. 11. On a certain test, the average grade for a class was 80. If 10 per cent of the class scored 95 and 20 per cent scored 90, what was the average grade for the remainder of the class?

(A) 65   (B) 70   (C) 72.5   (D) 75   (E) 80

II. 12. Of the following, which best approximates $\frac{(0.1667)(0.8333)(0.3333)}{(0.2222)(0.6667)(0.1250)}$?

(A) 2.00   (B) 2.40   (C) 2.43

(D) 2.50   (E) 3.43

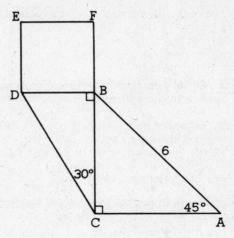

II. 13. In the figure above, what is the area of square DBFE ?

(A) 6   (B) 9   (C) $6\sqrt{2}$ (D) $6\sqrt{3}$

(E) It cannot be determined from the information given.

II. 14. When an object is dropped, the number of feet N that it falls is given by the formula $N = \frac{1}{2}gt^2$, where t is the time in seconds since it was dropped and g is 32.2. If it takes 5 seconds for the object to reach the ground, how many feet does it fall during the last 2 seconds?

(A) 64.4   (B) 96.6   (C) 161.0

(D) 257.6   (E) 402.5

II. 15. Two pipes A and B fill a swimming pool at constant rates of 10 gallons per minute and 15 gallons per minute, respectively. The pool can be filled in 60 hours, 40 hours, or 24 hours depending on whether pipe A alone, pipe B alone, or both pipes are used. If the pool is filled by using pipe B alone for half the time and both pipes for half the time, how many hours does it take to fill the pool?

(A) 15   (B) 30   (C) 38.7   (D) 42   (E) 50

GO ON TO THE NEXT PAGE.

II. 16. A salesman, whose commissions averaged $8,000 a year over a period of 20 years, earned 75 per cent or less of his average in 8 of those years. If his earnings in any one year did not exceed $13,000, what is the minimum number of years in which he <u>must</u> have earned <u>more</u> than $8,000 ?

(A) 1　(B) 4　(C) 5　(D) 8　(E) 9

II. 17. If a taxi driver charges x cents for the first quarter-mile of a trip and $\frac{x}{5}$ cents for each additional quarter-mile, what is the charge, in cents, for a trip whose distance in miles is the whole number y ?

(A) $\frac{x + xy}{125}$

(B) $\frac{4x + 4xy}{5}$

(C) $\frac{4x + xy}{500}$

(D) $\frac{4x + xy}{5}$

(E) $\frac{xy}{25}$

II. 18. A sum of money was invested at an annual simple interest rate of $3\frac{1}{2}$ per cent. At the end of 9 years, the amount was $8,613.25. How many dollars were invested?

(A) $4,675　(B) $5,000　(C) $6,550

(D) $6,725　(E) $7,500

II. 19. The weight of a container alone is 15 per cent of the weight of the container filled with a certain liquid. After some of the liquid has been removed, the weight of the container and the remaining liquid is 50 per cent of the original total weight. What fractional part of the liquid has been removed?

(A) $\frac{17}{20}$　(B) $\frac{10}{17}$　(C) $\frac{1}{2}$　(D) $\frac{7}{17}$　(E) $\frac{7}{20}$

II. 20. A certain car travels h miles on $\frac{p}{2}$ gallons of fuel. What is the total number of gallons of fuel that 5 such cars use if each car travels 250 miles?

(A) $\frac{125p}{h}$　(B) $\frac{625h}{p}$　(C) $\frac{625p}{h}$

(D) $\frac{1250p}{h}$　(E) $\frac{2500h}{p}$

II. 21. If the value of stock P is twice the average of 15 other stocks, what fraction of the total value of the 16 stocks is the value of stock P ?

(A) $\frac{1}{17}$　(B) $\frac{2}{17}$　(C) $\frac{1}{15}$　(D) $\frac{2}{15}$　(E) $\frac{3}{17}$

II. 22. A list of 18 different numbers is arranged from the least to the greatest. The average of the first n numbers in the list is x and the average of the remaining numbers is y. If the average of x and y is equal to the average of all 18 numbers, which of the following must be true?

(A) n = 1　(B) n = 9　(C) n = 17

(D) 1 < n < 9　(E) 9 < n < 17

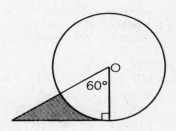

II. 23. In the figure above, if the circle with center O has radius 1, then the area of the shaded region is

(A) $\frac{\pi - \sqrt{3}}{2}$　(B) $\frac{6\sqrt{2} - \pi}{6}$　(C) $\frac{3\sqrt{2} - \pi}{2}$

(D) $\frac{\sqrt{3} - \pi}{2}$　(E) $\frac{3\sqrt{3} - \pi}{6}$

GO ON TO THE NEXT PAGE.

II. 24. A seesaw K feet long is supported at its center by a frame N feet high, where 2N is less than K. What is the greatest number of feet either end of the seesaw can rise above the ground?

(A) $\dfrac{K}{N}$ (B) N   (C) $\dfrac{K}{2}$ + N   (D) 2N   (E) KN

II. 25. If $1 < x < y < z$ and if $p = \dfrac{1}{x}$, $q = \dfrac{1}{\frac{1}{y}}$, and

$r = \dfrac{1}{\frac{1}{\frac{1}{z}}}$, then which of the following is true?

(A) $r < q < p$ (B) $p < q < r$ (C) $p < r < q$
(D) $q < r < p$ (E) $r < p < q$

II. 26. A, B, and C each drive 100-mile legs of a 300-mile course at speeds of 40, 50, and 60 miles per hour, respectively. What fraction of the total time does A drive?

(A) $\dfrac{15}{74}$ (B) $\dfrac{4}{15}$ (C) $\dfrac{15}{37}$ (D) $\dfrac{3}{5}$ (E) $\dfrac{5}{4}$

II. 27. An even number x divided by 7 gives some quotient plus a remainder of 6. Which of the following, when added to x, gives a sum which must be divisible by 14 ?

(A) 1   (B) 3   (C) 7   (D) 8   (E) 13

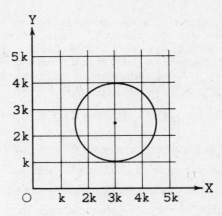

II. 28. If the area of the circle above is 64π, what is the value of k ?

(A) 2   (B) $\dfrac{8}{3}$ (C) 4   (D) $\dfrac{16}{3}$ (E) 12

II. 29. Abel owes Bob $4, Bob owes Charles $8, and Charles owes Abel a certain amount of money. If all three debts could be paid off by having Bob pay $1 to Abel and $3 to Charles, how many dollars does Charles owe Abel?

(A) 3   (B) 4   (C) 5   (D) 6   (E) 7

II. 30. The number of diagonals of a polygon of n sides is given by the formula $d = \dfrac{1}{2}n(n - 3)$. If a polygon has twice as many diagonals as sides, how many sides does it have?

(A) 3   (B) 5   (C) 6   (D) 7   (E) 8

END OF SAMPLE TEST II

PROBLEM SOLVING SAMPLE TEST III

Time—40 minutes

30 Questions

<u>Directions:</u> In this section solve each problem, using any available space on the page for scratchwork. Then indicate the <u>best</u> answer in the appropriate space on the answer sheet.

<u>Note:</u> Figures which accompany problems in this test are intended to provide information useful in solving the problems. They are drawn as accurately as possible EXCEPT when it is stated in a specific problem that its figure is not drawn to scale. All figures lie in a plane unless otherwise indicated.

All numbers used are real numbers.

III. 1. If $6x + 5 = 4x + 3$, then $x =$

(A) 5   (B) 4   (C) –1   (D) –2   (E) –3

III. 2. On the line segment RS above are 5 equally spaced dark segments, each with length 6. If x is the distance between dark segments and the length of RS is 42, then $x =$

(A) 2   (B) 3   (C) 6   (D) 12   (E) 30

III. 3. A crate of 96 oranges was opened and all but 24 oranges were sold. Which of the following must be true?

    I. Exactly $\frac{2}{3}$ of the oranges were sold.

    II. Fewer than 5 sales were made.

    III. More than 47 oranges were sold.

(A) None
(B) I only
(C) II only
(D) III only
(E) I and III

III. 4. There are 24 boys and 18 girls in a recreation program. Approximately what per cent of the children in the program are boys?

(A) 51%   (B) 54%   (C) 57%   (D) 60%   (E) 75%

III. 5. What are all real numbers x for which $(x - 3)^3 = 27$?

(A) 0   (B) 6   (C) 9

(D) 0 and 6   (E) 0 and 9

III. 6. $\dfrac{0.64}{0.005} \times \dfrac{0.125}{0.08} =$

(A)   2
(B)   20
(C)   200
(D) 2,000
(E) 20,000

III. 7. On a scale drawing, a rectangle 1 inch by $1\frac{1}{3}$ inches represents the floor of a room and the indicated scale is 1 inch equals 15 feet. How many square tiles 6 inches on a side will be needed to cover this floor?

(A) 40   (B) 70   (C) 120   (D) 700   (E) 1,200

III. 8. In 1970, Japan produced 20 per cent of the total world production of mineral K. If Japan produced 40 tons of mineral K, how many tons were produced by countries other than Japan?

(A) 32   (B) 120   (C) 140   (D) 160   (E) 200

GO ON TO THE NEXT PAGE.

III. 9. There are 4 card-processing machines in an office. The fastest of these machines processes x cards in 7 hours and the slowest processes x cards in 8 hours. Which of the following could NOT be the average time per machine for each of the 4 machines to process x cards?

(A) 7.2 (B) 7.3 (C) 7.5 (D) 7.6 (E) 7.7

III. 10. A certain organization has three committees. Only two persons are members of all three committees, but every pair of committees has three members in common. What is the LEAST possible number of members of any one committee?

(A) 4 (B) 5 (C) 6 (D) 7 (E) 8

III. 11. One bottle is half-full of oil and another bottle with twice the capacity is one-quarter full of oil. If water is added so that the bottles are full and the contents of both are then poured into a third bottle that is empty and large enough to hold the contents of both, what fraction of the contents in the third bottle is oil?

(A) $\frac{1}{4}$ (B) $\frac{1}{3}$ (C) $\frac{3}{8}$ (D) $\frac{2}{3}$ (E) $\frac{3}{4}$

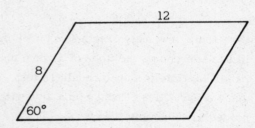

III. 12. In the figure above, the area of the parallelogram is

(A) 40 (B) $24\sqrt{3}$ (C) 72
(D) $48\sqrt{3}$ (E) 96

III. 13. How many prime numbers are integer multiples of 16 ?

(A) 0 (B) 1 (C) 2 (D) 4 (E) 16

III. 14. When a certain projector is 3 feet from the screen, the area of the picture on the screen is 6 square feet. If the projector is moved to a position n times as far away from the screen, then the picture will take up n^2 times as much space on the screen. When this projector is 5 feet from the screen, the area, in square feet, of the picture on the screen is

(A) $\frac{50}{3}$ (B) 24 (C) $\frac{100}{3}$ (D) 36 (E) 60

$$\begin{array}{r} 7\,3\,4 \\ 5\,\blacksquare\,8 \\ +\ 9\,\blacksquare\,2 \\ \hline 2,2\,\blacksquare\,4 \end{array}$$

III. 15. In the addition problem above, the number must be

(A) 5 (B) 6 (C) 7 (D) 8 (E) 9

III. 16. $\left(3 + \frac{1}{6}\right)^2 - 9 =$

(A) $\frac{1}{36}$ (B) $\frac{1}{6}$ (C) $\frac{19}{36}$ (D) $\frac{35}{36}$ (E) $\frac{37}{36}$

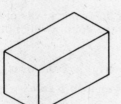

III. 17. If the length of each edge of the rectangular solid above is an integer, then the sum of the lengths of all the edges of the solid is necessarily divisible by which of the following?

(A) 3 (B) 4 (C) 5 (D) 7 (E) 11

III. 18. For the first 9 months of the year, a real estate investment trust reported earnings of $5.63 per share. The reported earnings per share for the third quarter were $2.21. If the number of shares listed did not change during the period, what were the average quarterly earnings for the first 2 quarters of the year?

(A) $1.71 (B) $1.88 (C) $2.81
(D) $3.42 (E) $3.92

GO ON TO THE NEXT PAGE.

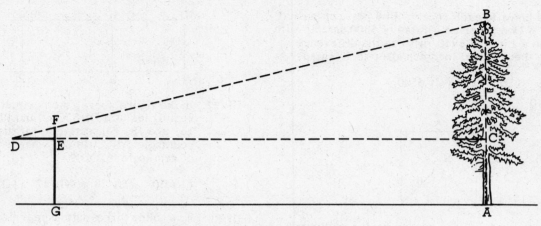

Note: Figure not drawn to scale.

III. 19. The height of a tree is measured by means of a cross-staff as shown in the figure above. The horizontal bar DE is adjusted up or down until points D, F, and B are in a straight line. Measured on level ground, DE is $1\frac{1}{2}$ feet, EF is $\frac{1}{2}$ foot, GE is 5 feet and GA is 60 feet. How tall is the tree?

(A) $20\frac{1}{2}$ ft.   (B) 22 ft.   (C) 24 ft.

(D) $25\frac{1}{2}$ ft.   (E) $26\frac{1}{2}$ ft.

III. 20. A man drove his automobile d_1 kilometers at the rate of r_1 kilometers per hour and an additional d_2 kilometers at the rate of r_2 kilometers per hour. In terms of d_1, d_2, r_1, and r_2, what was his average speed, in kilometers per hour, for the entire trip?

(A) $\dfrac{d_1 + d_2}{\dfrac{d_1}{r_1} + \dfrac{d_2}{r_2}}$

(B) $\dfrac{d_1 + d_2}{r_1 + r_2}$

(C) $\dfrac{\dfrac{d_1 + d_2}{r_1 + r_2}}{d_1 + d_2}$

(D) $\dfrac{\dfrac{d_1}{r_1} + \dfrac{d_2}{r_2}}{d_1 + d_2}$

(E) It cannot be determined from the information given.

III. 21. Printing press X can print an edition of a newspaper in 12 hours, whereas press Y can print the same edition in 18 hours. What is the total number of hours that it will take the two presses, working together but independently of one another, to print the same edition?

(A) 15   (B) 7.4   (C) 7.2   (D) 7.0   (E) 6.8

III. 22. If x is an integer and if $3 < x < 9$, $4 < x < 14$, $5 < x < 12$, and $7 < x < 16$, then x is

(A) 7   (B) 8   (C) 9   (D) 10   (E) 11

GO ON TO THE NEXT PAGE.

III. 23. Don and his wife each receive an 8 per cent annual raise. If Don receives a raise of $800 and his wife receives a raise of $840, what is the difference between their annual incomes after their raises?

(A) $40   (B) $460   (C) $500

(D) $540   (E) $580

III. 24. In the figure above, the square region is divided into four nonoverlapping triangular regions. If the area of the square region is 4, what is the sum of the perimeters of the four triangular regions?

(A) 8
(B) $8 + 4\sqrt{2}$
(C) 16
(D) $8 + 8\sqrt{2}$
(E) $16\sqrt{2}$

III. 25. If $\frac{1}{5}$ of the students in a class of 150 graduated with honors and $\frac{2}{3}$ of the students in the class were girls, what per cent of the girls in the class graduated with honors?

(A) 13%
(B) 20%
(C) 67%
(D) 87%
(E) It cannot be determined from the information given.

III. 26. In a student body the ratio of men to women was 1 to 4. After 140 additional men were admitted, the ratio of men to women became 2 to 3. How large was the student body after the additional men were admitted?

(A) 700   (B) 560   (C) 280   (D) 252   (E) 224

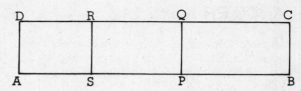

III. 27. In the figure above, the perimeters of the rectangles ASRD, SPQR, and PBCQ are 14, 16, and 18, respectively. If the perimeter of rectangle ABCD is 36, what is the perimeter of rectangle APQD ?

(A) 30   (B) 28   (C) 27   (D) 26   (E) 24

III. 28. How many three-digit numerals begin with a digit that represents a prime number and end with a digit that represents a prime number?

(A) 16   (B) 80   (C) 160   (D) 180   (E) 240

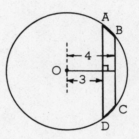

III. 29. The circle with center O in the figure above has radius 5. What is the area of the inscribed trapezoid ABCD ?

(A) $\frac{35}{2}$ (B) 14   (C) 10   (D) 7   (E) $\frac{7}{2}$

III. 30. A merchant sold two dresses for $24.00 each. He made a 25 per cent profit on one and lost 20 per cent on the other. What was his net gain or loss on the sale of the two dresses?

(A) $4.80 gain   (B) $1.20 gain   (C) $1.20 loss

(D) $4.80 loss   (E) $6.00 loss

END OF SAMPLE TEST III

ANSWER KEYS FOR SAMPLE TESTS

Answers followed by page numbers indicate questions discussed in detail in the explanatory material. These questions are used to illustrate kinds of problems common to the Problem Solving section of the GMAT. The page numbers indicate the pages on which the particular problems are discussed.

PROBLEM SOLVING

Sample Test I

I. 1 D	I.16 C (page 47)
I. 2 C	I.17 C
I. 3 C	I.18 E
I. 4 B (page 45)	I.19 A (page 43)
I. 5 E	I.20 E (page 45)
I. 6 C	I.21 E (page 43)
I. 7 A	I.22 A
I. 8 A	I.23 D (page 43)
I. 9 C	I.24 B (page 47)
I.10 B	I.25 A
I.11 E	I.26 B
I.12 D	I.27 E (page 44)
I.13 B	I.28 D
I.14 D	I.29 C
I.15 A (page 45)	I.30 B

Sample Test II

II. 1 D	II.16 B
II. 2 B	II.17 B (page 46)
II. 3 D	II.18 C
II. 4 E (page 44)	II.19 B
II. 5 B	II.20 C
II. 6 E	II.21 B
II. 7 C	II.22 B
II. 8 A	II.23 E
II. 9 A (page 46)	II.24 D
II.10 B	II.25 E
II.11 D	II.26 C (page 44)
II.12 D (page 44)	II.27 D (page 46)
II.13 A	II.28 D (page 48)
II.14 D (page 46)	II.29 C
II.15 B	II.30 D (page 48)

Sample Test III

III. 1 C	III.16 E
III. 2 B (page 46)	III.17 B
III. 3 D	III.18 A
III. 4 C	III.19 D
III. 5 B	III.20 A (page 47)
III. 6 C	III.21 C
III. 7 E	III.22 B
III. 8 D	III.23 D
III. 9 A (page 44)	III.24 D (page 48)
III.10 A (page 45)	III.25 E
III.11 B	III.26 B (page 47)
III.12 D (page 48)	III.27 E
III.13 A	III.28 C (page 45)
III.14 A	III.29 D
III.15 B (page 45)	III.30 C

EXPLANATORY MATERIAL: PROBLEM SOLVING

The following discussion is intended to familiarize you with the most efficient and effective approaches to the kinds of problems common to Problem Solving. The particular examples taken from the sample tests in this chapter are generally representative of the kinds of problems you will encounter in this section of the GMAT. Remember that it is the problem-solving strategy that is important, not the specific details of a particular problem. The explanations for Problem Solving problems are organized according to their content. Arithmetic problems are first, followed by algebra and geometry problems.

ARITHMETIC PROBLEMS

I.19 **The average of the five numbers x, 417, 524, 630, and 950 is what per cent of the sum of the five numbers?**

(A) 20%   **(B) 22%**   **(C) 25%**   **(D) 30%**
  (E) It cannot be determined from the information given.

The average of the five numbers is equal to one-fifth the sum of the five numbers: $\dfrac{x + 417 + 524 + 630 + 950}{5}$. One-fifth of the sum is equal to 20 percent of the sum and, therefore, the best answer is A. This is a moderately difficult question. (See Chapter II, Math Review, Section A.10.)

I.21 **A boy walking along a road at 3 kilometers per hour is overtaken by a truck traveling at 40 kilometers per hour. If the truck breaks down 1 kilometer beyond where it passes the boy, how many <u>minutes</u> after the breakdown does the boy reach the truck?**

(A) $21\dfrac{1}{2}$ **(B)** 20   **(C)** $18\dfrac{34}{37}$

(D) $18\dfrac{26}{43}$ **(E)** $18\dfrac{1}{2}$

The amount of time that it takes the boy to walk 1 kilometer is equal to $\dfrac{1 \text{ km}}{3 \text{ km/h}} = \dfrac{1}{3}$ hour or 20 minutes. The truck breaks down in $\dfrac{1 \text{ km}}{40 \text{ km/h}} = \dfrac{1}{40}$ hour or $1\dfrac{1}{2}$ minutes after it passes the boy. Therefore, the amount of time that elapses between when the truck breaks down and when the boy reaches the truck is $20 - 1\dfrac{1}{2} = 18\dfrac{1}{2}$ minutes, and the best answer is E. This is a difficult question. (See Chapter II, Math Review, Section D.1.)

I.23 **If x is the product of three consecutive positive integers, which of the following must be true?**

  I. x is an integer multiple of 3.
  II. x is an integer multiple of 4.
  III. x is an integer multiple of 6.

(A) I only   **(B) II only**   **(C) I and II only**
  (D) I and III only   **(E) I, II, and III**

For any three consecutive positive integers, one of the integers must be divisible by 3 and at least one of the integers must be divisible by 2 (e.g., 1, 2, 3; 9, 10, 11). Therefore, x must be a multiple of 3 and a multiple of 6. If two of the integers are even, then x must be a multiple of 4; however, if two of the integers are odd, x is not necessarily a multiple of 4. Therefore, the best answer is D. This is a moderately difficult question. (See Chapter II, Math Review, Section A.1.)

I.27 In order to give his customers a 25 per cent discount on the price and still net a 25 per cent profit on the cost of an item, at what price should a merchant mark an item if it cost him $16.80?

(A) $21.00   (B) $21.90   (C) $25.20
(D) $26.25   (E) $28.00

Remember that profit = selling price − cost. Here the profit, which is 25 percent of the cost, is equal to 0.25($16.80) = $4.20. The selling price after the 25 percent discount must be $16.80 + $4.20 = $21.00. Therefore, the price before the discount is $\frac{\$21}{0.75}$ = $28 (the price with the 25 percent discount is equal to 75 percent of the price before the discount) and the best answer is E. This is a difficult question. (See Chapter II, Math Review, Section A.7 and Section D.6.)

II.4 A certain type of concrete mixture is to be made of cement, sand, and gravel in a ratio 1:3:5 by weight. What is the greatest number of kilograms of this mixture that can be made with 5 kilograms of cement?

(A) $13\frac{1}{3}$ (B) 15   (C) 25   (D) 40   (E) 45

In the concrete mixture, 3 times as much sand as cement, or 15 kilograms of sand, is needed and 5 times as much gravel as cement, or 25 kilograms of gravel, is needed. The total weight of the mixture with 5 kilograms of cement would be 5 + 15 + 25 = 45 kilograms. Thus, the best answer is E. This is an easy question. (See Chapter II, Math Review, Section A.6.)

II.12 Of the following, which best approximates

$$\frac{(0.1667)(0.8333)(0.3333)}{(0.2222)(0.6667)(0.1250)}?$$

(A) 2.00   (B) 2.40   (C) 2.43
(D) 2.50   (E) 3.43

One way to approach this question is to recognize that the decimals in the expression are approximations of fractions. For example, 0.3333 is approximately $\frac{1}{3}$, and 0.1667, which is half of 0.3333, is approximately $\frac{1}{6}$. Thus the expression is approximately equal to $\dfrac{\left(\frac{1}{6}\right)\left(\frac{5}{6}\right)\left(\frac{1}{3}\right)}{\left(\frac{2}{9}\right)\left(\frac{2}{3}\right)\left(\frac{1}{8}\right)}$.

This fractional expression can be rewritten as

$$\left(\frac{1}{6}\right)\left(\frac{5}{6}\right)\left(\frac{1}{3}\right)\left(\frac{9}{2}\right)\left(\frac{3}{2}\right)\left(\frac{8}{1}\right).$$

(Dividing by a fraction is the same as multiplying by its reciprocal.) It is not necessary to multiply all numbers in this expression. Common factors in the numerator and denominator can be canceled:

$$\left(\frac{1}{\cancel{6}}\right)\left(\frac{5}{\cancel{6}}\right)\left(\frac{1}{\cancel{3}}\right)\left(\frac{\cancel{9}}{2}\right)\left(\frac{\cancel{3}}{\cancel{2}}\right)\left(\frac{\cancel{8}}{1}\right) = \frac{5}{2} = 2.5$$

Thus 2.50 best approximates the expression, and the best answer is D. This is a difficult question. (See Chapter II, Math Review, Section A.2 and Section A.3.)

II.26 A, B, and C each drive 100-mile legs of a 300-mile course at speeds of 40, 50, and 60 miles per hour, respectively. What fraction of the total time does A drive?

(A) $\frac{15}{74}$ (B) $\frac{4}{15}$ (C) $\frac{15}{37}$ (D) $\frac{3}{5}$ (E) $\frac{5}{4}$

The amount of time that A, B, and C each drove is $\frac{100}{40} = \frac{5}{2}$ hours, $\frac{100}{50} = 2$ hours, and $\frac{100}{60} = \frac{5}{3}$ hours, respectively. A drove $\dfrac{\frac{5}{2}}{\frac{5}{2} + 2 + \frac{5}{3}}$ of the total time.

$$\frac{\frac{5}{2}}{\frac{5}{2} + 2 + \frac{5}{3}} = \frac{\frac{5}{2}}{\frac{15 + 12 + 10}{6}} = \frac{5 \cdot 6}{2(37)} = \frac{15}{37}.$$

Thus, the best answer is C. This is a moderately difficult question. (See Chapter II, Math Review, Section D.1.)

III.9 There are 4 card-processing machines in an office. The fastest of these machines processes x cards in 7 hours and the slowest processes x cards in 8 hours. Which of the following could NOT be the average time per machine for each of the 4 machines to process x cards?

(A) 7.2   (B) 7.3   (C) 7.5   (D) 7.6   (E) 7.7

The total amount of time for the 4 machines to process x cards each is greater than or equal to 7 + 8 + 2(7) = 29 (the time it would take if the other 2 machines were as fast as the fastest) and less than 7 + 8 + 2(8) = 31 (the time it would take if the other 2 were as slow as the slowest). Therefore, the average time per machine is between $\frac{29}{4} = 7.25$ and $\frac{31}{4} = 7.75$, inclusive. Since 7.2 is less than 7.25, the average time could not be 7.2; thus, the best answer is A. This is a moderately difficult question. (See Chapter II, Math Review, Section A.10.)

III.10 A certain organization has three committees. Only two persons are members of all three committees, but every pair of committees has three members in common. What is the LEAST possible number of members of any <u>one</u> committee?

(A) 4   (B) 5   (C) 6   (D) 7   (E) 8

It is helpful to draw a diagram of the members on each committee. Let A and B be the members on all three committees.

I	II	III
AB	AB	AB

Let C be the third member common to I and II. C cannot be on III also, since that would give three members on all three committees; therefore, a third member common to II and III, D, is needed.

I	II	III
ABC	ABCD	ABD

D cannot be on I also, so a third member common to I and III, E, is needed.

I	II	III
ABCE	ABCD	ABDE

Every pair of committees has three members in common and the least possible number of members is four. Thus, the best answer is A. This is a moderately difficult question. (See Chapter II, Math Review, Section D.7.)

III.15
```
      734
      5 8
    + 9 2
    ─────
    2,2 4
```

In the addition problem above, the number ▨ must be

(A) 5   (B) 6   (C) 7   (D) 8   (E) 9

Note that a 1 is carried from the units' column to the tens' column and a 1 is also carried from the tens' column to the hundreds' column. Therefore, $4 + ▨ + ▨ = 10 + ▨$ or $▨ = 6$. Thus, the best answer is B. This is an easy question. (See Chapter II, Math Review, Section A.3.)

III.28 How many three-digit numerals begin with a digit that represents a prime number and end with a digit that represents a prime number?

(A) 16   (B) 80   (C) 160   (D) 180   (E) 240

The prime numbers that are digits are 2,3,5, and 7. There are 10 three-digit numerals that begin with 2 and end with 2 (202, 212, 222, . . ., 292) or a total of 40 that begin with 2 and end in a prime digit. There are also 40 such numerals beginning with each of the digits 3,5, and 7. Thus, the total number of three-digit numerals that begin and end with a digit that represents a prime number is $4(40) = 160$ and the best answer is C. This is a very difficult question. (See Chapter II, Math Review, Section A.1.)

ALGEBRA PROBLEMS

I.4 Audrey went shopping with D dollars. She spent 20 per cent of her money on a blouse and 25 per cent of what was left on a pair of shoes. What per cent of the original D dollars did she spend?

(A) 25%   (B) 40%   (C) 45%
(D) 47%   (E) 50%

Audrey spent 0.2D on the blouse and $0.25(1-0.2)D = 0.2D$ on the shoes. The total amount that she spent was 0.4D or 40% of the original D dollars. Thus, the best answer is B. This is an easy question. (See Chapter II, Math Review, Section A.7 and Section B, introduction.)

I.15 If $P = \dfrac{S}{1 + nr}$ and P, S, n, and r are positive numbers, then in terms of P, S, and r what does n equal?

(A) $\dfrac{S - P}{Pr}$ (B) $\dfrac{S}{rP} - 1$ (C) $\dfrac{S - P}{r}$

(D) $\dfrac{S}{P} - r$ (E) $\dfrac{Pr}{S} - 1$

To find the value of n in terms of P, S, and r, it is necessary to get n by itself on one side of the equation. The following algebraic manipulations can be done:

$P(1 + nr) = S$ (multiplying both sides by $1 + nr$)

$1 + nr = \dfrac{S}{P}$ (dividing by P)

$nr = \dfrac{S}{P} - 1 = \dfrac{S-P}{P}$ (subtracting 1 and getting a common denominator)

$n = \dfrac{S-P}{Pr}$ (dividing by r)

Therefore, the best answer is A. This is a moderately difficult question. (See Chapter II, Math Review, Section B.3.)

I.20 If x is a real number such that $\dfrac{4}{3}x^4 = \dfrac{27}{4}$, then x is

(A) $\dfrac{9}{4}$ (B) $\dfrac{3}{2}$ (C) $\dfrac{9}{4}$ or $-\dfrac{9}{4}$

(D) $\sqrt{3}$ or $-\sqrt{3}$ (E) $\dfrac{3}{2}$ or $-\dfrac{3}{2}$

If $\dfrac{4}{3}x^4 = \dfrac{27}{4}$, then $x^4 = \dfrac{27}{4} \cdot \dfrac{3}{4} = \dfrac{81}{16}$. To find the value of x, it is necessary to take the fourth root of $\dfrac{81}{16}$. This is the number that when raised to the fourth power is equal to $\dfrac{81}{16}$. Since $\dfrac{81}{16} = \left(\dfrac{3}{2}\right)\left(\dfrac{3}{2}\right)\left(\dfrac{3}{2}\right)\left(\dfrac{3}{2}\right) = \left(-\dfrac{3}{2}\right)\left(-\dfrac{3}{2}\right)\left(-\dfrac{3}{2}\right)\left(-\dfrac{3}{2}\right)$, the fourth roots of $\dfrac{81}{16}$ are $\dfrac{3}{2}$ and $-\dfrac{3}{2}$. Thus, the best answer is E.

Note that if the question asked for $\sqrt[4]{\frac{81}{16}}$, the best answer would be $\frac{3}{2}$ since $\sqrt[4]{x}$ denotes the positive fourth root of x. This is a moderately difficult question. (See Chapter II, Math Review, Section A.9 and Section B.6.)

II.9 **If x < 0, which of the following is NOT necessarily true?**

(A) $x^2 + x^3 < 0$ (B) $x^5 < x^2$ (C) $x^2 > 0$

(D) $\frac{1}{x} < 0$ (E) $\frac{1}{x^2} > 0$

In this question, the answer must be found by examining the choices. If x < 0, then x raised to an even integer power is positive and x raised to an odd integer power is negative. In A, then, $x^2 > 0$ and $x^3 < 0$; however, if $x = -\frac{1}{2}$,

$$x^2 + x^3 = \frac{1}{4} - \frac{1}{8} > 0.$$

Thus, A is not necessarily true, and the best answer is A. It can be shown as follows that the others must be true, but once you find a correct choice, you do not need to spend time verifying the others. Since $x^5 < 0$ and $x^2 > 0$, $x^5 < x^2$ and thus B and C are true. $\frac{1}{x}$ is negative since x is negative and $\frac{1}{x^2}$ is positive since x^2 is positive and D and E must also be true. This is a moderately difficult question. (See Chapter II, Math Review, Section A.5, Section A.9, and Section B.6.)

II.14 **When an object is dropped, the number of feet N that it falls is given by the formula $N = \frac{1}{2}gt^2$, where t is the time in seconds since it was dropped and g is 32.2. If it takes 5 seconds for the object to reach the ground, how many feet does it fall during the last 2 seconds?**

(A) 64.4   (B) 96.6   (C) 161.0
(D) 257.6   (E) 402.5

If it takes 5 seconds for the object to reach the ground, then by substituting 5 into the formula, you can find that it is dropped from a distance of $\frac{1}{2}(32.2)25 = 402.5$ feet above the ground.

Similarly, in the first 3 seconds the object falls $\frac{1}{2}(32.2)9 = 144.9$ feet. Therefore, in the last 2 seconds the object falls $402.5 - 144.9 = 257.6$ feet, and the best answer is D. This is a difficult question. (See Chapter II, Math Review, Section B.2.)

II.17 **If a taxi driver charges x cents for the first quarter-mile of a trip and $\frac{x}{5}$ cents for each additional quarter-mile, what is the charge, in cents, for a trip whose distance in miles is the whole number y?**

(A) $\frac{x + xy}{125}$ (B) $\frac{4x + 4xy}{5}$ (C) $\frac{4x + xy}{500}$

(D) $\frac{4x + xy}{5}$ (E) $\frac{xy}{25}$

The total number of quarter-miles in the trip is 4y. The charge for the first quarter-mile is x, and the charge for the remaining (4y − 1) quarter-miles is $(4y - 1)\frac{x}{5}$. The total charge for the trip is $x + \frac{4xy - x}{5} = \frac{5x + 4xy - x}{5} = \frac{4x + 4xy}{5}$.

The best answer is B. This is a difficult question. (See Chapter II, Math Review, Section B.2 and Section D.1.)

II.27 **An even number x divided by 7 gives some quotient plus a remainder of 6. Which of the following, when added to x, gives a sum which must be divisible by 14?**

(A) 1   (B) 3   (C) 7   (D) 8   (E) 13

The number x can be expressed as $x = 7q + 6$, where q is an integer. If the sum of x and another number is to be divisible by 14, then the sum must be even and the number added to x must also be even. The only even number given in the choices is 8. It can be shown as follows that x + 8 is divisible by 7.

$$x + 8 = 7q + 6 + 8$$
$$= 7q + 14$$
$$= 7(q + 2)$$

Thus, if x + 8 is divisible by 2 and by 7, it is also divisible by 14 and the best answer is D. This is a moderately difficult question. (See Chapter II, Math Review, Section A.1 and Section B.2.)

III.2

On the line segment RS above are 5 equally spaced dark segments, each with length 6. If x is the distance between dark segments and the length of RS is 42, then x =

(A) 2   (B) 3   (C) 6   (D) 12   (E) 30

The length of RS is equal to 42, which is equal to 5(6) + 4x. Thus, 4x = 12 and x is 3. The best answer is B. This is a very easy question. (See Chapter II, Math Review, Section B.3.)

III.20 A man drove his automobile d_1 kilometers at the rate of r_1 kilometers per hour and an additional d_2 kilometers at the rate of r_2 kilometers per hour. In terms of d_1, d_2, r_1, and r_2, what was his average speed, in kilometers per hour, for the entire trip?

(A) $\dfrac{d_1 + d_2}{\dfrac{d_1}{r_1} + \dfrac{d_2}{r_2}}$ (B) $\dfrac{d_1 + d_2}{r_1 + r_2}$

(C) $\dfrac{\dfrac{d_1 + d_2}{r_1 + r_2}}{d_1 + d_2}$ (D) $\dfrac{\dfrac{d_1}{r_1} + \dfrac{d_2}{r_2}}{d_1 + d_2}$

(E) It cannot be determined from the information given.

The average speed for the entire trip is equal to the total distance driven divided by the total time. The total distance driven is $d_1 + d_2$. Since rate $\times$ time = distance, time $= \dfrac{\text{distance}}{\text{rate}}$ and the total time is equal to $\dfrac{d_1}{r_1} + \dfrac{d_2}{r_2}$. Therefore, the average speed is $\dfrac{d_1 + d_2}{\dfrac{d_1}{r_1} + \dfrac{d_2}{r_2}}$ and the best answer is A. This is a difficult question. (See Chapter II, Math Review, Section D.1.)

III.26 In a student body the ratio of men to women was 1 to 4. After 140 additional men were admitted, the ratio of men to women became 2 to 3. How large was the student body _after_ the additional men were admitted?

(A) 700   (B) 560   (C) 280   (D) 252   (E) 224

Let m equal the original number of men; then 4m is the number of women. After 140 additional men are admitted, the ratio is 2:3, i.e., $\dfrac{m + 140}{4m} = \dfrac{2}{3}$. Cross multiplication results in the equation

$$3m + 420 = 8m$$
$$5m = 420$$
$$m = 84$$

The total number of students after the additional men were admitted is $m + 140 + 4m = 84 + 140 + 4(84) = 560$, and the best answer is B. This is a difficult question. (See Chapter II, Math Review, Section A.6 and Section B.3.)

GEOMETRY PROBLEMS

I.16 Both the length and width of a certain rectangle are even numbers, and the length is three times the width. Each of the following could be the perimeter of such a rectangle EXCEPT

(A) 32   (B) 64   (C) 120   (D) 160   (E) 192

If w is the width of the rectangle and 3w is its length, then the perimeter is 8w. Since w is even, the perimeter divided by 8 must be an even number. Dividing each of the given perimeters

by 8, you get an even number for all except C, $\dfrac{120}{8} = 15$. Thus, the best answer is C. This is a moderately difficult question. (See Chapter II, Math Review, Section C.7.)

I.24

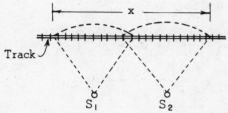

In the figure above, two searchlights S_1 and S_2 are located 10,000 feet apart; each covers an area of radius 10,000 feet, and each is located 8,000 feet from the railroad track. To the nearest 1,000 feet, what is the total length x of track spanned by the searchlights?

(A) 24,000   (B) 22,000   (C) 20,000
(D) 16,000   (E) 12,000

It is helpful to label the known distances on the figure.

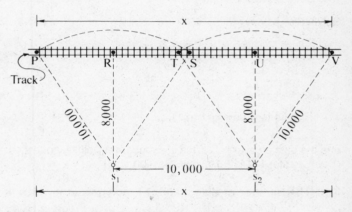

Using the Pythagorean theorem, you find that
$$(PR)^2 + (8{,}000)^2 = (10{,}000)^2$$

and get PR = RS = TU = UV = 6,000. Therefore, x is equal to PR + 10,000 + UV = 22,000, and the best answer is B. This is a difficult question. (See Chapter II, Math Review, Section C.6.)

II.28

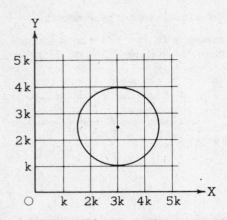

If the area of the circle above is 64π, what is the value of k?

(A) 2   (B) $\frac{8}{3}$ (C) 4   (D) $\frac{16}{3}$ (E) 12

Since the diameter of the circle is 4k − k = 3k, the radius in terms of k is $\frac{3}{2}$k; therefore, the area of the circle is

$$\pi\left(\frac{3}{2}k\right)^2 = 64\pi.$$

Solving for k, you get

$$\frac{9}{4}k^2 = 64$$

$$k^2 = \frac{256}{9}$$

$$k = \frac{16}{3}$$

and the best answer is D. This is a moderately difficult question. (See Chapter II, Math Review, Section C.8.)

II.30 The number of diagonals of a polygon of n sides is given by the formula d = $\frac{1}{2}$n(n − 3). If a polygon has twice as many diagonals as sides, how many sides does it have?

(A) 3   (B) 5   (C) 6   (D) 7   (E) 8

You want d to equal 2n or

$$\frac{1}{2}n(n - 3) = 2n$$

$$n^2 - 3n = 4n$$

$$n^2 = 7n$$

$$n = 7 \text{ since } n \neq 0.$$

Thus, the best answer is D. This is a difficult question. (See Chapter II, Math Review, Section B.2 and Section C.5.)

III.12

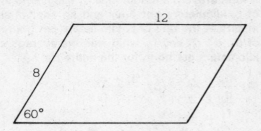

In the figure above, the area of the parallelogram is

(A) 40   (B) 24√3   (C) 72
(D) 48√3   (E) 96

The area of a parallelogram is equal to altitude × base. It is helpful to draw in an altitude:

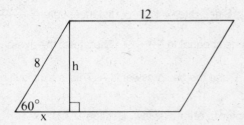

Since the triangle formed is a 30° − 60° − 90° triangle, x = 4 and h = 4√3. Thus, the area of the parallelogram is (4 √3)(12) = 48 √3, and the best answer is D. This is a difficult question. (See Chapter II, Math Review, Section C.6 and Section C.7.)

III.24

In the figure above, the square region is divided into four nonoverlapping triangular regions. If the area of the square region is 4, what is the sum of the perimeters of the four triangular regions?

(A) 8   (B) 8 + 4√2   (C) 16
(D) 8 + 8√2   (E) 16√2

If the area of the square region is 4, then each side of the square has length 2, and each diagonal has length 2√2. The lengths of the sides of each triangle are 2, √2, and √2, and the perimeter of each triangle is 2 + √2 + √2. Therefore, the sum of the four perimeters is equal to 4(2 + 2√2) = 8 + 8√2, and the best answer is D. This is a difficult question. (See Chapter II, Math Review, Section C.6 and Section C.7.)

IV Data Sufficiency

In this section of the GMAT, you are to classify each problem according to the five fixed answer choices, rather than find a solution to the problem. Each problem consists of a question and two statements. You are to decide whether the information in each statement alone is sufficient to answer the question or, if neither is, whether the information in the two statements together is sufficient.

The following pages include test-taking strategies, sample tests (with answer keys), and detailed explanations of selected problems from the sample tests. These explanations present possible problem-solving strategies for the examples. At the end of each explanation is a reference to the particular section(s) of Chapter II, Math Review, that you may find helpful in reviewing the mathematical concepts on which the problem is based. The sample problems are organized according to their content: arithmetic problems are first, followed by algebra and geometry problems.

TEST-TAKING STRATEGIES FOR DATA SUFFICIENCY

1. Do not waste valuable time solving a problem; you are only to determine whether sufficient information is given to solve the problem. After you have considered statement (1), make a check mark next to (1) if you can determine the answer and a cross mark if you cannot. Be sure to disregard all the information learned from statement (1) while considering statement (2). This is very difficult to do and often results in erroneously choosing answer C when the answer should be B or choosing B when the answer should be C. Suppose statement (2) alone is sufficient. Then a check mark next to (1) indicates that D is the correct answer; a cross mark next to (1) indicates that B is correct. Suppose statement (2) alone is not sufficient. A check mark next to (1) indicates that A is the correct answer; a cross mark next to (1) indicates that you must now consider whether the two statements taken together give sufficient information; if they do, the answer is C; if not, the answer is E.

2. If you determine that the information in statement (1) is sufficient to answer the question, the answer is necessarily either A or D. If you are not sure about statement (1) but you know that statement (2) alone is sufficient, the answer is necessarily either B or D. If neither statement taken alone is sufficient, the answer is either C or E. Thus, if you have doubts about certain portions of the information given but are relatively sure about other portions, you can logically eliminate two or three options and more than double your chances of guessing correctly.

3. Remember that when you are determining whether there is sufficient information to answer a question of the form, "What is the value of y?" the information given must be sufficient to find one and only one value for y. Being able to determine minimum or maximum values or an answer of the form $y = x + 2$ is not sufficient, because such answers constitute a range of values rather than "the value of y."

4. When geometric figures are involved, be very careful not to make unwarranted assumptions based on the figures. A triangle may appear to be isosceles, but can you detect the difference in the lengths of segments 1.8 inches long and 1.85 inches long? Furthermore, the figures are not necessarily drawn to scale; they are generalized figures showing little more than intersecting line segments and the betweenness of points, angles, and regions.

When you take the sample tests, use the answer spaces on the following page to mark your answers.

Answer Spaces for Sample Test I

1 Ⓐ Ⓑ Ⓒ Ⓓ Ⓔ   11 Ⓐ Ⓑ Ⓒ Ⓓ Ⓔ   21 Ⓐ Ⓑ Ⓒ Ⓓ Ⓔ
2 Ⓐ Ⓑ Ⓒ Ⓓ Ⓔ   12 Ⓐ Ⓑ Ⓒ Ⓓ Ⓔ   22 Ⓐ Ⓑ Ⓒ Ⓓ Ⓔ
3 Ⓐ Ⓑ Ⓒ Ⓓ Ⓔ   13 Ⓐ Ⓑ Ⓒ Ⓓ Ⓔ   23 Ⓐ Ⓑ Ⓒ Ⓓ Ⓔ
4 Ⓐ Ⓑ Ⓒ Ⓓ Ⓔ   14 Ⓐ Ⓑ Ⓒ Ⓓ Ⓔ   24 Ⓐ Ⓑ Ⓒ Ⓓ Ⓔ
5 Ⓐ Ⓑ Ⓒ Ⓓ Ⓔ   15 Ⓐ Ⓑ Ⓒ Ⓓ Ⓔ   25 Ⓐ Ⓑ Ⓒ Ⓓ Ⓔ
6 Ⓐ Ⓑ Ⓒ Ⓓ Ⓔ   16 Ⓐ Ⓑ Ⓒ Ⓓ Ⓔ   26 Ⓐ Ⓑ Ⓒ Ⓓ Ⓔ
7 Ⓐ Ⓑ Ⓒ Ⓓ Ⓔ   17 Ⓐ Ⓑ Ⓒ Ⓓ Ⓔ   27 Ⓐ Ⓑ Ⓒ Ⓓ Ⓔ
8 Ⓐ Ⓑ Ⓒ Ⓓ Ⓔ   18 Ⓐ Ⓑ Ⓒ Ⓓ Ⓔ   28 Ⓐ Ⓑ Ⓒ Ⓓ Ⓔ
9 Ⓐ Ⓑ Ⓒ Ⓓ Ⓔ   19 Ⓐ Ⓑ Ⓒ Ⓓ Ⓔ   29 Ⓐ Ⓑ Ⓒ Ⓓ Ⓔ
10 Ⓐ Ⓑ Ⓒ Ⓓ Ⓔ   20 Ⓐ Ⓑ Ⓒ Ⓓ Ⓔ   30 Ⓐ Ⓑ Ⓒ Ⓓ Ⓔ

Answer Spaces for Sample Test II

1 Ⓐ Ⓑ Ⓒ Ⓓ Ⓔ   11 Ⓐ Ⓑ Ⓒ Ⓓ Ⓔ   21 Ⓐ Ⓑ Ⓒ Ⓓ Ⓔ
2 Ⓐ Ⓑ Ⓒ Ⓓ Ⓔ   12 Ⓐ Ⓑ Ⓒ Ⓓ Ⓔ   22 Ⓐ Ⓑ Ⓒ Ⓓ Ⓔ
3 Ⓐ Ⓑ Ⓒ Ⓓ Ⓔ   13 Ⓐ Ⓑ Ⓒ Ⓓ Ⓔ   23 Ⓐ Ⓑ Ⓒ Ⓓ Ⓔ
4 Ⓐ Ⓑ Ⓒ Ⓓ Ⓔ   14 Ⓐ Ⓑ Ⓒ Ⓓ Ⓔ   24 Ⓐ Ⓑ Ⓒ Ⓓ Ⓔ
5 Ⓐ Ⓑ Ⓒ Ⓓ Ⓔ   15 Ⓐ Ⓑ Ⓒ Ⓓ Ⓔ   25 Ⓐ Ⓑ Ⓒ Ⓓ Ⓔ
6 Ⓐ Ⓑ Ⓒ Ⓓ Ⓔ   16 Ⓐ Ⓑ Ⓒ Ⓓ Ⓔ   26 Ⓐ Ⓑ Ⓒ Ⓓ Ⓔ
7 Ⓐ Ⓑ Ⓒ Ⓓ Ⓔ   17 Ⓐ Ⓑ Ⓒ Ⓓ Ⓔ   27 Ⓐ Ⓑ Ⓒ Ⓓ Ⓔ
8 Ⓐ Ⓑ Ⓒ Ⓓ Ⓔ   18 Ⓐ Ⓑ Ⓒ Ⓓ Ⓔ   28 Ⓐ Ⓑ Ⓒ Ⓓ Ⓔ
9 Ⓐ Ⓑ Ⓒ Ⓓ Ⓔ   19 Ⓐ Ⓑ Ⓒ Ⓓ Ⓔ   29 Ⓐ Ⓑ Ⓒ Ⓓ Ⓔ
10 Ⓐ Ⓑ Ⓒ Ⓓ Ⓔ   20 Ⓐ Ⓑ Ⓒ Ⓓ Ⓔ   30 Ⓐ Ⓑ Ⓒ Ⓓ Ⓔ

Answer Spaces for Sample Test III

1 Ⓐ Ⓑ Ⓒ Ⓓ Ⓔ   11 Ⓐ Ⓑ Ⓒ Ⓓ Ⓔ   21 Ⓐ Ⓑ Ⓒ Ⓓ Ⓔ
2 Ⓐ Ⓑ Ⓒ Ⓓ Ⓔ   12 Ⓐ Ⓑ Ⓒ Ⓓ Ⓔ   22 Ⓐ Ⓑ Ⓒ Ⓓ Ⓔ
3 Ⓐ Ⓑ Ⓒ Ⓓ Ⓔ   13 Ⓐ Ⓑ Ⓒ Ⓓ Ⓔ   23 Ⓐ Ⓑ Ⓒ Ⓓ Ⓔ
4 Ⓐ Ⓑ Ⓒ Ⓓ Ⓔ   14 Ⓐ Ⓑ Ⓒ Ⓓ Ⓔ   24 Ⓐ Ⓑ Ⓒ Ⓓ Ⓔ
5 Ⓐ Ⓑ Ⓒ Ⓓ Ⓔ   15 Ⓐ Ⓑ Ⓒ Ⓓ Ⓔ   25 Ⓐ Ⓑ Ⓒ Ⓓ Ⓔ
6 Ⓐ Ⓑ Ⓒ Ⓓ Ⓔ   16 Ⓐ Ⓑ Ⓒ Ⓓ Ⓔ   26 Ⓐ Ⓑ Ⓒ Ⓓ Ⓔ
7 Ⓐ Ⓑ Ⓒ Ⓓ Ⓔ   17 Ⓐ Ⓑ Ⓒ Ⓓ Ⓔ   27 Ⓐ Ⓑ Ⓒ Ⓓ Ⓔ
8 Ⓐ Ⓑ Ⓒ Ⓓ Ⓔ   18 Ⓐ Ⓑ Ⓒ Ⓓ Ⓔ   28 Ⓐ Ⓑ Ⓒ Ⓓ Ⓔ
9 Ⓐ Ⓑ Ⓒ Ⓓ Ⓔ   19 Ⓐ Ⓑ Ⓒ Ⓓ Ⓔ   29 Ⓐ Ⓑ Ⓒ Ⓓ Ⓔ
10 Ⓐ Ⓑ Ⓒ Ⓓ Ⓔ   20 Ⓐ Ⓑ Ⓒ Ⓓ Ⓔ   30 Ⓐ Ⓑ Ⓒ Ⓓ Ⓔ

DATA SUFFICIENCY SAMPLE TEST I

Time—30 minutes

30 Questions

<u>Directions</u>: Each of the data sufficiency problems below consists of a question and two statements, labeled (1) and (2), in which certain data are given. You have to decide whether the data given in the statements are <u>sufficient</u> for answering the question. Using the data given in the statements <u>plus</u> your knowledge of mathematics and everyday facts (such as the number of days in July or the meaning of <u>counterclockwise</u>), you are to blacken space

    A if statement (1) ALONE is sufficient, but statement (2) alone is not sufficient to answer the question asked;

    B if statement (2) ALONE is sufficient, but statement (1) alone is not sufficient to answer the question asked;

    C if BOTH statements (1) and (2) TOGETHER are sufficient to answer the question asked, but NEITHER statement ALONE is sufficient;

    D if EACH statement ALONE is sufficient to answer the question asked;

    E if statements (1) and (2) TOGETHER are NOT sufficient to answer the question asked, and additional data specific to the problem are needed.

<u>Note</u>: A figure in a data sufficiency problem will conform to the information given in the question, but will not necessarily conform to the additional information given in statements (1) and (2). All figures lie in a plane unless otherwise indicated.

<u>Example:</u>

In $\triangle PQR$, what is the value of x ?

(1) PQ = PR

(2) y = 40

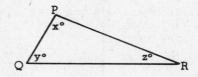

<u>Explanation:</u> According to statement (1), PQ = PR; therefore, $\triangle PQR$ is isosceles and y = z. Since x + y + z = 180, x + 2y = 180. Since statement (1) does not give a value for y, you cannot answer the question using statement (1) by itself. According to statement (2), y = 40; therefore, x + z = 140. Since statement (2) does not give a value for z, you cannot answer the question using statement (2) by itself. Using both statements together you can find y and z; therefore, you can find x, and the answer to the problem is C.

All numbers used are real numbers.

I. 1. This year the total enrollment of a certain school was 10 per cent higher than last year. What is this year's enrollment?

(1) Last year's total enrollment was 750.

(2) There are 30 transfer students enrolled this year.

I. 2. Both children's and adults' tickets were sold at the fair. How much money was collected from children's tickets?

(1) $504.10 was collected from the total sale of tickets.

(2) $0.30 was collected for each of the 347 children's tickets that was sold.

I. 3. If Alice and Bob receive raises of 10 per cent and 6 per cent, respectively, of their present salaries, what is the sum of their raises?

(1) Alice's new salary will be $17,600, and Bob's new salary will be $10,600.

(2) Alice's present salary is $16,000, and Bob's present salary is $10,000.

I. 4. How many gifts did David receive on his birthday this year?

(1) He received twice as many gifts as his age in years.

(2) He received four fewer gifts than he received on his third birthday.

GO ON TO THE NEXT PAGE.

A Statement (1) ALONE is sufficient, but statement (2) alone is not sufficient.
B Statement (2) ALONE is sufficient, but statement (1) alone is not sufficient.
C BOTH statements TOGETHER are sufficient, but NEITHER statement ALONE is sufficient.
D EACH statement ALONE is sufficient.
E Statements (1) and (2) TOGETHER are NOT sufficient.

I. 5. What is the average weekly pay of salesman X if he averages $1,400 a week in sales?

(1) He is paid a salary of $100 a week plus commission.

(2) He receives a commission based on weekly sales in excess of $1,000.

I. 6. P, Q, and R were the only candidates for the presidency of a certain club. If each candidate received at least one vote, which one received the most votes?

(1) P had $\frac{4}{3}$ as many votes as R.

(2) R had $\frac{2}{3}$ as many votes as Q.

I. 7. The cars loaded on an automobile transport vehicle range in weight from 2,200 to 3,400 pounds. How many cars are loaded on the vehicle?

(1) The maximum capacity of the transport vehicle is 14 tons.

(2) The total weight of the car shipment is 13.5 tons.

I. 8. If $x > 0$, then x is what per cent of y ?

(1) $x = \frac{1}{4}y$

(2) $x + y = 100$

COMPANY X REVENUES BY SOURCE

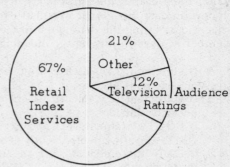

I. 9. To the nearest million dollars, how much revenue did Company X receive from television audience ratings?

(1) Company X received a total of 130.0 million dollars in revenues from retail index services.

(2) Company X received a total of 194.0 million dollars in revenues from all sources.

I. 10. A rectangle is defined to be "silver" if and only if the ratio of its length to its width is 2 to 1. If rectangle S is silver, is rectangle R silver?

(1) R has the same area as S.

(2) The ratio of one side of R to one side of S is 2 to 1.

I. 11. What was the total amount of money collected for a charity by John, Mary, Charles, and Beth?

(1) The average amount collected by each was $26.

(2) Mary collected twice as much as John; Charles and Beth each collected $13.

GO ON TO THE NEXT PAGE.

A Statement (1) ALONE is sufficient, but statement (2) alone is not sufficient.
B Statement (2) ALONE is sufficient, but statement (1) alone is not sufficient.
C BOTH statements TOGETHER are sufficient, but NEITHER statement ALONE is sufficient.
D EACH statement ALONE is sufficient.
E Statements (1) and (2) TOGETHER are NOT sufficient.

I.12. If $a > c$, is $ax - cx$ greater than $b - d$?

(1) $a - c > b - d$

(2) $x = 2$

I.13. If the radius of circle A is greater than 0, what is the radius of circle A?

(1) The area of A is equal to its radius times π.

(2) The circumference of A is 2π.

I.14. What is the volume of rectangular box R?

(1) The total surface area of R is 12 square meters.

(2) The height of R is 50 centimeters.

I.15. A motorist is trying to get to Town K by following unfamiliar roads. From his position at 1 p.m., he knew that Town K was in a direction that was halfway between north and west. What direction is Town K from his position at 3 p.m.?

(1) He went north at 30 miles per hour between 1 p.m. and 2 p.m. and west at 30 miles per hour between 2 p.m. and 3 p.m.

(2) At 1 p.m. he was 50 miles from K.

I.16. What is the value of $x^4 - y^2$?

(1) $x^2 + y = 10$

(2) $x^2 - y = 8$

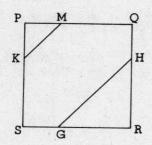

I.17. In square PQRS above, PK = PM. Is GH ∥ KM?

(1) $\dfrac{GH}{GR} = \sqrt{2}$

(2) $\dfrac{GH}{KM} = 3$

I.18. Did the average unit price of product X increase in 1976 by more than 20 per cent over that for 1975?

(1) The number of units sold in 1976 decreased 5 per cent from the number sold in 1975.

(2) The dollar value of sales of product X in 1976 increased by 22 per cent over that for 1975.

I.19. Is $xy < 0$?

(1) $x^2 y^3 < 0$

(2) $xy^2 > 0$

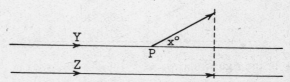

I.20. Cars Y and Z travel side by side at the same rate of speed along parallel roads as shown above. When car Y reaches point P, it forks to the left at angle $x°$, changes speed, and continues to stay even with car Z as shown by the dotted line. The speed of car Y beyond point P is what per cent of the speed of car Z?

(1) The speed of car Z is 50 miles per hour

(2) $x = 45$

I.21. If X and P denote the digits of a five-digit number XXXPP, is XXXPP divisible by 8?

(1) The three-digit number denoted by XPP is divisible by 8.

(2) The three-digit number denoted by XPP is divisible by 24.

I.22. If S is a sequence of 6 numbers in which each number after the 1st is x more than the preceding number, what is the sum of S?

(1) The sum of the 1st and 6th terms of S is 27.

(2) The sum of the 2nd and 5th terms of S is 27.

GO ON TO THE NEXT PAGE.

54

A Statement (1) ALONE is sufficient, but statement (2) alone is not sufficient.
B Statement (2) ALONE is sufficient, but statement (1) alone is not sufficient.
C BOTH statements TOGETHER are sufficient, but NEITHER statement ALONE is sufficient.
D EACH statement ALONE is sufficient.
E Statements (1) and (2) TOGETHER are NOT sufficient.

I. 23. Harry wants to telephone Jane, but he cannot recall the last four digits of her telephone number. He does recall that the sum of the four digits is 34 and that the first of these digits is the same as the last. What are the last four digits (in order) of Jane's telephone number?

(1) The sum of the first and the fourth digits is 18, and the second is the same as the third.

(2) The sum of the two middle digits is 16.

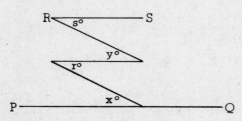

I. 24. In the figure above, is RS ∥ PQ ?

(1) $x = y$; $r = s$

(2) $x = r$; $y = s$

I. 25. If k is an integer less than 17 and $k - 1$ is the square of an integer, what is the value of k ?

(1) k is an even number.

(2) $k + 2$ is the square of an integer.

I. 26. If all of the 20 bolts of fabric on a shelf are either 100 per cent cotton, 100 per cent wool, or a mixture of cotton and wool, how many bolts are cotton and wool mixtures?

(1) Of the 20 bolts, 18 contain some wool and 14 contain some cotton.

(2) Of the 20 bolts, 6 are 100 per cent wool.

I. 27. If $x = y^2$, what is the value of $y - x$?

(1) $x = 4$

(2) $x + y = 2$

I. 28. The Celsius temperature, $C°$, of a gas is increased 10 degrees. If the pressure remains the same, what is the difference between the new volume and the old volume?

(1) New volume $= \left(\dfrac{\text{new } C° + 273°}{\text{old } C° + 273°} \right) \times$ old volume

(2) The old volume was 100 cubic centimeters.

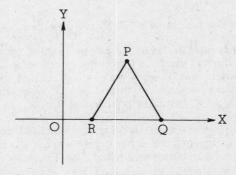

I. 29. In the figure above, R and Q are points on the X-axis. What is the area of equilateral $\triangle PQR$?

(1) The coordinates of point P are (6, $2\sqrt{3}$).

(2) The coordinates of point Q are (8, 0).

I. 30. If x, y, and z are the lengths of the three sides of a triangle, is $y > 4$?

(1) $z = x + 4$

(2) $x = 3$ and $z = 7$

END OF SAMPLE TEST I

DATA SUFFICIENCY SAMPLE TEST II

Time—30 minutes

30 Questions

Directions: Each of the data sufficiency problems below consists of a question and two statements, labeled (1) and (2), in which certain data are given. You have to decide whether the data given in the statements are <u>sufficient</u> for answering the question. Using the data given in the statements <u>plus</u> your knowledge of mathematics and everyday facts (such as the number of days in July or the meaning of <u>counterclockwise</u>), you are to blacken space

- A if statement (1) ALONE is sufficient, but statement (2) alone is not sufficient to answer the question asked;
- B if statement (2) ALONE is sufficient, but statement (1) alone is not sufficient to answer the question asked;
- C if BOTH statements (1) and (2) TOGETHER are sufficient to answer the question asked, but NEITHER statement ALONE is sufficient;
- D if EACH statement ALONE is sufficient to answer the question asked;
- E if statements (1) and (2) TOGETHER are NOT sufficient to answer the question asked, and additional data specific to the problem are needed.

Note: A figure in a data sufficiency problem will conform to the information given in the question, but will not necessarily conform to the additional information given in statements (1) and (2). All figures lie in a plane unless otherwise indicated.

Example:

In $\triangle PQR$, what is the value of x ?

(1) PQ = PR

(2) y = 40

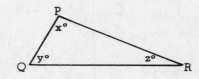

Explanation: According to statement (1), PQ = PR; therefore, $\triangle PQR$ is isosceles and y = z. Since x + y + z = 180, x + 2y = 180. Since statement (1) does not give a value for y, you cannot answer the question using statement (1) by itself. According to statement (2), y = 40; therefore, x + z = 140. Since statement (2) does not give a value for z, you cannot answer the question using statement (2) by itself. Using both statements together you can find y and z; therefore, you can find x, and the answer to the problem is C.

All numbers used are real numbers.

II. 1. How many hours did it take the secretary to type 65 pages?

(1) There were 30 lines on each page.

(2) It took the secretary an average of 12 minutes per page.

II. 2. Is 16 per cent of x equal to 48 ?

(1) 16 per cent of y is 96.

(2) y = 2x

II. 3. How many miles did Bill walk on a certain day?

(1) If Bill had walked exactly 1 mile less, he would have walked a total of 2 miles on that day.

(2) If Bill had walked for exactly 1 more hour, he would have walked a total of 5 miles on that day.

II. 4. What is the 1st term in sequence S ?

(1) The 3rd term in S is 2.

(2) The 2nd term in S is twice the 1st, and the 3rd term is three times the 2nd.

GO ON TO THE NEXT PAGE.

A if statement (1) ALONE is sufficient, but statement (2) alone is not sufficient to answer the question asked;

B if statement (2) ALONE is sufficient, but statement (1) alone is not sufficient to answer the question asked;

C if BOTH statements (1) and (2) TOGETHER are sufficient to answer the question asked, but NEITHER statement ALONE is sufficient;

D if EACH statement ALONE is sufficient to answer the question asked;

E if statements (1) and (2) TOGETHER are NOT sufficient to answer the question asked, and additional data specific to the problem are needed.

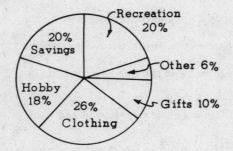

II. 5. The chart above shows how Jeff spent his earnings for one year. How much did Jeff spend for clothing?

(1) He spent $18 during the year on tennis balls.

(2) He spent $190 during the year on recreation.

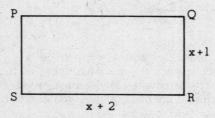

II. 6. Is the area of rectangle PQRS above an integer?

(1) x is an integer greater than 1.

(2) x = 3

II. 7. Is it cheaper to buy a round-trip ticket instead of two one-way tickets?

(1) A round-trip ticket costs twice as much as a one-way ticket.

(2) A round-trip ticket costs $8.20.

II. 8. If p and q are between 0 and 1, is $p + q > 1$?

(1) $p = \frac{1}{2}$

(2) $p - q < 0$

II. 9. How many full pitchers are needed to fill the punch bowl?

(1) Each pitcher holds $1\frac{1}{2}$ liters.

(2) Four full pitchers fill $\frac{2}{3}$ of the bowl.

II. 10. Exactly how many bonds does Bob have?

(1) Of Bob's bonds, exactly 21 are worth at least $5,000 each.

(2) Of Bob's bonds, exactly 65 per cent are worth less than $5,000 each.

II. 11. Is $x + 1$ positive?

(1) $x + 3$ is positive.

(2) x is negative.

II. 12. What is the area of circular region C ?

(1) C has radius 5.

(2) C has circumference 10π.

II. 13. What was the difference in degrees Fahrenheit between the highest and lowest temperatures recorded in Sea City during a certain month?

(1) The greatest difference in temperature recorded in Sea City on any one day in that month was 30° Fahrenheit.

(2) The lowest temperature recorded in Sea City in that month was 32° Fahrenheit.

II. 14. John is one of exactly 15 boys and 6 girls standing in single file at a movie theater. How many of those children are ahead of John?

(1) There are exactly 9 children behind John.

(2) There are exactly 8 boys ahead of John and exactly 3 girls behind him.

GO ON TO THE NEXT PAGE.

A if statement (1) ALONE is sufficient, but statement (2) alone is not sufficient to answer the question asked;

B if statement (2) ALONE is sufficient, but statement (1) alone is not sufficient to answer the question asked;

C if BOTH statements (1) and (2) TOGETHER are sufficient to answer the question asked, but NEITHER statement ALONE is sufficient;

D if EACH statement ALONE is sufficient to answer the question asked;

E if statements (1) and (2) TOGETHER are NOT sufficient to answer the question asked, and additional data specific to the problem are needed.

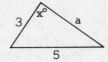

II.15. What is the area of the triangle above?

(1) $a^2 + 9 = 25$

(2) $x = 90$

II.16. What is the remainder when the positive integer x is divided by 2 ?

(1) x is an odd integer.

(2) x is a multiple of 3.

II.17. If $xz \neq 0$, what is the value of $\dfrac{x^5 \sqrt{z^4}}{(x^2)^2 z^2}$?

(1) $x = 2$

(2) $z = 3$

II.18. A car left point A and arrived at point C sometime later. A second car left point B and arrived at point C at the same time as the first car. If neither car reversed its direction or stopped along its way, which traveled faster on the average?

(1) The distance from A to C is greater than the distance from B to C.

(2) The second car started an hour before the first car.

II.19. Does line ℓ bisect $\angle ABC$?

(1) ℓ intersects the sides of $\angle ABC$ at B and only at B.

(2) If p is a point on ℓ, then any line through p that is perpendicular to AB cannot be perpendicular to BC.

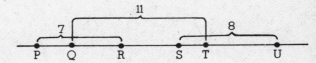

II.20. Six points are graphed on the number line above, and the lengths of three segments are indicated. What is the sum of the lengths of QR and ST ?

(1) PU has length 20.

(2) PT has length 14.

II.21. If the ratio of men to women employed by Company S in 1975 was $\frac{1}{2}$, what is the ratio of men to women employed by Company S in 1976 ?

(1) Company S employed 20 more women in 1976 than in 1975.

(2) Company S employed 20 more men in 1976 than in 1975.

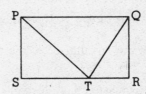

II.22. In the figure above, if PQRS is a rectangle and T is a point on side SR, what is the ratio $\dfrac{\text{area of } \triangle QRT}{\text{area of } \triangle PTS}$?

(1) The area of $\triangle PQT$ is 8.

(2) $ST = \frac{2}{3} SR$

GO ON TO THE NEXT PAGE.

A if statement (1) ALONE is sufficient, but statement (2) alone is not sufficient to answer the question asked;

B if statement (2) ALONE is sufficient, but statement (1) alone is not sufficient to answer the question asked;

C if BOTH statements (1) and (2) TOGETHER are sufficient to answer the question asked, but NEITHER statement ALONE is sufficient;

D if EACH statement ALONE is sufficient to answer the question asked;

E if statements (1) and (2) TOGETHER are NOT sufficient to answer the question asked, and additional data specific to the problem are needed.

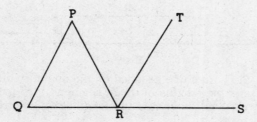

II. 23. In the figure above, QRS is a straight line and line TR bisects ∠PRS. Is it true that lines TR and PQ are parallel?

(1) PQ = PR

(2) QR = PR

II. 24. Are there exactly 3 code symbols used in code language Q ?

(1) The code groups in language Q are all of the horizontal arrangements of one or more distinct code symbols.

(2) There are exactly 15 code groups in language Q.

II. 25. What was the circulation of the Daily Star newspaper 10 years ago?

(1) Its circulation has increased by 10,000 for each of the last 10 years.

(2) Today its circulation is 2 per cent more than it was 1 year ago.

II. 26. What is the value of $\frac{x}{y}$?

(1) $\frac{2}{3} = \frac{x(x + 3)}{xy + 3y}$

(2) $\frac{2p}{3q} = \frac{px}{qy}$ and $pq \neq 0$

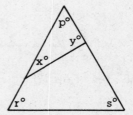

II. 27. In the triangle above, what is the value of p ?

(1) x = 40

(2) s = 50

II. 28. How long did it take a man to make a 180-mile trip?

(1) He took the same amount of time to travel the first 90 miles as to travel the second 90 miles.

(2) If he had taken 3 hours less, his average rate would have been twice as fast.

II. 29. If the sum of n consecutive integers is zero, is 3 the greatest of these integers?

(1) n = 7

(2) The least of these integers is −3.

II. 30. What is the value of x − y ?

(1) x − y = y − x

(2) $x - y = x^2 - y^2$

END OF SAMPLE TEST II

DATA SUFFICIENCY SAMPLE TEST III
Time—30 minutes

30 Questions

<u>Directions:</u> Each of the data sufficiency problems below consists of a question and two statements, labeled (1) and (2), in which certain data are given. You have to decide whether the data given in the statements are <u>sufficient</u> for answering the question. Using the data given in the statements <u>plus</u> your knowledge of mathematics and everyday facts (such as the number of days in July or the meaning of <u>counterclockwise</u>), you are to blacken space

- A if statement (1) ALONE is sufficient, but statement (2) alone is not sufficient to answer the question asked;
- B if statement (2) ALONE is sufficient, but statement (1) alone is not sufficient to answer the question asked;
- C if BOTH statements (1) and (2) TOGETHER are sufficient to answer the question asked, but NEITHER statement ALONE is sufficient;
- D if EACH statement ALONE is sufficient to answer the question asked;
- E if statements (1) and (2) TOGETHER are NOT sufficient to answer the question asked, and additional data specific to the problem are needed.

<u>Note:</u> A figure in a data sufficiency problem will conform to the information given in the question, but will not necessarily conform to the additional information given in statements (1) and (2). All figures lie in a plane unless otherwise indicated.

<u>Example.</u>

In $\triangle PQR$, what is the value of x ?

(1) PQ = PR

(2) y = 40

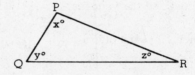

Explanation: According to statement (1), PQ = PR; therefore, $\triangle PQR$ is isosceles and y = z. Since x + y + z = 180, x + 2y = 180. Since statement (1) does not give a value for y, you cannot answer the question using statement (1) by itself. According to statement (2), y = 40; therefore, x + z = 140. Since statement (2) does not give a value for z, you cannot answer the question using statement (2) by itself. Using both statements together you can find y and z; therefore, you can find x, and the answer to the problem is C.

All numbers used are real numbers.

III. 1. How much money did Ms. Stewart save in three years?

(1) She saved 5 per cent of her salary over that period.

(2) She saved an average of $25 a month over that period.

III. 2. Does y equal 1 ?

(1) x = 2y

(2) x = 2

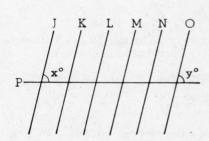

III. 3. In the figure above, line P is crossed by six other lines. Does x = y ?

(1) J ‖ L ‖ N

(2) K ‖ M ‖ O

GO ON TO THE NEXT PAGE.

A Statement (1) ALONE is sufficient, but statement (2) alone is not sufficient.
B Statement (2) ALONE is sufficient, but statement (1) alone is not sufficient.
C BOTH statements TOGETHER are sufficient, but NEITHER statement ALONE is sufficient.
D EACH statement ALONE is sufficient.
E Statements (1) and (2) TOGETHER are NOT sufficient.

III. 4. Is $x > y$?

(1) $0 < x < 0.75$

(2) $0.25 < y < 1.0$

III. 5. If Mrs. White's monthly paycheck after deductions is $523.50, what is her monthly salary?

(1) Fifteen per cent of her monthly salary over $50.00 is withheld for income tax.

(2) All deductions except income tax amount to 6 per cent of her monthly salary.

III. 6. If there are 13 boys in club X, what is the average age of these boys?

(1) The oldest boy is 13 years old and the youngest boy is 9 years old.

(2) Eleven of the boys are either 10 years old or 11 years old.

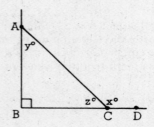

III. 7. In the figure above, ABC is a triangle and BCD is a line. What is the value of x ?

(1) AB = BC

(2) $y = z$

III. 8. If $pq \neq 0$, what per cent of q is p ?

(1) q is 200 per cent of p.

(2) $3q = 6p$

III. 9. Car X and car Y ran a 500-kilometer race. What was the average speed of car X ?

(1) Car X completed the race in 6 hours and 40 minutes.

(2) Car Y, at an average speed of 100 kilometers per hour, completed the race 1 hour and 40 minutes before car X crossed the finish line.

III. 10. In a refinery, the capacity of oil tank A is 70 per cent of the capacity of oil tank B. How many more gallons of oil are in tank A than in tank B ?

(1) Tank A is 90 per cent full; tank B is 50 per cent full.

(2) When full, tank A contains 50,000 gallons of oil.

III. 11. If Betty and Dick together have saved $1,000, how much has each saved?

(1) Dick saved more than twice as much as Betty.

(2) Betty has saved exactly $400 less than Dick.

III. 12. If the sum of 2 different integers is 5, what is the lesser number?

(1) Both integers are positive.

(2) The integers have a difference of 3.

III. 13. Is $x > y$?

(1) $x^2 > y^2$

(2) $x - y > 0$

III. 14. If $xy \neq 0$, what is the value of $\dfrac{x - y}{y} + \dfrac{y - x}{x}$?

(1) $x = y$

(2) $x = 2$

GO ON TO THE NEXT PAGE.

A Statement (1) ALONE is sufficient, but statement (2) alone is not sufficient.
B Statement (2) ALONE is sufficient, but statement (1) alone is not sufficient.
C BOTH statements TOGETHER are sufficient, but NEITHER statement ALONE is sufficient.
D EACH statement ALONE is sufficient.
E Statements (1) and (2) TOGETHER are NOT sufficient.

III. 15. Which weighs more, a cubic unit of water or a cubic unit of liquid X ?

(1) A cubic unit of water weighs more than $\frac{1}{3}$ cubic unit of liquid X.

(2) A cubic unit of liquid X weighs less than 3 cubic units of water.

III. 16. What is the value of the two-digit number x ?

(1) The sum of the two digits is 4.

(2) The difference between the two digits is 2.

III. 17. What is the value of $y + z$?

(1) $x + y + z = x - y - z + 2$

(2) $x - y - z = 5$

III. 18. How many books will fit into a drawer?

(1) Each book has a volume of 10 cubic centimeters.

(2) The drawer is 300 centimeters by 30 centimeters by 20 centimeters and has the shape of a rectangular solid.

III. 19. If $xy \neq 0$, what is the value of $\dfrac{x^4y^2 - (xy)^2}{x^3y^2}$?

(1) $x = 2$

(2) $y = 8$

III. 20. How many minutes long is time period X ?

(1) Time period X is 3 hours long.

(2) Time period X starts at 11 p.m. and ends at 2 a.m.

III. 21. What is the value of $x^2 + y^2$?

(1) $xy = 16$

(2) $x + y = 10$

III. 22. What is the area of circle O ?

(1) The ratio of the area of the square circumscribed about circle O to the square inscribed in it is 2 to 1.

(2) The ratio of the length of a side of the square circumscribed about circle O to the diameter of O is 1 to 1.

III. 23. If all the employees of a company fall into one and only one of 3 groups, X, Y, or Z, with 250, 100, and 20 members in each group, respectively, what is the average (arithmetic mean) weekly salary of all the employees of this company, if all employees are paid every week of the year?

(1) The average (arithmetic mean) annual salary of the employees in Group X is $10,000, in Group Y $15,000, and in Group Z $20,000.

(2) The total annual payroll is $4,400,000.

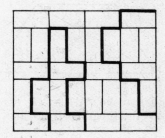

III. 24. As shown above, a rectangle is divided into smaller rectangles of the same size and shape. What is the perimeter of the large rectangle?

(1) The length of the darkened path on the right is 36.

(2) The length of the darkened path on the left is 54.

GO ON TO THE NEXT PAGE.

A Statement (1) ALONE is sufficient, but statement (2) alone is not sufficient.
B Statement (2) ALONE is sufficient, but statement (1) alone is not sufficient.
C BOTH statements TOGETHER are sufficient, but NEITHER statement ALONE is sufficient.
D EACH statement ALONE is sufficient.
E Statements (1) and (2) TOGETHER are NOT sufficient.

III. 25. In a particular 8-hour period, how many revolutions did the rotor of a certain generator make?

(1) The rotor made a total of 50 revolutions every second that it ran in that period.

(2) The generator ran a total of 20 minutes out of every hour of that period.

III. 26. What is the area, in square feet, of parallelogram PQRS ?

(1) The perimeter of PQRS is 60 feet.

(2) The base QR is 10 feet.

III. 27. If x is an integer, is $\frac{x}{2}$ an <u>even</u> integer?

(1) x is a multiple of 2.

(2) x is a multiple of 4.

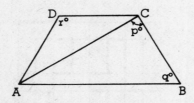

III. 28. In the figure above, AB ∥ CD, AD is not parallel to BC, and the lengths of AD and BC are equal. What is the value of r ?

(1) q = 60

(2) p = 90

AGE OF LICENSED DRIVERS IN THE UNITED STATES IN YEAR X

Age (in years)	Number (in thousands)	Per Cent
Under 20	*	*
20-24	9,650	10.6
25-29	10,650	11.7
30-34	11,100	12.2
35-39	10,750	11.8
40-44	9,850	10.8
45-49	8,550	9.4
50-54	7,300	8.0
55-59	5,900	6.5
60-64	4,550	5.0
65-69	3,100	3.4
70-74	1,800	2.0
75 or Over	*	*
Total of all United States drivers	91,000	100.0

* Information NOT provided.

III. 29. With reference to the table above, what per cent of all drivers in the United States in year X were 75 years old or over?

(1) The number of drivers under age 20 in year X was 6,461,000.

(2) The number of drivers under age 20 in year X was 7.1 per cent of the total number of drivers.

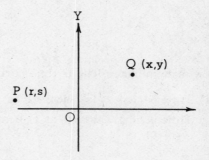

III. 30. In the figure above, Q and P are points in the first and second quadrants, respectively. Does the Y-axis bisect segment PQ ?

(1) −r = x

(2) y = s

END OF SAMPLE TEST III

ANSWER KEYS FOR SAMPLE TESTS

Answers followed by page numbers indicate questions discussed in detail in the explanatory material. These questions are used to illustrate kinds of problems common to the Data Sufficiency section of the GMAT. The page number indicates the page on which the particular problem is discussed.

DATA SUFFICIENCY

Sample Test I

I.1	A	I.16	C
I.2	B	I.17	A
I.3	D	I.18	C
I.4	E	I.19	C (page 65)
I.5	E	I.20	B (page 67)
I.6	C	I.21	D (page 65)
I.7	E	I.22	D
I.8	A	I.23	A
I.9	D	I.24	B
I.10	E (page 66)	I.25	B
I.11	A	I.26	A (page 63)
I.12	C	I.27	C (page 65)
I.13	D	I.28	E
I.14	E (page 66)	I.29	A (page 67)
I.15	C	I.30	D (page 67)

Sample Test II

II.1	B	II.16	A (page 64)
II.2	C	II.17	A
II.3	A	II.18	C
II.4	C (page 65)	II.19	E
II.5	B (page 64)	II.20	A
II.6	D	II.21	E (page 64)
II.7	A	II.22	B
II.8	C	II.23	B (page 68)
II.9	B	II.24	C (page 64)
II.10	C (page 64)	II.25	C
II.11	E	II.26	D
II.12	D	II.27	E
II.13	E	II.28	B
II.14	D	II.29	D
II.15	D (page 67)	II.30	A (page 66)

Sample Test III

III.1	B	III.16	E (page 65)
III.2	C	III.17	A
III.3	E	III.18	E
III.4	E (page 66)	III.19	A (page 66)
III.5	C	III.20	A (page 65)
III.6	E	III.21	C
III.7	D	III.22	E (page 68)
III.8	D	III.23	D
III.9	D (page 64)	III.24	D
III.10	C (page 65)	III.25	C
III.11	B	III.26	E
III.12	B	III.27	B (page 65)
III.13	B (page 66)	III.28	A
III.14	A	III.29	D
III.15	E	III.30	A

EXPLANATORY MATERIAL: DATA SUFFICIENCY

The following discussion of Data Sufficiency is intended to familiarize you with the most efficient and effective approaches to the kinds of problems common to Data Sufficiency. The particular examples taken from the sample tests in this chapter are generally representative of the kinds of questions you will encounter in this section of the GMAT. Remember that it is the problem-solving strategy that is important, not the specific details of a particular question. The explanations for Data Sufficiency are organized according to the content of the question. Arithmetic questions are first, followed by algebra and geometry questions.

ARITHMETIC PROBLEMS

I.26 **If all of the 20 bolts of fabric on a shelf are either 100 per cent cotton, 100 per cent wool, or a mixture of cotton and wool, how many bolts are cotton and wool mixtures?**

   (1) Of the 20 bolts, 18 contain some wool and 14 contain some cotton.

   (2) Of the 20 bolts, 6 are 100 per cent wool.

One way to solve this problem is to draw a circle diagram.

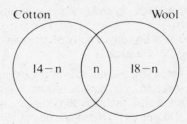

From (1), if n is the number of bolts that are cotton and wool mixtures, then $(14-n) + n + (18-n) = 20$, and $n = 12$. Therefore, (1) is sufficient to answer the question, and the answer must be A or D. From (2),

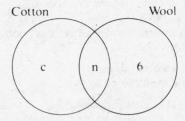

if c is the number of bolts that are 100 percent cotton, then $c + n + 6 = 20$. Since the number of bolts that are 100 percent cotton cannot be determined, the question cannot be answered from (2) alone. Therefore, the best answer is A. This is a difficult question. (See Chapter II, Math Review, Section D.7.)

II.5

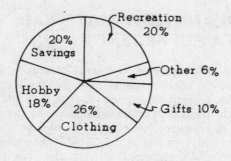

The chart above shows how Jeff spent his earnings for one year. How much did Jeff spend for clothing?

(1) He spent $18 during the year on tennis balls.
(2) He spent $190 during the year on recreation.

From (1) you know that Jeff spent at least $18 on "recreation" expenses. Since you do not know what additional expenses are included in that 20 percent recreation expense, (1) alone is not sufficient to answer the question. Thus, the answer must be B, C, or E. From (2), you know that $190 is equal to 20 percent of Jeff's earnings. You can compute Jeff's earnings and the amount spent on clothing. Therefore, the best answer is B. This is an easy question. (See Chapter II, Math Review, Section A.7.)

II.10 Exactly how many bonds does Bob have?

(1) Of Bob's bonds, exactly 21 are worth at least $5,000 each.
(2) Of Bob's bonds, exactly 65 per cent are worth less than $5,000 each.

Statement (1) tells you the number of bonds that Bob has that are worth at least $5,000, but you do not know how many of Bob's bonds are worth less than $5,000 each; the answer must be B, C, or E. Statement (2) alone is also not sufficient, because it only gives the percent of Bob's bonds that are worth less than $5,000 each. However, (2) does tell you that 35 percent of Bob's bonds are worth at least $5,000 each. From (1) and (2) together you know that 35 percent of Bob's bonds is equal to 21, and the best answer is C. This is a moderately difficult question. (See Chapter II, Math Review, Section A.7.)

II.16 What is the remainder when the positive integer x is divided by 2?

(1) x is an odd integer.
(2) x is a multiple of 3.

Statement (1) is sufficient because from (1) you know that the remainder is 1; whenever an odd integer is divided by 2, the remainder is 1. Thus, the answer is A or D. The question cannot be answered from (2) alone because x could be odd (e.g., 3) or could be even (e.g., 6). Therefore, the best answer is A. This is a moderately difficult question. (See Chapter II, Math Review, Section A.1.)

II.21 If the ratio of men to women employed by Company S in 1975 was $\frac{1}{2}$, what is the ratio of men to women employed by Company S in 1976?

(1) Company S employed 20 more women in 1976 than in 1975.
(2) Company S employed 20 more men in 1976 than in 1975.

Clearly, neither (1) nor (2) alone is sufficient to determine the ratio for 1976. Thus, the answer must be C or E. If n is the number of men employed in 1975, then from (1) and (2) together the ratio of men to women employed in 1976 is $\frac{n + 20}{2n + 20}$. Since you do not know the value of n, you cannot determine the ratio for 1976, and the best answer is E. This is a moderately difficult question. (See Chapter II, Math Review, Section A.6.)

II.24 Are there exactly 3 code symbols used in code language Q?

(1) The code groups in language Q are all of the horizontal arrangements of one or more distinct code symbols.
(2) There are exactly 15 code groups in language Q.

Statement (1) tells you what code groups are, but it does not say anything about the number of symbols. For example, if there is only one symbol, a, there is just one code group; but if there are 2 symbols, a and b, there are 4 code groups, a, b, ab, and ba. Thus (1) is not sufficient, and the answer must be B, C, or E. Statement (2) alone is insufficient since it does not specify what code groups are, and so the answer must be C or E. From (1) and (2) and the examples given above, you know that there must be more than 2 symbols if there are to be 15 code groups. If there are 3 symbols, a, b, and c, then the code groups are a, b, c, ab, ba, ac, ca, bc, cb, abc, acb, bac, bca, cab, cba; i.e., there are 15 code groups. Clearly, if there were 4 or more symbols, there would be more than 15 code groups. Thus, the best answer is C. This is a difficult question. (See Chapter II, Math Review, Section D.7.)

III.9 Car X and car Y ran a 500-kilometer race. What was the average speed of car X?

(1) Car X completed the race in 6 hours and 40 minutes.
(2) Car Y, at an average speed of 100 kilometers per hour, completed the race 1 hour and 40 minutes before car X crossed the finish line.

Statement (1) is sufficient because from statement (1) the average speed of car X can be determined by dividing 500 kilometers by $6\frac{2}{3}$ hours; thus, the answer is A or D. Statement (2) implies that car Y took 5 hours to complete the race and car X took $6\frac{2}{3}$ hours. Therefore, (2) alone is sufficient to determine the average speed of car X, and the best answer is D. This is an easy question. (See Chapter II, Math Review, Section D.1.)

III.10 In a refinery, the capacity of oil tank A is 70 per cent of the capacity of oil tank B. How many more gallons of oil are in tank A than in tank B?

  (1) Tank A is 90 per cent full; tank B is 50 per cent full.
  (2) When full, tank A contains 50,000 gallons of oil.

Since you do not know the number of gallons in either tank A or tank B, (1) alone is not sufficient; the answer must be B, C, or E. From (2) alone, you can determine the capacities of tanks A and B, but you do not know whether the tanks are full, so the answer must be C or E. Using (1) and (2) together, you can determine the number of gallons in A and B; therefore, the best answer is C. This is a moderately difficult question. (See Chapter II, Math Review, Section A.7.)

III.16 What is the value of the two-digit number x?

  (1) The sum of the two digits is 4.
  (2) The difference between the two digits is 2.

Statement (1) implies that x is 13, 22, 31, or 40; thus, (1) alone is insufficient, and the answer must be B, C, or E. Statement (2) implies that x could have any one of a number of values, including 13, 24, 31, 42, ... From (1) and (2) together there are still two possibilities for x, 13 and 31; therefore, the best answer is E. This is a moderately difficult question. (See Chapter II, Math Review, Section A.1.)

III.20 How many minutes long is time period X?

  (1) Time period X is 3 hours long.
  (2) Time period X starts at 11 p.m. and ends at 2 a.m.

Statement (1) is sufficient because from (1) you can determine that time period x is 180 minutes long; thus, the answer must be A or D. Statement (2) alone is not sufficient to answer the question because you do not know whether the two times given are for the same day. This is a question that depends not on calculation but on your analysis of the assumptions made or not made by the statement. Therefore, the best answer is A. This is a very difficult question.

III.27 If x is an integer, is $\frac{x}{2}$ an <u>even</u> integer?

  (1) x is a multiple of 2.
  (2) x is a multiple of 4.

Statement (1) implies that x is an even integer, but not that $\frac{x}{2}$ is necessarily even. For example, if $x = 8$, $\frac{x}{2}$ is even, but if $x = 6$, $\frac{x}{2}$ is odd; in both cases, (1) is satisfied. Thus, the answer is B, C, or E. Statement (2) implies that $x = 2 \cdot 2 \cdot n$, where n is an integer. Hence, $\frac{x}{2} = 2n$ and 2n is even. Therefore, the best answer is B. This is a difficult question. (See Chapter II, Math Review, Section A.1.)

ALGEBRA PROBLEMS

I.19 Is xy $<$ 0?

  (1) $x^2y^3 < 0$
  (2) $xy^2 > 0$

Statement (1) implies that $x \neq 0$ and $y \neq 0$ since the product is not equal to zero. x^2 must be greater than zero because the square of any nonzero number is positive. A positive number times a negative number is a negative number; thus, $y^3 < 0$ since $x^2y^3 < 0$. Likewise, if $y^3 < 0$, $y < 0$. However, (1) is not sufficient to determine whether xy $<$ 0 because you do not know whether $x > 0$ or $x < 0$; thus, the answer is B, C, or E. Similarly, from (2) alone you know that $x > 0$ since $xy^2 > 0$ and $y^2 > 0$, but you do not know whether $y > 0$ or $y < 0$. Combining the information from (1) and (2) you know $y < 0$ and $x > 0$, so xy $<$ 0; the best answer is C. This is a difficult question. (See Chapter II, Math Review, Section A.5.)

I.21 If X and P denote the digits of a five-digit number XXXPP, is XXXPP divisible by 8?

  (1) The three-digit number denoted by XPP is divisible by 8.
  (2) The three-digit number denoted by XPP is divisible by 24.

Statement (1) implies that XXXPP is divisible by 8 for the following reason. The number XXXPP is equal to

$$XX000 + XPP = XX(1,000) + XPP$$

Since XPP and 1,000 are both divisible by 8, XXXPP is divisible by 8. Therefore, the answer is A or D. Since (2) says that XPP is divisible by 24, XPP is divisible by 8, implying (1), and, since (1) alone is sufficient, (2) alone is also sufficient. Thus, the best answer is D. This is a difficult question. (See Chapter II, Math Review, Section A.1.)

I.27 If $x = y^2$, what is the value of y $-$ x?

  (1) $x = 4$
  (2) $x + y = 2$

From (1) you find that $y = 2$ or $y = -2$, but which of these values y has cannot be determined. Therefore, (1) alone is not sufficient to answer the question asked, and the answer is B, C, or E. Substituting y^2 for x in (2), you find that $y = 1$ or $y = -2$; therefore, (2) alone is not sufficient, and the answer is C or E. Using (1) and (2) together you find that $x = 4$, $y = -2$, and $y - x = -2 - 4 = -(2 + 4) = -6$. Therefore, the best answer is C. This is a difficult question. (See Chapter II, Math Review, Section B.5.)

II.4 What is the 1st term in sequence S?

  (1) The 3rd term in S is 2.
  (2) The 2nd term in S is twice the 1st, and the 3rd term is three times the 2nd.

It is clear that (1) offers no help in determining the first term in S. Thus, the answer is B, C, or E. Although (2) gives the relationships among the first three terms in S, it is not sufficient to answer the question asked, and the answer must be C or E.

From (1) and (2) together it can be determined that the 2nd term is $\frac{1}{3}$ the 3rd term $\left(\frac{1}{3}(2) = \frac{2}{3}\right)$ and the 1st term is $\frac{1}{2}$ the 2nd term $\left(\frac{1}{2}\left(\frac{2}{3}\right) = \frac{1}{3}\right)$. Therefore, the best answer is C. This is an easy question. (See Chapter II, Math Review, Section B.2.)

II.30 What is the value of x − y?

    (1) x − y = y − x
    (2) x − y = x² − y²

From (1) you know that $2x = 2y$ or $x = y$ and $x - y = 0$; thus, the answer is A or D. Statement (2) can be reexpressed as $x - y = (x - y)(x + y)$, which implies that $x - y = 0$, or $x + y = 1$; however, this is not sufficient to determine the value of $x - y$. For example, if $x = y = \frac{1}{2}$, $x - y = 0$, but if $x = 2$ and $y = -1$, $x - y = 3$. Therefore, the best answer is A. This is a difficult question. (See Chapter II, Math Review, Section B.1 and Section B.4.)

III.4 Is x > y?

    (1) 0 < x < 0.75
    (2) 0.25 < y < 1.0

Clearly neither (1) nor (2) alone is sufficient to determine whether $x > y$; thus, the answer must be C or E. Statements (1) and (2) together are also not sufficient to answer the question. For example, if $x = 0.6$ and $y = 0.5$, $x > y$; but, if $x = 0.6$ and $y = 0.9$, $x < y$. Both these examples are consistent with (1) and (2); therefore, the best answer is E. This is an easy question. (See Chapter II, Math Review, Section B.8.)

III.13 Is x > y?

    (1) x² > y²
    (2) x − y > 0

Statement (1) is insufficient to determine whether $x > y$ because (1) implies nothing about the signs of x and y. For example, if $x = 3$ and $y = 2$, $x > y$, but if $x = -3$ and $y = 2$, $x < y$. Thus, the answer is B, C, or E. By adding y to both sides of (2), you get $x > y$; therefore, the best answer is B. This is a moderately difficult question. (See Chapter II, Math Review, Section A.9 and Section B.8.)

III.19 If xy ≠ 0, what is the value of $\frac{x^4y^2 - (xy)^2}{x^3y^2}$?

    (1) x = 2
    (2) y = 8

It is helpful to simplify the expression in the question:

$$\frac{x^4y^2 - (xy)^2}{x^3y^2} = \frac{y^2(x^4 - x^2)}{x^3y^2} = \frac{x^4 - x^2}{x^3}$$

$$= \frac{x^2(x^2 - 1)}{x^2(x)} = \frac{x^2 - 1}{x}.$$

Since statement (1) gives the value of x, the value of the expression can be determined, and the answer is A or D. Statement

(2) alone is insufficient to answer the question asked because the value of x is not given and is not deducible. Hence, the value of the expression cannot be determined from (2), and the best answer is A. This is a difficult question. (See Chapter II, Math Review, Section B.1.)

GEOMETRY PROBLEMS

I.10 A rectangle is defined to be "silver" if and only if the ratio of its length to its width is 2 to 1. If rectangle S is silver, is rectangle R silver?

    (1) R has the same area as S.
    (2) The ratio of one side of R to one side of S is 2 to 1.

Statement (1) alone is not sufficient to answer the question because R could have the same dimensions as S (e.g., 4×2) and be silver, or R could have different dimensions (e.g., 8×1) and not be silver. Thus, the answer is B, C, or E. Statement (2) alone does not tell anything about the relationship between the other sides of R and S, and so it is not sufficient; the answer must be C or E. The logic applied to (1) can also be applied to the information given in (2); thus, (1) and (2) together are not sufficient, and the best answer is E. This is a moderately difficult question. (See Chapter II, Math Review, Section C.7.)

I.14 What is the volume of rectangular box R?

    (1) The total surface area of R is 12 square meters.
    (2) The height of R is 50 centimeters.

For this problem it may be helpful to draw a diagram:

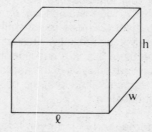

From (1) you know that $2(\ell w + wh + \ell h) = 12$, but since you do not know ℓ, w, or h, (1) is not sufficient to determine the volume of the box ($\ell \times w \times h$), and the answer must be B, C, or E. Since (2) gives just one dimension of the box, it is not sufficient to determine the volume, and the answer must be C or E. From (1) and (2) together you know that

$$\ell w + \frac{w}{2} + \frac{\ell}{2} = 6,$$

because 50 centimeters $= \frac{1}{2}$ meter, but you still need to know either the length or the width of the box to determine its volume. The best answer is E. This is a moderately difficult question. (See Chapter II, Math Review, Section C.10.)

I.20

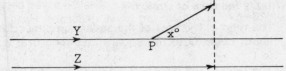

Cars Y and Z travel side by side at the same rate of speed along parallel roads as shown above. When car Y reaches point P, it forks to the left at angle x°, changes speed, and continues to stay even with car Z as shown by the dotted line. The speed of car Y beyond point P is what per cent of the speed of car Z?

(1) The speed of car Z is 50 miles per hour.
(2) x = 45

This is a rate/distance problem; it is helpful to keep in mind that rate × time = distance (i.e., symbolically $r \times t = d$). In this case the times for Y and Z are equal, and so you have the equation $\frac{d_y}{r_y} = \frac{d_z}{r_z}$. Since (1) does not give any information about the distances traveled, it is not sufficient, and the answer must be B, C, or E. Since the triangle formed is a $45° - 45° - 90°$ triangle and d_y is the hypotenuse of the triangle, (2) implies that $d_y = \sqrt{2}\, d_z$. Therefore, $\frac{\sqrt{2}\, d_z}{r_y} = \frac{d_z}{r_z}$. From this information it can be determined that $r_y = \sqrt{2}\, r_z$, and therefore the speed of car Y beyond point P is $100 \sqrt{2}$ percent of the speed of car Z. Thus, the best answer is B. This is a difficult question. (See Chapter II, Math Review, Section A.7, Section C.6, and Section D.1.)

I.29

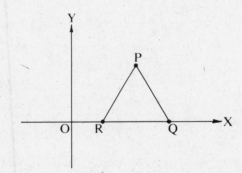

In the figure above, R and Q are points on the X-axis. What is the area of equilateral ΔPQR?

(1) The coordinates of point P are (6, 2√3).
(2) The coordinates of point Q are (8, 0).

Statement (1) gives the height of triangle PQR, and, since ΔPQR is equilateral, its other dimensions can be determined:

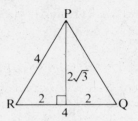

Thus, the area of ΔPQR is $\frac{(2\sqrt{3})(4)}{2}$, and the answer is A or D. Since (2) does not give any information about the coordinates of either of the other points, the length of RQ cannot be determined, and (2) is insufficient. Therefore, the best answer is A. This is a difficult question. (See Chapter II, Math Review, Section C.6 and Section C.13.)

I.30 If x, y, and z are the lengths of the three sides of a triangle, is y > 4?

(1) z = x + 4
(2) x = 3 and z = 7

The sum of the lengths of any two sides of a triangle is always greater than the length of the third side; therefore, $x + y > z$. Statement (1) implies $x + y > x + 4$, and $y > 4$. Therefore, the answer must be A or D. Statement (2) implies $3 + y > 7$ and $y > 4$. Thus, the best answer is D. This is a very difficult question. (See Chapter II, Math Review, Section B.8 and Section C.6.)

II.15

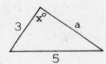

What is the area of the triangle above?

(1) a² + 9 = 25
(2) x = 90

Statement (1) implies that a = 4. Thus, the figure shows a 3-4-5 triangle, so x = 90. Therefore, the area of the triangle is $\frac{(3)(4)}{2}$, and the answer is A or D. Statement (2) indicates that the triangle is a right triangle. Therefore, since a = 4, the area is $\frac{(3)(4)}{2}$, and the best answer is D. This is a moderately difficult question. (See Chapter II, Math Review, Section C.6.)

II.23

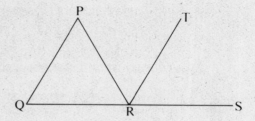

In the figure above, QRS is a straight line and line TR bisects ∠PRS. Is it true that lines TR and PQ are parallel?

(1) PQ = PR
(2) QR = PR

Let the angles of the figure have the following measures:

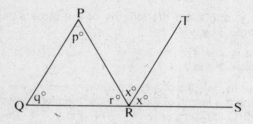

Since QRS is a straight line, $r + 2x = 180$. For PQ ∥ TR, x must equal p. From (1) you know that $q = r$, but there is no way to determine whether $p = x$. So the answer must be B, C, or E. From (2) you know that $q = p$ and that $r + 2p = 180 = r + 2x$ and thus $p = x$. Therefore, PQ ∥ TR, and the best answer is B. This is a very difficult question. (See Chapter II, Math Review, Section C.4 and Section C.5.)

III.22 What is the area of circle O?

   (1) The ratio of the area of the square circumscribed about circle O to the square inscribed in it is 2 to 1.
   (2) The ratio of the length of a side of the square circumscribed about circle O to the diameter of O is 1 to 1.

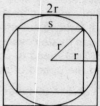

Using the sketch above, you see that the area of the circumscribed square is $4r^2$ and the area of the inscribed square is s^2. Since r is one-half the diameter of the inscribed square, $s\sqrt{2} = 2r$ or $s = r\sqrt{2}$. In terms of r, the area of the inscribed square is $(r\sqrt{2})^2 = 2r^2$. Thus, for any circle, the ratio of the area of the circumscribed square to the inscribed square is 2 to 1; so (1) does not provide any additional information and is not sufficient. Thus, the answer must be B, C, or E. In like manner, (2) is true for all circles and so (2) is not sufficient either. Since (1) and (2) together offer no additional information, the best answer is E. This is a moderately difficult question. (See Chapter II, Math Review, Section C.6, Section C.7, and Section C.8.)

V Reading Comprehension

There are six kinds of Reading Comprehension questions, each of which tests a different reading skill. The following pages include descriptions of the various question types, test-taking strategies, sample tests (with answer keys), and detailed explanations of selected questions from the sample tests. The explanations further illustrate the ways in which Reading Comprehension questions evaluate basic reading skills.

Reading Comprehension questions include:

1. Questions that ask about the main idea of a passage

Each Reading Comprehension passage in the GMAT is a unified whole—that is, the individual sentences and paragraphs support and develop one main idea or central point. Sometimes you will be told the central point in the passage itself, and sometimes it will be necessary for you to determine the central point from the overall organization or development of the passage. You may be asked in this kind of question to recognize a correct restatement, or paraphrase, of the main idea of a passage; to identify the author's primary purpose, or objective, in writing the passage; or to assign a title that summarizes briefly and pointedly the main idea developed in the passage.

2. Questions that ask about the supporting ideas presented in a passage

These questions measure your ability to comprehend the supporting ideas in a passage and to differentiate those supporting ideas from the main idea. The questions also measure your ability to differentiate ideas that are *explicitly stated* in a passage from ideas that are *implied* by the author but are not explicitly stated. You may be asked about facts cited in a passage, or about the specific content of arguments presented by the author in support of his or her views, or about descriptive details used to support or elaborate on the main idea. Whereas questions about the main idea ask you to determine the meaning of a passage *as a whole,* questions about supporting ideas ask you to determine the meanings of individual sentences and paragraphs that *contribute to* the meaning of the passage as a whole. One way to think about these questions is to see them as questions asking for the main point of *one small part* of the passage.

3. Questions that ask for inferences based on information presented in a passage

These questions ask about ideas that are not explicitly stated in a passage but are *strongly implied* by the author. Unlike questions about supporting details, which ask about information that is directly stated in a passage, inference questions ask about ideas or meanings that must be inferred from information that is directly stated. Authors often make their points in indirect ways, suggesting ideas without actually stating them. These questions measure your ability to infer an author's intended meaning in parts of a passage where the meaning is only suggested. The questions do not ask about meanings or implications that are remote from the passage but about meanings that are developed indirectly or implications specifically suggested by the author. To answer these questions, you may have to carry statements made by the author one step beyond their literal meanings, or recognize the *opposite* of a statement made by the author, or identify the intended meaning of a word used figuratively in a passage. If a passage explicitly states an effect, for example, you may be asked to infer its cause. If the author compares two phenomena, you may be asked to infer the basis for the comparison. You may be asked to infer the characteristics of an old policy from an explicit description of a new one. When you read a passage, therefore, you should concentrate not only on the explicit meaning of the author's words, but also on the more subtle meaning implied by those words.

4. Questions that ask how information given in a passage can be applied to a context outside the passage itself

These questions measure your ability to discern the relationships between situations or ideas presented by the author and other situations or ideas that might parallel those in the passage. In this kind of question, you may be asked to identify a hypothetical situation that is comparable to a situation presented in the passage, or to select an example that is similar to an example provided in the passage, or to apply ideas given in the passage to a situation not mentioned by the author, or to recognize ideas that the author would probably agree or disagree with on the basis of statements made in the passage. Unlike inference questions, these questions use ideas or situations *not* taken from the passage. Ideas and situations given in the question are *like* those given in the passage, and they parallel ideas and situations given in the passage. Therefore, to answer the question, you must do more than recall what you read. You must recognize the essential attributes of ideas and situations presented in the passage when they appear in different words and in an entirely new context.

5. Questions that ask about the logical structure of a passage

These questions ask you to analyze and evaluate the organization and the logic of a passage. They may ask how a passage is constructed: for instance, does it define, does it compare or contrast, does it present a new idea, does it refute an idea. They may also ask how the author persuades readers to accept his or her assertions, or about the reason behind the author's use of any particular supporting detail. You may also be asked to identify assumptions that the author is making, to assess the strengths and weaknesses of the author's arguments, or to recognize appropriate counterarguments. These questions measure your ability not only to comprehend a passage but to evaluate it critically. However, it is important for you to realize that these questions do not rely on any kind of formal logic nor do they require that you be familiar with specific terms of logic or argumentation. You can answer these questions using only the information in the passage and careful reasoning.

6. Questions that ask about the style and tone of a passage

These questions ask about the language of a passage and about the ideas in a passage that may be expressed through its language. You may be asked to deduce the author's attitude toward an idea, a fact, or a situation from the words that he or she uses to describe it. You may also be asked to select a word that accurately describes the tone of a passage—for instance, "critical," "questioning," "objective," or "enthusiastic." To answer this type of question, you will have to consider the language of the passage as a whole: it takes more than one pointed critical word to make the tone of an entire passage "critical." Sometimes, these questions ask what audience the passage was probably intended for or what type of publication it probably appeared in. Style and tone questions may apply to one small part of the passage or to the passage as a whole. To answer them, you must ask yourself what meanings are contained in the words of a passage beyond their literal meanings. Were such words selected because of their emotional content, or because of their suggestiveness, or because a particular audience would expect to hear them? Remember, these questions measure your ability to discern meaning expressed by the author through his or her choice of words.

TEST-TAKING STRATEGIES FOR READING COMPREHENSION

1. You should not expect to be completely familiar with any of the material presented in Reading Comprehension passages. You may find some passages easier to understand than others, but all passages are designed to present a challenge. If you have some familiarity with the material being presented in a passage, do not let this knowledge influence your choice of answers to the questions. Answer all questions on the basis of what is *stated* or *implied* in the passage itself.

2. Since the questions require specific and detailed understanding of the material in a passage, analyze each passage carefully the first time you read it. There are approximately 1,500 words of text in the entire Reading Comprehension section. This means that, even if you read at the relatively slow rate of 250 words per minute, you will be able to read the passages in about 6 minutes and will have about 24 minutes left for answering the questions. You should, of course, be sure to allow sufficient time to work on each passage and its questions. There are other ways of approaching Reading Comprehension passages: some test-takers prefer to skim the passages the first time through or even to read the questions before reading the passages. You should choose the method most suitable for you.

3. Underlining parts of a passage may be helpful to you. Focus on key words and phrases and try to follow exactly the development of separate ideas. In the margins, note where each important idea, argument, or set of related facts begins. Make every effort to avoid losing the sense of what is being discussed. If you become lost, you will have to go back over the material, and that wastes time. Keep the following in mind:

   - Note how each fact relates to an idea or an argument.
   - Note where the passage moves from one idea to the next.
   - Separate main ideas from supporting ideas.
   - Determine what conclusions are reached and why.

4. Read the questions carefully, making certain that you understand what is being asked. An answer choice may be incorrect, even though it accurately restates information given in the passage, if it does not answer the question. If you need to, refer back to the passage for clarification.

5. Read all the choices carefully. Never assume that you have selected the best answer without first reading all the choices.

6. Select the choice that best answers the question in terms of the information given in the passage. Do not rely on outside knowledge of the material for answering the questions.

7. Remember that understanding, not speed, is the critical factor in reading comprehension.

When you take the sample tests, use the answer spaces on the following page to mark your answers.

Answer Spaces for Sample Test I

1 Ⓐ Ⓑ Ⓒ Ⓓ Ⓔ	6 Ⓐ Ⓑ Ⓒ Ⓓ Ⓔ	11 Ⓐ Ⓑ Ⓒ Ⓓ Ⓔ	16 Ⓐ Ⓑ Ⓒ Ⓓ Ⓔ	21 Ⓐ Ⓑ Ⓒ Ⓓ Ⓔ
2 Ⓐ Ⓑ Ⓒ Ⓓ Ⓔ	7 Ⓐ Ⓑ Ⓒ Ⓓ Ⓔ	12 Ⓐ Ⓑ Ⓒ Ⓓ Ⓔ	17 Ⓐ Ⓑ Ⓒ Ⓓ Ⓔ	22 Ⓐ Ⓑ Ⓒ Ⓓ Ⓔ
3 Ⓐ Ⓑ Ⓒ Ⓓ Ⓔ	8 Ⓐ Ⓑ Ⓒ Ⓓ Ⓔ	13 Ⓐ Ⓑ Ⓒ Ⓓ Ⓔ	18 Ⓐ Ⓑ Ⓒ Ⓓ Ⓔ	23 Ⓐ Ⓑ Ⓒ Ⓓ Ⓔ
4 Ⓐ Ⓑ Ⓒ Ⓓ Ⓔ	9 Ⓐ Ⓑ Ⓒ Ⓓ Ⓔ	14 Ⓐ Ⓑ Ⓒ Ⓓ Ⓔ	19 Ⓐ Ⓑ Ⓒ Ⓓ Ⓔ	24 Ⓐ Ⓑ Ⓒ Ⓓ Ⓔ
5 Ⓐ Ⓑ Ⓒ Ⓓ Ⓔ	10 Ⓐ Ⓑ Ⓒ Ⓓ Ⓔ	15 Ⓐ Ⓑ Ⓒ Ⓓ Ⓔ	20 Ⓐ Ⓑ Ⓒ Ⓓ Ⓔ	25 Ⓐ Ⓑ Ⓒ Ⓓ Ⓔ

Answer Spaces for Sample Test II

1 Ⓐ Ⓑ Ⓒ Ⓓ Ⓔ	6 Ⓐ Ⓑ Ⓒ Ⓓ Ⓔ	11 Ⓐ Ⓑ Ⓒ Ⓓ Ⓔ	16 Ⓐ Ⓑ Ⓒ Ⓓ Ⓔ	21 Ⓐ Ⓑ Ⓒ Ⓓ Ⓔ
2 Ⓐ Ⓑ Ⓒ Ⓓ Ⓔ	7 Ⓐ Ⓑ Ⓒ Ⓓ Ⓔ	12 Ⓐ Ⓑ Ⓒ Ⓓ Ⓔ	17 Ⓐ Ⓑ Ⓒ Ⓓ Ⓔ	22 Ⓐ Ⓑ Ⓒ Ⓓ Ⓔ
3 Ⓐ Ⓑ Ⓒ Ⓓ Ⓔ	8 Ⓐ Ⓑ Ⓒ Ⓓ Ⓔ	13 Ⓐ Ⓑ Ⓒ Ⓓ Ⓔ	18 Ⓐ Ⓑ Ⓒ Ⓓ Ⓔ	23 Ⓐ Ⓑ Ⓒ Ⓓ Ⓔ
4 Ⓐ Ⓑ Ⓒ Ⓓ Ⓔ	9 Ⓐ Ⓑ Ⓒ Ⓓ Ⓔ	14 Ⓐ Ⓑ Ⓒ Ⓓ Ⓔ	19 Ⓐ Ⓑ Ⓒ Ⓓ Ⓔ	24 Ⓐ Ⓑ Ⓒ Ⓓ Ⓔ
5 Ⓐ Ⓑ Ⓒ Ⓓ Ⓔ	10 Ⓐ Ⓑ Ⓒ Ⓓ Ⓔ	15 Ⓐ Ⓑ Ⓒ Ⓓ Ⓔ	20 Ⓐ Ⓑ Ⓒ Ⓓ Ⓔ	25 Ⓐ Ⓑ Ⓒ Ⓓ Ⓔ

Answer Spaces for Sample Test III

1 Ⓐ Ⓑ Ⓒ Ⓓ Ⓔ	6 Ⓐ Ⓑ Ⓒ Ⓓ Ⓔ	11 Ⓐ Ⓑ Ⓒ Ⓓ Ⓔ	16 Ⓐ Ⓑ Ⓒ Ⓓ Ⓔ	21 Ⓐ Ⓑ Ⓒ Ⓓ Ⓔ
2 Ⓐ Ⓑ Ⓒ Ⓓ Ⓔ	7 Ⓐ Ⓑ Ⓒ Ⓓ Ⓔ	12 Ⓐ Ⓑ Ⓒ Ⓓ Ⓔ	17 Ⓐ Ⓑ Ⓒ Ⓓ Ⓔ	22 Ⓐ Ⓑ Ⓒ Ⓓ Ⓔ
3 Ⓐ Ⓑ Ⓒ Ⓓ Ⓔ	8 Ⓐ Ⓑ Ⓒ Ⓓ Ⓔ	13 Ⓐ Ⓑ Ⓒ Ⓓ Ⓔ	18 Ⓐ Ⓑ Ⓒ Ⓓ Ⓔ	23 Ⓐ Ⓑ Ⓒ Ⓓ Ⓔ
4 Ⓐ Ⓑ Ⓒ Ⓓ Ⓔ	9 Ⓐ Ⓑ Ⓒ Ⓓ Ⓔ	14 Ⓐ Ⓑ Ⓒ Ⓓ Ⓔ	19 Ⓐ Ⓑ Ⓒ Ⓓ Ⓔ	24 Ⓐ Ⓑ Ⓒ Ⓓ Ⓔ
5 Ⓐ Ⓑ Ⓒ Ⓓ Ⓔ	10 Ⓐ Ⓑ Ⓒ Ⓓ Ⓔ	15 Ⓐ Ⓑ Ⓒ Ⓓ Ⓔ	20 Ⓐ Ⓑ Ⓒ Ⓓ Ⓔ	25 Ⓐ Ⓑ Ⓒ Ⓓ Ⓔ

READING COMPREHENSION SAMPLE TEST I

Time—30 minutes

25 Questions

Each passage in this group is followed by questions based on its content. After reading a passage, choose the best answer to each question and blacken the corresponding space on the answer sheet. Answer all questions following a passage on the basis of what is stated or implied in that passage.

Frequently there is a time lag between the statement of a managerial policy and the implementation of that policy. This appears to be particularly true with regard to the acceptance of women in management positions. According to our survey findings, women interested in management or professional careers still face social and psychological barriers, despite recent changes in policies on the employment of women.

The responses we received to the case examples reflect two general patterns of sex discrimination: (1) there is greater organizational concern for the careers of men than there is for those of women, and (2) there is a degree of skepticism about women's abilities to balance work and family demands. Underlying these patterns of discrimination there is an assumption that is not at first apparent from the survey findings: it appears that women are expected to change to satisfy the organization's demands. For example, written comments from participating managers often suggest that women must become more assertive and independent before they can succeed in some of the situations described in the case examples in the survey. These managers do not see the organization as having any obligation to alter its attitudes toward women. Neither, apparently, are organizations about to change their expectations of men. Perhaps because it is expected that the job will eventually "win out" over the family, a man is given the time and opportunity to resolve conflicts between home and job. This in itself says a great deal about how organizations might conceive of a man's relationship with his family.

Another conclusion we can draw is that when information is scant and the situation ambiguous, managers tend to fall back on traditional concepts of male and female roles. Only when there are clear rules and qualifications do both women and men stand a chance of breaking out of the stereotyped parts usually reserved for them.

When the results of this survey are extrapolated to the total population of American managers, even a small bias against women could represent a great many unintentional discriminatory acts that potentially affect thousands of career women. The end result of these various forms of bias might be great personal damage for individuals and costly underutilization of human resources. If managers are sincere in wanting to encourage all employees equally, they ought to examine their own organizations' implicit expectations of both men and women to see whether these expectations reflect some of the same traditional notions revealed by the survey. Identification of these biases would help managers to move toward the goal of equal employment opportunity for all.

I. 1. Which of the following best expresses the main idea of the passage?

(A) The barriers to careers in management for women will be broken down within a few years.
(B) Although organizations provide similar opportunities for men and women, men and women do not advance at equal rates.
(C) Most organizations do not sincerely attempt to achieve equal employment opportunity for men and women.
(D) The findings of a recent survey contradict previously held beliefs about women in management.
(E) Implicit attitudes toward women may prevent women from succeeding in careers in management.

I. 2. It can be inferred that the survey mentioned in line 5 required respondents to

(A) make evaluations based on the information given in case studies
(B) describe discrimination that they encountered in becoming managers
(C) provide specific cases as examples to illustrate their views
(D) give opinions as to why discrimination in hiring occurs
(E) explain how discrimination against women can best be remedied

I. 3. The author suggests that most discrimination against women is primarily a result of managers'

(A) past experiences with female employees
(B) failure to identify their own deep-rooted biases
(C) misunderstanding of the wishes of their employers
(D) desire to maintain their own positions by discouraging competition
(E) inability to identify the qualities that characterize good managers

GO ON TO THE NEXT PAGE.

I. 4. The author refers to the written comments made by managers primarily in order to

(A) show how managers can prevent discrimination against women
(B) show how managers' statements differ from their actions
(C) show how women are expected to adapt to organizations' expectations
(D) illustrate managers' attitudes toward women with families
(E) illustrate recent changes in attitudes toward women in management

I. 5. It can be inferred that the author would describe the attitudes revealed by the survey as

(A) justified
(B) militant
(C) uncommon
(D) irremediable
(E) pervasive

I. 6. The author is primarily concerned with

(A) interpreting the results of a survey
(B) discussing the role of women in management
(C) describing recent changes in hiring practices
(D) recommending that women change their attitudes toward employment
(E) suggesting reasons for recent changes in managerial policies

I. 7. With which of the following conclusions would the author be most likely to agree?

(A) Further information is needed before action can be taken.
(B) Policies cannot be implemented until managers' attitudes change.
(C) Discrimination will not end until women assert their rights.
(D) The attitudes of a few should not encourage condemnation of many.
(E) Bias against women is more harmful to organizations than to women themselves.

I. 8. The tone of the author's closing remarks can best be described as

(A) humorous
(B) indifferent
(C) indecisive
(D) admonitory
(E) indignant

GO ON TO THE NEXT PAGE.

The enjoyment and understanding of music are dominated in a most curious way by the prestige of the masterpiece. Neither the theater nor the cinema nor poetry nor narrative fiction pays
(5) allegiance to its ideal of excellence in the tyrannical way that music does. They recognize no unbridgeable chasm between "great work" and lesser efforts. Even the world of painting, though also a victim of "appreciation" rackets based on the
(10) concept of gilt-edged quality, is more penetrable to reason in this regard. But music in our time seems committed to the idea that first-class work in composition is separable from the rest of music-writing by a distinction as
(15) radical as that recognized in theology between the elect and the damned. Or at the very least by as rigorous an exclusion from glory as that which formerly marked the difference between Mrs. Astor's Four Hundred and the rest of the human
(20) race.

This snobbish definition of excellence is opposed to the classical concept of a republic of letters. It reposes, rather, on the theocratic idea that inspiration is less a privilege of the
(25) private citizen than of the ordained prophet. Its weakness lies in the fact that music is not a religion. Music does not deal in general ideas or morality or salvation. It is an art. It expresses private sentiments through skill and sincerity,
(30) both of which are a privilege, a duty, of the private citizen, and no monopoly of the prophetically inclined.

Originally a "masterpiece" was merely a graduation piece which marked the student's advance from
(35) apprenticeship to master status. Later it referred to any artist's most accomplished work, the high point of his production. Nowadays most people understand by it a piece differing from the run of the repertory by a degree of concentration in its
(40) expressivity that establishes a difference of kind. The idea that any composer, however gifted and skillful, is merely a masterpiece factory would have been repellent to Bach or Haydn or Handel or Mozart. But all the successors of Beethoven
(45) who aspired to his position quite consciously imbued their music with the "masterpiece" tone. This tone is lugubrious, portentous, world-shaking; and length, as well as heavy instrumentation, is essential to it. The masterpiece cult tends to
(50) substitute an impressive manner for specific expression, just as oratory does. That music should stoop to the procedures and techniques of contemporary political harangue is deplorable.

There are occasions (funerals, for instance)
(55) where the tone of a discourse is more important than its content, but the concert is not one of them. The concert is a habitual thing like a meal; the ceremonial is only incidental to it. And restricting its menu to what observes the fictitious "master-
(60) piece" tone is like limiting one's nourishment to the heavier party foods. If the idea can be got rid of that a proper concert should consist only of "masterpieces," either historic or contemporary, our programs will cease to be repetitive and monotonous.

I. 9. The primary purpose of the passage is to

(A) explain the history of musical masterpieces
(B) describe the steps in the creation of musical masterpieces
(C) expose the fallacy inherent in a current attitude toward musical masterpieces
(D) provide a new standard for composers to follow
(E) compare music criticism with criticism of the other arts

I. 10. According to the passage, a "masterpiece" is characterized by all of the following EXCEPT

(A) ceremoniousness
(B) lengthiness
(C) orchestration
(D) political overtones
(E) heaviness and pomposity

I. 11. According to the passage, music now differs from other arts in terms of

(A) its range of quality
(B) the goals of its creators
(C) its public rather than private nature
(D) the nature of the people who criticize it
(E) the standards used to judge its quality

I. 12. The "classical concept of a republic of letters" (lines 22-23) can best be interpreted as meaning that

(A) each work of art should be appreciated for its own merits
(B) the arts should be separate from religion
(C) the arts should be measured, if at all, by the criteria of classical times
(D) in a republic, literature should set the standard for all the arts
(E) in a republic, no exclusionary standards should be applied to the arts

I. 13. It can be inferred that the chief difference between older and current conceptions of a musical masterpiece is that in former times the production of a masterpiece

(A) was not viewed as an accomplishment
(B) required an impressive style
(C) was not viewed by major composers as being necessary
(D) required enthusiastic public support
(E) received immediate critical acclaim

GO ON TO THE NEXT PAGE.

I. 14. It can be inferred that a commitment to the idea of musical masterpieces has resulted in

(A) less integration of music with other arts
(B) a limited concert repertory
(C) less understanding of music
(D) less popular music
(E) fewer contemporary composers

I. 15. Funerals are mentioned (line 54) in order to

(A) illustrate metaphorically the death of inspiration in music
(B) predict the future of music if present misconceptions continue
(C) provide a legitimate instance of the domination of tone over content
(D) link music with other aspects of life
(E) show the varied uses of music

I. 16. The tone of the passage can best be described as

(A) argumentative
(B) noncommittal
(C) ambivalent
(D) hortatory
(E) enthusiastic

I. 17. With which of the following statements would the author be LEAST likely to agree?

(A) Art cannot exist without inspiration.
(B) Sincerity is an essential ingredient of art.
(C) Content is at least as important as form in art.
(D) Standards by which art is judged should be codified.
(E) Individual works of art are specific rather than general expressions.

GO ON TO THE NEXT PAGE.

(This passage was written in 1966.)

Nearly twenty years ago, biochemists found that a separable constituent of the cell—deoxyribonucleic acid or DNA—appeared to guide the cell's protein-synthesizing machinery. The internal structure of DNA seemed to represent a set of coded instructions which dictated the pattern of protein synthesis. Experiments indicated that in the presence of appropriate enzymes each DNA molecule could form a replica, a new DNA molecule, containing the specific guiding message present in the original. This idea, when added to what was already known about the cellular mechanisms of heredity (especially the knowledge that DNA is localized in chromosomes), appeared to establish a molecular basis for inheritance.

Proponents of the theory that DNA was a "self-duplicating" molecule, containing a code that by itself determined biological inheritance, introduced the term "central dogma" into scientific literature in order to describe the principles that were supposed to explain DNA's governing role. The dogma originally involved an admittedly unproven assumption: that whereas nucleic acids can guide the synthesis of other nucleic acids and of proteins, the reverse effect is impossible, that is, proteins cannot guide the synthesis of nucleic acids. But actual experimental observations deny the second and crucial part of this assumption. Other test-tube experiments show that agents besides DNA have a guiding influence. The kind of protein made may depend on the specific organism from which the necessary enzyme is obtained. It also depends on the test tube's temperature, the degree of acidity, and the amount of metallic salts present.

The central dogma banishes from consideration the interactions among the numerous molecular processes that have been discovered in cells or in their extracted fluids. In the living cell, molecular processes—the synthesis of nucleic acids and proteins or the oxidation of food substances—are not separate but interact in exceedingly complex ways. No matter how many ingredients the biochemists' test tubes may contain, the mixtures are nonliving; but these same ingredients, organized by the subtle structure of the cell, constitute a system which is alive.

Consider an example from another field. At ordinary temperatures, electricity flows only so long as a driving force from a battery or generator is imposed on the circuit. At temperatures near absolute zero, metals exhibit superconductivity, a unique property that causes an electric current to flow for months after the voltage is cut off. Although independent electrons exist in a metal at ordinary temperatures, at very low temperatures they interact with the metal's atomic structure in such a way as to lose their individual identities and form a coordinated, collective system which gives rise to superconductivity.

Such discoveries of modern physics show that the unique properties of a complex system are not necessarily explicable solely by the properties that can be observed in its isolated parts. We can expect to find a similar situation in the complex chemical system of the living cell.

I. 18. The author is primarily concerned with

(A) proposing that a new philosophical foundation for modern biochemistry be developed
(B) describing the various processes that take place in a living cell
(C) drawing analogies between different scientific fields
(D) revealing a discrepancy between a scientific theory and some experimental results
(E) questioning the assumptions behind experimental methods in science

I. 19. The author provides information that would answer which of the following questions?

I. What have test-tube experiments revealed about the role of DNA?
II. What cellular mechanisms influence heredity?
III. What methods have been developed to allow scientists to observe a living cell?

(A) I only
(B) II only
(C) I and III only
(D) II and III only
(E) I, II, and III

I. 20. The author's argument is directed against which of the following?

I. The use of test-tube experimentation alone to establish the validity of scientific theories
II. The exclusion of experimental facts from the formation of scientific theories
III. The observation of certain cellular components in isolation

(A) I only
(B) I and II only
(C) I and III only
(D) II and III only
(E) I, II, and III

I. 21. The author refers to the results of test-tube experiments involving the replication of DNA primarily in order to

(A) question the validity of experimental results that describe the structure of DNA
(B) provide evidence to contradict the theory that DNA alone governs protein synthesis
(C) show the way in which DNA acts as a self-duplicating molecule
(D) explain the internal structure of DNA
(E) reveal how nucleic acid can influence the synthesis of proteins

GO ON TO THE NEXT PAGE.

I. 22. According to the passage, a metal cannot become superconductive unless

(A) the voltage through the metal is increased
(B) the metal's atomic structure has been destroyed
(C) the metal is exposed to very low temperatures
(D) electrons in the metal interact with one another at ordinary temperatures
(E) electrical flow is provided by a battery

I. 23. The author suggests that the most important difference observed between a dead cell and a living cell results primarily from the

(A) differences in the chemical elements present in each
(B) differences in the degree of acidity present in each
(C) biochemical procedures used to examine each cell
(D) varying temperatures at which cells are examined
(E) integrating mechanism thought to exist within the structure of the living cell

I. 24. The experimental results mentioned in the passage suggest that biological inheritance depends on

(A) instructions contained in a single molecule within the cell
(B) processes that are guided by specific enzymes
(C) genetic information contained in metallic salts
(D) interactions among several molecular processes in the cell
(E) replicative processes within the chemistry of protein synthesis

I. 25. The author presents his argument primarily by

(A) contrasting two fields of science
(B) providing experimental evidence against a point of view
(C) criticizing proponents of other theories
(D) stating a new theory and its important implications
(E) comparing two theories of cellular structure

END OF SAMPLE TEST I

READING COMPREHENSION SAMPLE TEST II

Time—30 minutes

25 Questions

Each passage in this group is followed by questions based on its content. After reading a passage, choose the best answer to each question and blacken the corresponding space on the answer sheet. Answer all questions following a passage on the basis of what is stated or implied in that passage.

The great challenge to public health services in economically poor countries lies in providing primary health care to satisfy the minimum health needs of rural populations. Assistance from
(5) advanced nations, however, has often adversely influenced the development of health services because most aid programs do not recognize the priorities involved in the health needs of developing countries.
(10) Assistance programs, with their concern for visibility, not infrequently include spectacular but ill-adapted showpieces such as large hospitals, advanced technical apparatus, and specialized training in clinical medicine and surgery. In
(15) promoting such complicated and expensive projects, outside aid programs dissipate local resources and skilled manpower and perpetuate the dependency of poorer nations on the advanced nations. Developing countries basically need to
(20) improve their sanitary systems, provide for adequate nutrition, and immunize their people against communicable diseases. Experience has shown that even programs only partially meeting these needs result in a dramatic reduction of in-
(25) fant mortality and an increase in life expectancy.
A crucial factor for the success of such programs is the ability to provide large numbers of minimally trained individuals who can mobilize the self-help capacities of the people themselves
(30) and who can maximize the benefits of whatever health resources are available. A pyramidal structure with a wide base of minimally trained workers, covering even remote rural areas, with referral of more serious cases to progressively
(35) more complex medical institutions, leading to an apex of highly specialized medical and surgical facilities, would provide the health care system most appropriate to developing countries.
In training physicians from the developing
(40) countries, the major error has been the insistence on levels of competence and areas of study relevant to the advanced countries. Both the medical schools and the authorities of the countries that provide such training have failed to recognize that
(45) advanced countries have medical needs markedly different from those of the developing countries. This has led to a significant loss of physicians in the developing countries because of the frustrations highly skilled physicians feel upon returning to
(50) countries that are unable economically or organizationally to satisfy their misplaced expectations. The answer surely lies in promoting medical education in the developing countries which is appropriate to the priorities and essential needs of those countries.

II. 1. The author uses the image of a pyramid to suggest that

(A) the financial aid sent to developing countries is not distributed evenly
(B) the ratio of large, complex facilities to small clinics in developing countries is very high
(C) a small number of administrators can control a large number of medical programs
(D) the number of highly specialized physicians needed in developing countries is relatively small
(E) small investments in advanced medical technology yield large returns

II. 2. According to the passage, a successful medical system in a developing country will have a large number of

(A) physicians specializing in urban diseases
(B) men or women with limited medical training
(C) administrators with experience in managing hospitals and clinics
(D) dentists specializing in oral surgery
(E) technicians familiar with the latest laboratory equipment

II. 3. The author condemns complex medical assistance programs for developing countries because they are

(A) expensive and limit the number of countries that can receive such programs
(B) wasteful and prolong the developing country's reliance on external resources
(C) corrupt and permit the donating country to exploit the developing country
(D) extravagant and exhaust the financial resources of the donating country
(E) shortsighted and overemphasize the current needs of the developing country

GO ON TO THE NEXT PAGE.

II. 4. It can be inferred that the author's objective in the passage is to

(A) indict the administrators of large medical schools
(B) advocate reform of the medical education systems of advanced countries
(C) undermine suggestions that a country's resources should be used for political rather than medical reform
(D) advocate the development of mutual exchange programs between developing and advanced countries
(E) urge that all citizens in developing countries be provided with minimal medical assistance

II. 5. The author's statements on infant mortality and life expectancy (lines 22-25) are apparently supported by evidence that is

(A) fragmented
(B) economic
(C) hypothetical
(D) empirical
(E) biased

II. 6. If a developing country had $500,000 to spend on medical services, which of the following projects would the author of the passage be likely to support?

I. Food distribution in rural areas
II. Research on the effect of refined sugar on infant growth
III. Instruction in simple methods of sewage disposal
IV. Classes to train medical technicians to read x-ray pictures

(A) I only
(B) I and III only
(C) II and III only
(D) II and IV only
(E) III and IV only

II. 7. Which of the following statements, if true, would most seriously undermine the author's arguments against expensive assistance programs?

(A) People in developing countries have illnesses that are different from those that people in advanced countries have.
(B) Advanced countries contribute to a more equal distribution of wealth when they donate medical facilities to other countries.
(C) Expensive assistance programs provide useful technical knowledge for use in developing countries.
(D) Expensive assistance programs train highly qualified doctors and technicians from both advanced and developing countries.
(E) Expensive assistance programs improve all medical services available in developing countries.

GO ON TO THE NEXT PAGE.

Amiri Baraka's importance in Afro-American literature is in his far-reaching exposition of the doctrine of cultural nationalism, a composite of attitudes that led him to the most uncompromising
(5) examination of black American culture yet developed. A disciple of the beat generation and of the avant-garde culture of the 1950's, Baraka was trained to rebel, grounding his art on the principle of self-revelation as the source of primary artistic
(10) truth. Added to this was a powerful gift for political inquiry that depended for its development on his eventual recognition of empiricism and historicity as the keys to political analysis. Baraka long resisted that recognition because of his native
(15) tendency toward idealism as a personal attitude and lyricism as his most expressive mode. He shared, usually with discomfort, the disdain of the avant-garde for political commitment. But in their thematic and technical concerns, the beat
(20) avant-garde and their successors provided cultural analogues recognizable to the black artist politically troubled and enmeshed in reactionary cultural forms. Baraka enlisted in the brigade of poetic rebels distinguished by their scorn for traditional
(25) descriptions of Western culture as fundamentally moral and humanitarian.

From the outset, Baraka rejected any proposition that could not be directly translated into a force or an act, preferring the dramatic and em-
(30) phatic gesture to the elusiveness of implied meaning. That aspiration to concreteness had been only fitfully expressed in Afro-American literature before Baraka. It was Baraka who broke most vigorously with the traditional desire for complicity
(35) between the black artist and his reticent, if not hostile, white counterpart: it was Baraka who assaulted the matrix of philosophic assumptions with which bourgeois culture can surround and stifle the black writer. Baraka exposed the failure of intelli-
(40) gence that linked writers of an oppressed group to such notions as Christian piety as a substitute for secular power, the necessary and inherent vagueness of moral inquiry, the romantic essence of love and death, and the pastoral or nightmarish
(45) interpretations of the natural world. In other words, he rebelled against the imposition on black writing of the typical and often pernicious translation of the history of the white middle class into the laws of immutable human nature, an imposition
(50) that practically guaranteed the mediocrity of black literary art by securing the marginality of its rela-

tionship to black experience. Trying to give meaning to the spiritual African base of his people's hybrid culture, Baraka dramatized the conflict
(55) between the African roots and the grafted colonialist features of Afro-American art. He revived the central debate of the Afro-American experience— whether or not the black is assimilable into American culture—and powerfully asserted the negative
(60) position, often violently and vindictively expressing his antipathies.

His great achievement was the gradual imposition of dialectical discipline on a romantic sensibility continually nourished by his sense of ethnic and
(65) political identity. Realizing that a marked degree of nationalism is the base on which the black American must build all durable structures of humanistic understanding, he made his own character and history his principal focus.

II. 8. The passage is primarily concerned with

(A) detailing the evolutionary steps in Baraka's development as an artist
(B) comparing Baraka with black writers who came before him
(C) contrasting the work of black writers with that of white middle-class writers
(D) outlining the ways in which Baraka departed from black literary tradition
(E) describing the cultural roots of Baraka's writing

II. 9. According to the passage, one of Baraka's most significant contributions to black literature is his

(A) insistence that black writing be founded on black experience
(B) incorporation of African culture into his writing
(C) fusion of African experience with American experience in his writing
(D) linking of art with politics in America
(E) setting forth of a credo for other black writers

GO ON TO THE NEXT PAGE.

II.10. It can be inferred from the passage that Baraka shared which of the following with the beat generation avant-garde culture of the 1950's ?

(A) An attempt to bridge the gap between two different but equally oppressed groups
(B) An insistence on separating art from social institutions that were outmoded
(C) A recognition that the usual forms of writing were inadequate for and irrelevant to his concerns
(D) A commitment to using writing as a means of shaping society
(E) A disillusionment about the ability of any art to flourish in a corrupt society

II.11. According to the passage, with which of the following statements is Baraka most likely to agree?

(A) The black writer must reject his or her past and focus on the present and future.
(B) The black writer must reject idealized abstractions and deal with concrete realities.
(C) Oppressed groups must win their freedom and equality by adopting the techniques used by their oppressors.
(D) Politics rather than art must become the means by which oppressed peoples express their concerns.
(E) The essence of all literature is in its rebellion against traditional themes and modes.

II.12. The "complicity" (line 34) between the black artist and his white counterpart can best be described as

(A) a perception by others that the two are similar
(B) the stifling of both by bourgeois culture
(C) an attempt by both to rebel against standard cultural forms
(D) collusion between the two in undermining Western tradition
(E) an expression by both of the same point of view

II.13. The author cites "the romantic essence of love and death" (lines 43-44) primarily as an example of

(A) an abstract notion that has little relationship to the realities of black life
(B) a concept that has been traditionally ignored by black writers
(C) an assumption compatible with avant-garde writing but not with black writing
(D) an outmoded theme that is irrelevant to any writing
(E) a motif that is not legitimately translatable into literature

II.14. It can be inferred that Baraka embraced political commitment largely because of

(A) the political models espoused by the beat generation avant-garde culture, who were his predecessors
(B) his original and continuing distaste for traditional literary modes
(C) the concreteness and empiricism characteristic of practical politics
(D) his natural tendency toward political inquiry and analysis
(E) the sense of ethnic identity provided by his past history

II.15. It can be inferred that the author believes that the imposition of white middle-class history on black writing is pernicious (lines 46-49) because such an imposition

(A) portrays black writers unfavorably
(B) undermines the unity of the black population
(C) creates psychological conflicts within the black artist
(D) has deleterious effects on black literature
(E) destroys the ethnic and political identity of all writers

II.16. The primary purpose of the passage is to

(A) describe and analyze a point of view
(B) provide a historical context for a movement
(C) present a hypothesis to account for a set of beliefs
(D) reconcile two opposing points of view
(E) promote a new method of analysis

II.17. The tone of the passage is primarily

(A) neutral in weighing Baraka's successes and shortcomings
(B) commendatory of Baraka's achievement and impact
(C) hostile toward the ideas Baraka is promoting
(D) uncertain about Baraka's goals
(E) pessimistic about the chances for Baraka's ultimate success

GO ON TO THE NEXT PAGE.

Scientists believe that hypertension, or high blood pressure, is one factor responsible for heart attacks and strokes. High blood pressure, in turn, seems to be an inevitable result of the rapid pace of Western life—a pace that gives no indication of slowing down. Since our present standard of living is generally believed to depend on keeping up that pace, it is likely that many people would not want it to slow down. It appears, then, that everyday situations of stress, which require physiological adjustments that may lead to hypertension and subsequent heart failure, are a permanent part of Western life, and that people's only recourse lies in learning how to counteract the harmful effects of their physiological responses to such situations.

In general, a person can counteract such effects by regularly eliciting, by psychological means, what is called a "relaxation response." The relaxation response is an innate, integrated set of physiological changes that are the opposites of the changes involved in the "fight-or-flight" response associated with hypertension. One particularly well-known method of relaxing, called transcendental meditation (TM), decreases the activity of the sympathetic nervous system and thus effectively counterbalances the harmful, environmentally induced fight-or-flight response.

Techniques that elicit the relaxation response should not be confused with biofeedback. Using the biofeedback method, subjects can be made aware of physiological functions that are normally performed unconsciously and can learn to consciously alter those functions. For instance, when a monitoring device "feeds back" to the subject information corresponding to each heartbeat, the subject becomes aware of changes in heart rate and can gain at least partial control over the changes. While biofeedback requires special equipment to monitor physiological processes and can usually focus on only one function at a time, TM requires no monitoring equipment and affects several functions simultaneously. Meditation is known to cause a simultaneous decrease in heart rate and the rates of metabolism and breathing.

Although blood pressure remains unchanged during actual periods of meditation, it has been found that the blood pressure of meditators is, in general, lower than the blood pressure of people who do not practice TM. Recently, individuals with elevated blood pressure who were attending an introductory TM lecture were asked to participate in a study to determine the effects of meditation on high blood pressure. The selected group was asked to postpone the regular practice of meditation for six weeks, so that each person's exact "premeditation" blood pressure could be established. At the end of this period, the subjects began to practice TM on a regular basis. After nine weeks, it was found that the average blood pressure of the group had dropped from what is considered borderline hypertensive to what is considered a normal range.

II. 18. The author is primarily concerned with

(A) discussing a remedy
(B) explaining a predicament
(C) evaluating a study
(D) outlining a proposal
(E) countering an argument

II. 19. Which of the following, if true, would most seriously weaken the conclusions of the experiment described in the last paragraph?

(A) Two weeks after subjects had stopped meditating, they again exhibited blood pressures in the hypertensive range.
(B) Persons who had not volunteered for the experiment but who had practiced TM for 9 weeks also experienced lowered blood pressures.
(C) A group of people who were of the same age as the subjects in the experiment but who had not been trained in TM exhibited normal blood pressures.
(D) Many of the subjects were unable to elicit the relaxation response during the 9-week training period.
(E) Persons who had not volunteered for the experiment but who had signed up for TM training had a higher average blood pressure than did the volunteers.

II. 20. According to the passage, changes in which of the following occur during meditation?

  I. Heart rate
  II. Blood pressure
  III. Metabolic rate

(A) I only
(B) II only
(C) III only
(D) I and III only
(E) I, II, and III

GO ON TO THE NEXT PAGE.

II. 21. It can be inferred that the author discusses biofeed-back primarily in order to

(A) provide the reader with another definition of the relaxation response
(B) provide the reader with information necessary for understanding the experiment described
(C) show that TM is the most widely used means of eliciting the relaxation response
(D) provide more detailed information about the ideas already discussed
(E) contrast TM with another means of altering physiological functions

II. 22. According to the passage, biofeedback techniques permit subjects to

(A) elicit the relaxation response
(B) suppress the fight-or-flight response
(C) consciously control physiological functions
(D) gain better control over their environments
(E) better understand their mental states

II. 23. According to the passage, all of the following were true of the people who participated in the experiment described in the last paragraph EXCEPT:

(A) They were all volunteers.
(B) They all had high blood pressures.
(C) They were all inexperienced in meditation.
(D) They had all expressed interest in learning about TM.
(E) They were all helped by the practice of TM.

II. 24. The author suggests that the most practical way for people to avoid hypertension is to learn to

(A) reverse the effects of stress situations
(B) inhibit their fight-or-flight responses
(C) stay away from stress situations
(D) deliberately control physiological processes
(E) alter their daily environments

II. 25. The author's attitude toward the pace of Western life can best be described as one of

(A) anxiety
(B) apology
(C) resignation
(D) indignation
(E) unconcern

END OF SAMPLE TEST II

READING COMPREHENSION SAMPLE TEST III

Time—30 minutes

25 Questions

Each passage in this group is followed by questions based on its content. After reading a passage, choose the best answer to each question and blacken the corresponding space on the answer sheet. Answer all questions following a passage on the basis of what is stated or implied in that passage.

(This passage was written in 1974.)

Like student activism, ethnicity—the assertion of distinctiveness—is on the rise throughout the world. The black movement in the United States has found an echo among other ethnic groups in the United States, such as the Puerto Rican, Mexican-American, American Indian, Oriental, Italian, Irish, and Polish groups. The original circumstances of all of these groups varied greatly. Some had been conquered, some had emigrated from colonies and some from free countries, and some had met substantial prejudice and discrimination. Yet the notion of a unified ethnic group seemed, in some degree, to satisfy individuals from every ethnic background. The black revolution has had as widespread a resonance abroad as at home. A black power movement developed in the West Indies, a civil rights movement in Northern Ireland, and a Black Panther group in Israel. The Catholics of Northern Ireland did not need the black example to teach them that they were aggrieved—their miseries in relation to the Protestant majority go back farther in history than those of American blacks. Nor did the Oriental Jews of Israel need the American blacks to remind them that something was amiss with their position. Nevertheless, the black example exerted its influence around the world, just as certain developments abroad influenced American blacks. The American civil rights movement, for example, avowedly and explicitly adopted techniques developed in twentieth-century India during the struggle against British rule.

It seems clear that, in the last twenty years, ethnic identity has become more salient, ethnic self-assertion stronger, and ethnic conflict more marked everywhere. The natural concomitant of increased ethnic awareness is the development of ethnic groups as political forces. In those economic systems characteristic of the twentieth century, where the state becomes a crucial and direct influence on the individual's economic well-being and political status, it is inevitable that ethnopolitical coalitions form. The assertion of claims on behalf of large but loosely aggregated groups, such as "workers," "peasants," or "blue-collar employees," is insufficient because claims of this order are too broad and the benefits too diffuse to affect the individual noticeably. Smaller interest groups, however, like the ethnic group, can have a significant effect within the relatively limited range of their concerns.

The growing heterogeneity of national populations and international systems of communication have also contributed to the growth of ethnic groups as political interest groups. In fact, ethnicity has recently been referred to as part of the "refeudalization" of society, the return of given or ascribed, rather than achieved, characteristics as determinants of social stratification. Ethnicity is a phenomenon intimately and organically bound up with major developments in modern societies.

III. 1. The author suggests that student activism has

(A) inspired the rise of ethnicity
(B) effected economic changes
(C) resulted from class conflict
(D) created conflict between ethnic groups
(E) been international in scope

III. 2. The author mentions twentieth-century India in order to show that

(A) the Indians were successful in their struggle against British rule
(B) the efforts of blacks in the United States affected ethnic groups in non-European states
(C) American blacks were influenced by a foreign movement
(D) Indians encouraged and advised American civil rights leaders
(E) ethnic groups gained political power in India

III. 3. Which of the following questions does the author answer in the passage?

(A) Has ethnic conflict been characterized by violence?
(B) Has ethnic conflict intensified in recent years?
(C) Is ethnic protest as effective in American as in European states?
(D) When will the political power of ethnic groups decline?
(E) What is a satisfactory definition of ethnicity?

GO ON TO THE NEXT PAGE.

III. 4. Which of the following would be logically appropriate topics for the author to consider in a continuation of the passage?

    I. The relationship between the rise of ethnicity and modern communication systems
    II. Ethnicity as a distinctively Western development
    III. The possible results of an increase in ethnic awareness

(A) I only
(B) II only
(C) I and II only
(D) I and III only
(E) I, II, and III

III. 5. The author implies that the black revolution in the United States influenced foreign ethnic groups partly because the foreign groups

(A) needed an effective model for seeking power
(B) shared the same racial background as blacks in the United States
(C) generally looked to the United States for leadership
(D) were previously unaware that they were unjustly treated
(E) were suffering under unusually oppressive conditions

III. 6. According to the author, the rise of ethnicity has been due partly to

(A) inflated expectations of improvements in the standard of living
(B) the failure of totalitarianism to check the outbreak of dissidence
(C) an application of the concept of individual freedoms to groups of individuals
(D) an emotional need created by the overwhelming size and impersonality of inflexible political systems
(E) the increasing influence of the state on the economic and political status of its citizens

III. 7. The author mentions not only similarities but also differences between

(A) systems of government
(B) experiences of ethnic groups
(C) political and economic forces
(D) workers and their leaders
(E) richer and poorer nations of the world

III. 8. The primary purpose of the passage is to

(A) discuss a trend
(B) analyze a system
(C) deplore a blunder
(D) recommend a solution
(E) defend a stance

III. 9. The development discussed in the passage is mainly

(A) technical
(B) philosophical
(C) political
(D) psychological
(E) methodological

GO ON TO THE NEXT PAGE.

If viewed from the outside, our galaxy would appear to be a giant pinwheel made up of billions of stars rotating slowly around a compact, brilliant nucleus. The spherical volume of space

(5) above and below the pinwheel is not empty but is filled with billions of much fainter stars, and scattered about in this "halo" are some 200 fuzzy but brightly glowing globules. Each globule consists of from 100,000 to a million stars, most of

(10) which are of low luminosity. These are the globular clusters. If one could collapse hundreds of millions of years into a few minutes, one would see that the 200 clusters are traveling in giant elliptical orbits around the nucleus of the galaxy.

(15) The entire system thus closely resembles the old-fashioned picture of electrons whirling around the nucleus of an atom.

Globular clusters are fascinating astronomical objects, and what has pushed them to the front of

(20) theoretical interest has been the recognition that their stars are extremely old and contain clues concerning the early history of the universe. Some of the first estimates of the age of globular-cluster stars were so high (20 to 25 billion years) that they

(25) could not be reconciled with the apparently much younger age of the universe, as indicated by the recession velocities of distant galaxies. The velocity measurements imply that all the galaxies emerged from a primordial fireball no more than

(30) 12 to 13 billion years ago.

Astronomers are currently constructing theoretical models for stars of various initial masses and compositions to determine in what manner and how rapidly such stars would evolve as their

(35) nuclear fuel is consumed. From these studies astronomers hope to refine estimates of the ages of globular-cluster stars, to establish whether their ages are really inconsistent with the estimated age of the universe, and to draw some inferences

(40) about the cosmological conditions surrounding their origin. Initial research suggests that the globular-cluster stars are about as old as the universe is thought to be and that the initial quantity of helium in the stars is remarkably close to

(45) that predicted by "big bang" models of the universe. Hence, cluster stars provide evidence that the universe has expanded from a tremendously hot primeval atom that was formed in one event 12 or 13 billion years ago.

(50) Direct observation of individual cluster stars provides just enough information to make comparison with theoretical models worthwhile. Although one can determine none of the bulk properties (mass, radius, or intrinsic brightness), one can

(55) estimate the surface temperature from the star's color and judge whether the star is more or less luminous than its neighbors. From the star's spectrum one can also estimate the quantities present of elements heavier than helium. The

(60) heavier elements, being readily excited, yield considerable spectroscopic information. It appears that cluster stars are strikingly deficient in heavy elements; they contain only from a tenth to a hundredth as many heavy atoms as do stars of

(65) equal mass in the disk of the galaxy. Moreover, the farther a cluster star is from the center of the galaxy, the more deficient it seems to be in heavy elements.

III. 10. Which of the following is the most important reason for scientific interest in globular-cluster stars?

(A) They have an inexplicably high helium content.
(B) Their age is probably equivalent to that of the universe.
(C) They can be considered as representing the history of the universe collapsed into a few minutes.
(D) They seem to be traveling in orbits that have the nucleus of our own galaxy as their center.
(E) Direct observation of them makes possible comparison with various theoretical models.

III. 11. It can be inferred from the passage that the author holds which of the following beliefs concerning the origin of the universe?

(A) It occurred approximately 20 to 25 billion years ago.
(B) It can be explained by the model of electrons orbiting a nucleus.
(C) It antedated by millions of years the origin of globular-cluster stars.
(D) It is plausibly explained by the "big bang" theory.
(E) It occurred in a series of stages rather than as a single event.

GO ON TO THE NEXT PAGE.

III. 12. Which of the following best describes the relation-ship between globular-cluster stars and halo stars?

(A) Globular-cluster stars move at a higher velocity than do halo stars.
(B) Globular-cluster stars are older than halo stars.
(C) Globular-cluster stars are one kind of halo star.
(D) Halo stars are one kind of globular-cluster star.
(E) Halo stars surround globular-cluster stars.

III. 13. According to the passage, all of the following properties of a globular-cluster star can be determined EXCEPT

(A) intrinsic brightness
(B) surface temperature
(C) color
(D) velocity
(E) relative luminosity

III. 14. Which of the following titles best describes the content of the passage?

(A) How the Universe Began
(B) Theoretical Star Models
(C) The Age of the Universe
(D) Telling Time from the Stars
(E) Globular Clusters in Our Galaxy

III. 15. When the author says that "the universe has ex-panded from a tremendously hot primeval atom" (lines 46-48), in what sense is he apparently using the word "atom"?

(A) Literally, in the same sense that it is used in modern physics to describe a molecular component
(B) Literally, but in a sense designed to convey the explosive force of an atom bomb
(C) Humorously, since it is inconceivable that the entire universe could arise from a single particle
(D) Figuratively, to indicate only that the universe originated from very basic elements
(E) Figuratively, to indicate that the original size of the universe was relatively small

III. 16. It can be inferred that which of the following constitute an important basis for estimating the age of the universe?

(A) Calculations of the ratio of helium to heavy elements in globular-cluster stars
(B) Computations of the velocity of globular-cluster stars within our galaxy
(C) Observations of the velocity at which galaxies far from us are receding
(D) Measurements of the rate at which the surface temperatures of stars are changing
(E) Studies of theoretical models of the universe constructed by astronomers

III. 17. The author's primary purpose is to

(A) discredit techniques that determine the age of the universe through velocity measure-ments
(B) demonstrate the value of cluster stars in helping to determine the age of the universe
(C) question the validity of theoretical models of the evolution of stars
(D) defend the use of spectroscopic data in describing star clusters
(E) explain the mechanical structure of our galaxy

GO ON TO THE NEXT PAGE.

Mass culture is an urban product. Confined to the close spaces of a city, members of an industrial society must always face the disturbing problem of what to do with their leisure time, how to organize it in relation to their work day.

One thing seems certain: except during brief revolutionary intervals, the quality of leisure-time activity cannot vary too sharply from that of the work day. If it did, office or factory workers would be exposed to terrible dualities of feeling that would make it difficult for them to adjust to their jobs. They want no part of such difficulties. Following the dictum of industrial society that anonymity is a key to safety, they seek the least troublesome solution: mass culture.

Whatever its manifest content, mass culture must therefore not subvert the basic patterns of industrial life. Leisure time must be so organized as to bear a factitious relationship to working time: apparently different, actually the same. It must provide relief from work monotony without making the return to work too unbearable; it must provide amusement without insight and pleasure without disturbance—as distinct from art, which gives pleasure through disturbance.

Mass culture is thus oriented toward a central aspect of industrial society: the depersonalization of the individual. On the one hand, it diverts workers from their disturbing reduction to semi-robot status by arranging "relaxing" amusements for them. The need for such amusements explains the ceaseless and hectic quest for novelty in the mass-culture industries. On the other hand, mass culture reinforces those emotional attitudes that seem inseparable from existence in modern society—passivity and boredom. The frenetic chase after novelty, after something new that might rise above routine experience, is simply another means of molding leisure-time activity according to work-time patterns. What is supposed to deflect us from the reduction of our personalities actually reinforces it.

If only because it must conform to the psychological patterns created by life in an industrial society, mass culture is inseparable from common experience. The notion that it concocts a world of irrelevant fantasy is nonsense spread by those whose only complaint about Hollywood is that it is not "realistic" enough. In actuality, the audience accepts both mass culture and daily experience precisely to the degree that the two blend.

Mass culture elicits the most conservative responses possible from its audience. So long as the audience feels that it must continue to live as it does, it has little desire to see its passivity and deep-seated (though hardly conscious) boredom upset; it wants to be titillated and amused, but not disturbed. For those molded in the image of contemporary society, art has many dangers: its effects are unpredictable and its demands tremendous. Art demands effort, a creative response from the audience. But mass culture is safe, for its end is already present in its beginning.

III. 18. The primary purpose of the passage is to

(A) analyze the different components of mass culture
(B) examine the ways in which leisure-time activities divert people
(C) explore the ways in which people engage in leisure-time activities
(D) describe the role of mass culture in modern society
(E) outline the history of mass culture in urban life

III. 19. According to the passage, most people in an industrial society find mass culture more satisfying than art because art

(A) makes too many demands on people
(B) does not provide relief from the boredom of work
(C) is too difficult to understand
(D) does not offer enough novelty
(E) gives insight but no enjoyment

III. 20. The last sentence in the passage, "But mass culture is safe, for its end is already present in its beginning," means that mass culture

(A) has always existed and will continue to exist
(B) tempts people because it holds out the promise of something different
(C) is attractive only because it is short-lived
(D) should not trouble anyone because it is temporary by its very nature
(E) neither threatens nor taxes people because it is predictable

III. 21. Which of the following best describes the tone of the passage?

(A) Tentative and inquisitive
(B) Ambivalent and confused
(C) Critical and analytical
(D) Optimistic and whimsical
(E) Ill-tempered and harsh

GO ON TO THE NEXT PAGE.

III. 22. It can be inferred that an item of mass culture will be successful only to the extent that it

(A) ostensibly mimics the process of the assembly line
(B) adopts the problems of urban living as its subject matter
(C) reminds its audience that escape from reality is possible
(D) attempts to change basic patterns of living
(E) resembles the everyday experiences of its audience

III. 23. With which of the following statements would the author be LEAST likely to agree?

(A) The nature of leisure-time activity must fundamentally resemble the nature of work.
(B) Mass culture allows the worker to escape from the monotony imposed by work.
(C) Art and mass culture differ primarily in the nature of the responses they require from their audiences.
(D) Contemporary society has created cultural forms that only appear to be different from life.
(E) Contemporary workers are unwilling to be troubled by their leisure-time activities.

III. 24. The author's argument assumes an absolute dichotomy between

(A) leisure time and working time
(B) novelty and conservatism
(C) art and mass culture
(D) amusement and depersonalization
(E) insight and disturbance

III. 25. According to the passage, mass culture is a direct outgrowth of

(A) a revolt against depersonalization
(B) a revolt against intellectualism
(C) the need for fantasy
(D) the industrialization of society
(E) psychological imbalances

END OF SAMPLE TEST III

ANSWER KEYS FOR SAMPLE TESTS

Answers preceded by asterisks indicate questions discussed in detail in the explanatory material. This discussion is designed to provide you with the best preparation for Reading Comprehension questions on the GMAT. Therefore, it is less important that you focus on the individual explanation of a particular answer than that you study the discussion as a whole in order to grasp the underlying principles of Reading Comprehension questions.

READING COMPREHENSION

Sample Test I

*I. 1. E	*I.14. B
I. 2. A	*I.15. C
I. 3. B	I.16. A
I. 4. C	I.17. D
I. 5. E	*I.18. D
I. 6. A	I.19. A
I. 7. B	*I.20. E
*I. 8. D	I.21. B
I. 9. C	I.22. C
*I.10. D	I.23. E
I.11. E	I.24. D
I.12. A	*I.25. B
I.13. C	

Sample Test II

II. 1. D	II.14. C
*II. 2. B	II.15. D
II. 3. B	*II.16. A
II. 4. E	II.17. B
II. 5. D	II.18. A
*II. 6. B	II.19. D
*II. 7. E	*II.20. D
II. 8. D	II.21. E
II. 9. A	II.22. C
*II.10. C	II.23. E
II.11. B	*II.24. A
II.12. E	*II.25. C
II.13. A	

Sample Test III

*III. 1. E	*III.14. E
III. 2. C	III.15. E
III. 3. B	III.16. C
*III. 4. D	III.17. B
III. 5. A	III.18. D
III. 6. E	III.19. A
III. 7. B	III.20. E
III. 8. A	*III.21. C
III. 9. C	III.22. E
III.10. B	*III.23. B
III.11. D	*III.24. C
*III.12. C	III.25. D
III.13. A	

EXPLANATORY MATERIAL: READING COMPREHENSION

The following discussion of Reading Comprehension is intended to familiarize you with the most efficient and effective approaches to the kinds of problems common to Reading Comprehension. The particular examples taken from the sample tests in this chapter are generally representative of the kinds of questions you will encounter in this section of the GMAT. Remember that it is the problem-solving strategy that is important, not the specific details of a particular question. References in the explanatory material to questions from the sample tests are indicated by the Roman numeral of the particular sample test followed by the Arabic numeral of the particular question.

QUESTIONS ABOUT THE MAIN IDEA

I.1. Which of the following best expresses the main idea of the passage?

(A) The barriers to careers in management for women will be broken down within a few years.
(B) Although organizations provide similar opportunities for men and women, men and women do not advance at equal rates.
(C) Most organizations do not sincerely attempt to achieve equal employment opportunity for men and women.
(D) The findings of a recent survey contradict previously held beliefs about women in management.
(E) Implicit attitudes toward women may prevent women from succeeding in careers in management.

This is a straightforward question that asks you to select the one sentence that fully and accurately expresses the main idea of the passage. In approaching such a question, you should first determine whether or not the author has explicitly stated the main idea anywhere in the passage. In the first and last paragraphs of the passage, the author states that barriers to the acceptance of women in managerial positions still exist despite overt changes in employment policy, that long-held beliefs about women in management still prevail in the business community, and that, unless such beliefs change, the barriers are likely to remain. These three ideas are the ones summarized in choice E, the best answer to this moderately difficult question.

Choices A and D are relatively easy to eliminate because they say exactly the opposite of what the passage says. Choices B and C may seem attractive, but they do not say precisely what is said in the passage. The last sentence of the passage makes it clear that the author does not consider opportunities in management to be equal for men and women, so B is not acceptable. Choice C attributes the lack of equal employment opportunity to insincerity on the part of organizations; however, in the last paragraph of the passage, the author concedes that managers may be sincere in their desire for equality. He encourages them to eliminate their built-in biases so that the equality they say they desire may quickly become a reality.

Questions like I.1, which ask you to recognize a correct restatement, or paraphrase, of the main idea or central point of a passage, are asking you what the passage *as a whole* is saying. The best answer to such questions is always the choice that summarizes *all* of the most important ideas in a passage in a few well-chosen words.

I.18. The author is primarily concerned with

   (A) proposing that a new philosophical foundation for modern biochemistry be developed
   (B) describing the various processes that take place in a living cell
   (C) drawing analogies between different scientific fields
   (D) revealing a discrepancy between a scientific theory and some experimental results
   (E) questioning the assumptions behind experimental methods in science

This is a question that asks not for the main idea of a passage but rather for the author's primary *purpose* or *objective* in writing the passage. To answer a "primary purpose" question correctly, you must pay careful attention to the initial words in the five choices. Is the author actually *proposing, describing, drawing analogies, revealing a discrepancy,* or *questioning assumptions*? The passage does not actually describe any of the processes, such as protein synthesis, that take place within the living cell, so choice B can be eliminated. Also, although the author does draw an analogy in the last two paragraphs between modern biochemistry and modern physics, that analogy is only indirectly related to the central point of the passage, which concerns the adequacy of the "central dogma" as an explanation of protein synthesis. Choices A, D, and E, however, suggest possibilities that go beyond information explicitly given in the passage. Since the author never literally says, "I propose," or "I question," you must infer his purpose from the language of the passage and from the arguments advanced in it.

The central idea of the passage on which this question is based is that experimental results have called into question the "central dogma." Once you have recognized this central idea, you can eliminate choice E because it is too general. The author is not questioning the assumptions behind all scientific experimentation but only the assumptions behind one particular scientific theory. According to the passage, "experimental methods" have actually helped to discredit the questionable theory, and the author supports them enthusiastically. Choices A and D, however, are both consistent with the central idea of the passage, so choosing the best answer to this question requires careful discrimination. The "central dogma" is limited in this passage to DNA research and it is not the basis for all of modern biochemistry, so choice A is too general. Also, the passage deals with research in science rather than with the philosophy of science. Thus, A can be eliminated on the grounds that it is too general and does not concern the area of science emphasized in the passage. The best answer to this question of above-average difficulty is choice D: "revealing a discrepancy between a scientific theory and some experimental results."

One way in which this question measures your ability to discern the primary purpose of a passage is by asking you to differentiate between the primary objective of the author and any secondary objectives he may wish to achieve. Since authors frequently communicate their objectives to readers only indirectly, you must approach a "primary purpose" question by asking yourself what the author is *doing* in the passage. The language of a passage and its organization often provide the best clues to whether the author is "proposing," "describing," or "questioning." Though the author of a passage may not explicitly state his or her purpose, you will find that purpose strongly implied in the kind of language used in a passage to express important ideas.

II.16. The primary purpose of the passage is to

   (A) describe and analyze a point of view
   (B) provide a historical context for a movement
   (C) present a hypothesis to account for a set of beliefs
   (D) reconcile two opposing points of view
   (E) promote a new method of analysis

Question II.16, like I.18, asks for the author's primary purpose, and you can best approach it by considering the appropriateness of the words that begin the five choices and by asking yourself what the language and the organization of the passage suggest about the author's primary purpose. This question, however, is more difficult than I.18 because it asks about the purpose of the passage only in the most general terms, without referring specifically to the actual content of the passage itself. The best answer to question II.16 is A; the passage as a whole describes Amiri Baraka's view of culture and art—the doctrine of cultural nationalism—and analyzes his view in the light of views held by other artists and by other Black Americans.

Choice B can be eliminated because the passage is about the point of view of an individual, not about a movement, although some details of the historical context within which Baraka wrote are given. Likewise, choice D can be eliminated on the grounds that only one point of view—Baraka's—is discussed. The passage is concerned with how Baraka resolved opposing tendencies within himself, not with the reconciliation of Baraka's point of view and those of other writers. There is no evidence in the passage that the author's analysis of Baraka represents a new way of analyzing culture or art, so E can also be eliminated. Choice C is tempting, since the passage is clearly about a set of beliefs, but because the information about Baraka is presented by the author as fact, the primary purpose cannot be "to present a hypothesis." You may wish to compare question II.16 with question II.8, which asks about the primary purpose of that same passage in different words, offering five answer choices that are different from the answer choices given in question II.16.

Questions I.18, II.8, and II.16 are differently worded versions of the same type of "primary purpose" question. These questions do not ask what the passage itself is saying, but what the author is *doing* in the passage—that is, they ask whether the author is describing and analyzing, providing a historical context, presenting a hypothesis, and so forth. Often, a set of questions about a passage will contain both a question that asks what the passage is saying and a question that asks what the author is doing. Question I.1, for instance, has a "primary purpose" counterpart in question I.6.

III.14 Which of the following titles best describes the content of the passage?

    (A) How the Universe Began
    (B) Theoretical Star Models
    (C) The Age of the Universe
    (D) Telling Time from the Stars
    (E) Globular Clusters in Our Galaxy

This question asks you to select a title for the passage that accurately and succinctly summarizes the ideas developed throughout the entire passage. The passage begins with a description of globular clusters and the stars composing them, gives the principal reason why astronomers have found them fascinating, and then describes some of the theoretical and empirical research now being done. Of the five answer choices, only E is broad enough to encompass all of those subtopics. Choices A, B, and C each concern only one subtopic in the passage, so their scope is necessarily narrower than the scope of E. Choices A, B, and C might make appropriate titles for *parts* of the passage, but none of them is appropriate as a title for the passage as a whole, particularly since none of them specifically mentions globular clusters. Choice D is incorrect because the passage makes no mention of using the stars to tell time. Therefore, the best answer to this moderately difficult question is E.

"Title" questions, "primary purpose" questions, and "main idea" questions may seem different, but they all ask for the same thing. These types of questions all ask what the passage *as a whole* is about. To answer these questions, you must consider every aspect of the passage—ideas explicitly stated by the author, ideas implied by the author, arguments presented by the author in support of his or her views, and the style and tone used by the author to express those views. Other types of Reading Comprehension questions ask about each of these aspects of a passage individually.

QUESTIONS ABOUT SUPPORTING IDEAS

I.10 According to the passage, a "masterpiece" is characterized by all of the following EXCEPT

    (A) ceremoniousness
    (B) lengthiness
    (C) orchestration
    (D) political overtones
    (E) heaviness and pomposity

Question I.10, a moderately easy question, asks you to gather from various parts of the passage all of the characteristics that the author attributes to music in the self-conscious "masterpiece" style. "Lengthiness," "pomposity," and "heavy instrumentation" (a kind of orchestration) can be found in lines 47-49. The word "heavy" in line 48 and the phrase "the heavier party foods" in line 61 add "heaviness." Lines 54-58 establish the "masterpiece" tone as "ceremonial." While lines 51-53 suggest that empty political rhetoric and self-conscious musical "masterpieces" may have something in common, the passage does not imply that a musical composition itself has any political overtones. Therefore, the best answer to the question is D.

Questions that ask you about several specific details given by an author in different parts of a passage are often phrased like question I.10, using the words "all of the following EXCEPT." Other examples of similar questions include questions II.23 and III.13. You may approach such questions in either of two ways: as in the example above, you may locate the place in the passage where the author mentions each of the four choices, thus eliminating those four and identifying the one choice not mentioned in the passage, or as in question III.13, you may find an explicit statement that identifies one choice as the *exception* in the group.

II.2 According to the passage, a successful medical system in a developing country will have a large number of

    (A) physicians specializing in urban diseases
    (B) men or women with limited medical training
    (C) administrators with experience in managing hospitals and clinics
    (D) dentists specializing in oral surgery
    (E) technicians familiar with the latest laboratory equipment

This question asks for a specific supporting detail presented in the passage. It is an easy question about the point being made in a single sentence—in this case, lines 26-31, in which the author asserts that, to be successful, health delivery programs in developing countries must "provide large numbers of minimally trained individuals." This assertion is accurately given in choice B. Choice A is not correct because the opening lines of the passage explicitly state that the needs of rural populations of developing nations are not being met. Choices C and D may safely be eliminated because the third paragraph of the passage suggests that developing countries need relatively few large hospitals with surgical facilities. Choice E is incorrect because, in lines 13-14, the author strongly rejects the idea that "advanced technical apparatus" is necessary to the success of the medical system in a developing nation.

Supporting-detail questions that ask for a restatement or paraphrase of an idea in the passage are very common. (See, for example, questions I.22, II.3, II.22, and III.19.) Similar to these questions are those that ask for an idea as it might be formulated by the author. This formulation is based on statements made throughout the passage. Questions I.11 and III.25 fall into this category. These questions do not repeat statements made by the author, but the ideas they ask for are based on statements in the passage and are consistent with the author's views. Many questions that restate information in the passage prove to be easy, but that is not always the case. The best answer to question III.19, for instance, is given explicitly in the passage, but the information on which the answer is based is not emphasized or repeated by the author; therefore, you cannot locate it easily if you are merely skimming. This is why it is important to read a passage carefully, concentrating on understanding the material, to ensure that you do not miss *any* of the supporting details provided by the author.

II.20 According to the passage, changes in which of the following occur during meditation?

    I. Heart rate
   II. Blood pressure
  III. Metabolic rate

 (A) I only
 (B) II only
 (C) III only
 (D) I and III only
 (E) I, II, and III

Question II.20 brings together information from more than one part of the passage, and the question is difficult because the answer has several parts. You must consider each possible part of the answer, indicated by Roman numerals, separately and carefully. According to the third paragraph of the passage, both heart rate and metabolic rate decrease during meditation, so I and III must be part of the best answer: therefore choices A, B, and C can be eliminated. To decide between D and E, you must determine whether or not blood pressure also changes during meditation. The first lines of the concluding paragraph state that there is no change in blood pressure "during actual periods of meditation," so II is not part of the best answer, and E can be eliminated. The best answer to this question of average difficulty is D.

You must approach a question like II.20 by weighing each Roman numeral part individually. This same approach is necessary when, as in questions I.19 and III.3, the choices consist of a series of independent questions that may or may not be answerable on the basis of information given in the passage. Questions I.10, I.19, II.20, and III.3 all require that you understand the entire passage; it is advisable to read all of a passage before you begin answering the questions based on it.

III.12 Which of the following best describes the relationship between globular-cluster stars and halo stars?

 (A) Globular-cluster stars move at a higher velocity than do halo stars.
 (B) Globular-cluster stars are older than halo stars.
 (C) Globular-cluster stars are one kind of halo star.
 (D) Halo stars are one kind of globular-cluster star.
 (E) Halo stars surround globular-cluster stars.

Question III.12 asks you for an interpretation of information explicitly provided in the passage. This comparatively difficult question is based on only one small part of the passage, the definition and description of globular-cluster stars with which the passage begins. In lines 4-11, globular clusters are described by the author as "scattered about in [a] 'halo' " that surrounds our galaxy. The halo is itself composed of faint stars interspersed with globular clusters that are composed of low-luminosity stars. Nothing is said in the passage about the velocity or the relative ages of globular-cluster stars and halo stars, so choices A and B can be eliminated. Lines 5-7 specifically describe the stars that make up the halo, and lines 8-10 make a clear distinction between the halo stars and the stars that make up the globular clusters within the halo. Thus, a halo star is not considered a cluster star, and choice D is incorrect. Choice E is attractive, since the passage indicates that the halo is com-

posed of stars and that globular clusters, and the stars that form them, are "scattered about" in the halo. However, although it is accurate to say that halo stars surround the globular clusters, it is not accurate to say that halo stars surround individual globular-cluster stars, and E is not correct. Finally, since the clusters are part of the halo, cluster stars are a kind of halo star, and thus choice C is the best answer.

Questions II.9 and III.7 are similar to this question. They ask about individual statements made by the author as part of a discussion that occupies an entire paragraph. When you read a passage, you should note not only the general discussion but the details that contribute to that general discussion.

INFERENCE QUESTIONS

I.14 It can be inferred that a commitment to the idea of musical masterpieces has resulted in

 (A) less integration of music with other arts
 (B) a limited concert repertory
 (C) less understanding of music
 (D) less popular music
 (E) fewer contemporary composers

Inference questions like I.14 require that you understand ideas not explicitly developed in the passage. Question I.14 requires that you recognize how an analogy works to develop and reinforce a point being made by the author. When the author of a passage uses an analogy, he or she is developing an idea indirectly and, in order to understand fully, you must make an inference. The basis for the inference in this question is found in lines 57-65 of the passage. In those lines, the author uses the analogy with eating habits to imply that the number of musical compositions considered appropriate for a "proper concert" is quite limited—restricted, in fact, to historic or contemporary compositions with the "masterpiece" tone. Nowhere in the passage is there evidence to suggest that the "snobbish definition of excellence" (line 21) of which the author disapproves has led to A, less integration of music with the other arts, to D, less popular music, to E, fewer contemporary composers, or even to C, less understanding of music. The domination of the "masterpiece cult" has led only to a "repetitive and monotonous" concert "menu." Since a menu that is repetitive and monotonous is necessarily limited, the best answer to this moderately difficult question is B.

Question I.14 provides an illustration of what is legitimately inferrable from a passage and what is not inferrable. It is possible the author thinks that less understanding of music has resulted from overemphasis on the "masterpiece." It may be that some people are too biased to appreciate musical compositions lacking the "masterpiece" tone. But nowhere in the passage does the author actually imply that condemnation of nonmasterpieces by music lovers results from a lack of understanding of such compositions. In fact, lines 11-16 suggest that those who differentiate masterpieces and nonmasterpieces do so with a clear understanding of the differences. Always remember, therefore, that an inference must be based on substantial, though indirect, evidence. An answer choice in an inference question is incorrect if the passage does not provide accurate and logical information to justify the choice.

Inference questions that, like I.14, ask you to comprehend analogies and other figurative language are well represented in the sample tests. Questions I.12, II.1, II.12, and III.20 all ask you to recognize the implications of the language used in a passage. They do not ask about the contribution of the language of a passage to its tone, but rather about the contribution of the language to the development of an idea.

II.10 It can be inferred from the passage that Baraka shared which of the following with the beat generation avant-garde culture of the 1950's?

    (A) An attempt to bridge the gap between two different but equally oppressed groups

    (B) An insistence on separating art from social institutions that were outmoded

    (C) A recognition that the usual forms of writing were inadequate for and irrelevant to his concerns

    (D) A commitment to using writing as a means of shaping society

    (E) A disillusionment about the ability of any art to flourish in a corrupt society

To make the inference required in this question you must read the first paragraph of the passage carefully. The question asks you to infer a belief or point of view held by both Baraka and the beat generation of the 1950's. In lines 7-10, the author states that Baraka's involvement with the beat generation trained him "to rebel, grounding his art on the principle of self-revelation as the source of primary artistic truth." In lines 18-23, the author asserts a reason for the attraction of the beat avant-garde for an artist like Baraka: they "provided cultural analogues recognizable to the black artist politically troubled and enmeshed in reactionary cultural forms." Finally, in lines 23-26, the author explains that Baraka allied himself with "poetic rebels distinguished by their scorn for traditional descriptions of Western culture as fundamentally moral and humanitarian."

The inference in choice A can be eliminated because it is not supported by the author's assertion in lines 18-23, which says only that the beat avant-garde "provided cultural analogues" recognized by artists like Baraka, but does not say that the beat avant-garde's rebellion against traditional forms was motivated by any desire to bridge a gap between oppressed groups. Choice B can be eliminated because there is no mention in the passage of social institutions or their influence on art. Choice E can be eliminated because the passage says nothing about the ability of art to flourish in any society, corrupt or not. This is not an issue the author deals with at all in the passage. Choice D is harder to eliminate, because lines 27-31 imply that Baraka himself was committed to concrete acts, to creating art that functioned as a dramatic gesture of self-assertion and independence from prevailing White cultural and literary standards. However, the question asks which of the choices expresses a belief "shared" by Baraka and the beat avant-garde, and nothing in the passage indicates that the beat avant-garde were committed to "using writing as a means to shaping society"; rather, the passage indicates that they were committed to rejection of traditional literary standards. Choice C, the best answer, can be inferred from the author's assertions in lines 7-10 and 18-26. In lines 7-10, he makes clear that Baraka and the beat poets rebelled against the usual basis of art by espousing "the principle of self-

revelation as the source of primary artistic truth." In lines 18-23, the author mentions the "thematic and technical concerns" of the beat avant-garde as a source for Baraka's sense that they offered an alternative to "reactionary cultural forms." And, finally, in lines 23-26, the author asserts that Baraka and the other poetic rebels with whom he identified were distinguished, as artists, by their scornful rejection of the traditional belief that Western culture was "fundamentally moral and humanitarian."

II.24 The author suggests that the most practical way for people to avoid hypertension is to learn to

    (A) reverse the effects of stress situations

    (B) inhibit their fight-or-flight responses

    (C) stay away from stress situations

    (D) deliberately control physiological processes

    (E) alter their daily environments

Question II.24 asks you to make a generalization for which the author has provided the necessary supporting evidence. According to the passage, hypertension is one result of physiological adjustment to the everyday situations of stress created by the rapid pace of Western life. In the first paragraph, the author states that "people's only recourse lies in learning how to counteract the harmful effects of their physiological responses to such situations." Therefore, the best answer to this difficult question is choice A. In describing situations of stress as "everyday," "permanent," and "inevitable," the author clearly implies that it is *not* practical for people to stay away from stressful situations or alter their daily environments, and so choices C and E can be eliminated. Choice B seems attractive, since the author recommends in the second paragraph that people try to counterbalance the harmful "fight-or-flight" response, but he does not suggest here that the response can be inhibited, only that it can be counteracted. Choice D is even more difficult to eliminate because the author states in the second paragraph that the physiological "relaxation response" can be deliberately elicited by psychological means. Note, once more, that the question asks for "the most practical way." In the second paragraph of the passage, the author notes that some physiological functions can be controlled, but he goes on to say that the control is only partial, and usually limited to only one physiological function at a time. Finally, this control requires the use of special monitoring equipment. Thus, though deliberate control is possible, it does not seem altogether practical, and choice D can be eliminated.

Questions I.3, II.4, and III.10 also ask you to make a generalization based on supporting evidence from the passage. Question III.22 asks for just the opposite; in that question you are asked to infer the specific attributes of a specific item of mass culture on the basis of generalizations made by the author about the nature of mass culture as a whole. The relationships between particular supporting details in a passage and generalizations based on those details are often the basis for inference questions.

III.1 The author suggests that student activism has

    (A) inspired the rise of ethnicity

    (B) effected economic changes

    (C) resulted from class conflict

    (D) created conflict between ethnic groups

    (E) been international in scope

This is another example of an inference question based on an analogy. To answer the question, you must first look for the specific mention of student activism. In the opening lines, the author uses student activism as part of a comparison between such activism and the rise of ethnicity; ethnicity is described as being "on the rise throughout the world." This comparison strongly implies that student activism, too, is "on the rise throughout the world"; therefore, the best answer to the question is E. There is nothing in the passage to suggest that student activism preceded ethnicity as an international movement, so choice A can be eliminated. Moreover, no connection is drawn in the passage between student activism and economic change, class conflict, or conflict between ethnic groups, although those phenomena are discussed in relation to ethnicity. Thus, the passage does not support the inferences given in B, C, and D. Choice E is the best response, because it contains the only inference that is supported by the passage.

APPLICATION QUESTIONS

II.6 If a developing country had $500,000 to spend on medical services, which of the following projects would the author of the passage be likely to support?

> I. Food distribution in rural areas
> II. Research on the effect of refined sugar on infant growth
> III. Instruction in simple methods of sewage disposal
> IV. Classes to train medical technicians to read x-ray pictures

> (A) I only
> (B) I and III only
> (C) II and III only
> (D) II and IV only
> (E) III and IV only

Question II.6 is typical of questions that ask you to apply information given in the passage in a new context. The projects described in the question do not actually appear in the passage, but the passage gives information that tells you how the author would probably feel about such projects. Lines 19-22 describe three public health goals that, in the author's opinion, should carry the very highest priority in developing nations. Distribution of food in rural areas would help to provide for adequate nutrition, so the author would probably support project I. Similarly, since sewage disposal training would improve sanitation, project III would probably also receive the author's endorsement. However, neither research into the effect of refined sugar on infant growth nor training in x-ray technology would directly improve nutrition, sanitation, or resistance to communicable diseases; therefore, projects II and IV would not be likely to receive the author's support for high-priority funding. Choice B, then, is the best answer to this comparatively easy question.

III.4 Which of the following would be logically appropriate topics for the author to consider in a continuation of the passage?

> I. The relationship between the rise of ethnicity and modern communication systems
> II. Ethnicity as a distinctively Western development
> III. The possible results of an increase in ethnic awareness

> (A) I only
> (B) II only
> (C) I and II only
> (D) I and III only
> (E) I, II, and III

Question III.4 asks you for extensions of ideas introduced in the passage. To answer this question of average difficulty, you must consider the passage as a whole. An appropriate continuation of the passage would be an elaboration of an idea introduced or suggested in the passage but not fully discussed there. Topic I proposes a further discussion of a causal relationship between the rise of ethnicity and international systems of communication suggested in the final paragraph. Since, in the last sentence of the passage, the author contends that "ethnicity is a phenomenon intimately and organically bound up with major developments in modern societies," it would be appropriate for the paragraph following the passage to contain a detailed discussion of the role played by one such development—modern communication systems—in the rise of ethnicity. Thus, I is part of the best answer and B can be eliminated. Topic II—ethnicity as a distinctively Western development—is explicitly contradicted by the passage; in the first sentence, the author asserts that the rise of ethnicity is an international phenomenon. Therefore, choices B, C, and E, which contain topic II, can be eliminated. To choose between A and D, you must determine whether or not topic III is also a logically appropriate continuation for the passage. In the second paragraph, the author states that ethnic awareness has increased in recent years, then adds that an increase in political activity by ethnic groups is a "natural concomitant" of such an increase in awareness. He stops just short of outlining the possible specific effects of increased ethnopolitical activity, but he does imply that "significant" effects are not unlikely. Therefore, a discussion of what those effects might be is a logical extension of information already in the passage. The best answer to the question, then, is choice D: "I and III only."

III.23 With which of the following statements would the author be LEAST likely to agree?

> (A) The nature of leisure-time activity must fundamentally resemble the nature of work.
> (B) Mass culture allows the worker to escape from the monotony imposed by work.
> (C) Art and mass culture differ primarily in the nature of the responses they require from their audiences.
> (D) Contemporary society has created cultural forms that only appear to be different from life.
> (E) Contemporary workers are unwilling to be troubled by their leisure-time activities.

Question III.23 is typical of questions that ask you to determine, on the basis of ideas presented in the passage, what the author would probably think about ideas *not* in the passage. To answer this particular question, which is quite difficult, you must consider each of the choices in the context of statements made in the passage. Of the choices, C and E are relatively easy to eliminate. In the last paragraph, the author contrasts art and mass culture on the basis of the demands they place on their audiences: mass culture "elicits the most conservative responses possible" while art "demands effort, a creative response." Therefore, the author would agree with the statement presented in choice C. Choice E can be eliminated because the author specifically states in the last paragraph that the mass-culture audience "wants to be titillated and amused, but not disturbed." Choice A is also explicitly stated in the passage; the author argues in the second paragraph that, in an industrial society, the quality of leisure time cannot differ too greatly from the quality of working time. Choices B and D concern this same argument, as it is continued in the third paragraph. The author states: "Leisure time must be so organized as to bear a factitious relationship to working time: apparently different, actually the same." On the basis of this statement, choice D can be eliminated because it restates this idea. Only choice B, the best answer, presents an idea with which the author would disagree. In the fifth paragraph, the author states that "mass culture is inseparable from common experience" and that men and women accept mass culture and daily experience "to the degree that the two blend." Since both statements emphasize the similarity between mass culture and daily (work) experience, and since the author believes mass culture actually reinforces passivity and boredom, it is least likely that the author would believe that mass culture allows the worker to escape the monotony imposed by work.

In approaching application questions, you should keep in mind that they differ from other types of Reading Comprehension questions in that the material in a question is *not* taken from the passage. To answer these questions correctly, you must concentrate on the logical relationships between information given in the passage and choices given in the questions. You will be able to locate in the passage not only the information that ensures the correctness of one answer choice, but also the information that ensures the incorrectness or inappropriateness of the other answer choices.

QUESTIONS ABOUT LOGICAL STRUCTURE

I.15 Funerals are mentioned (line 54) in order to

    (A) illustrate metaphorically the death of inspiration in music

    (B) predict the future of music if present misconceptions continue

    (C) provide a legitimate instance of the domination of tone over content

    (D) link music with other aspects of life

    (E) show the varied uses of music

Question I.15 asks you to supply the reason for the author's choice of a particular supporting detail in the passage. The author brings up the subject of funerals to ensure that his readers understand that, in his opinion, the domination of tone over content is not necessarily always wrong; emphasis on tone is simply inappropriate in selecting material for a concert. Choice C, the best answer to this very easy question, is almost a restatement of that reason as it is given in the passage. Since the author explicitly states his reason for mentioning funerals in the passage, A, B, D, and E can be easily eliminated.

The logical reason governing an author's choice of a particular example or a particular piece of supporting evidence is also important in questions I.4, I.21, II.13, II.21, and III.2. Questions about the relationship between the supporting evidence and the argument being presented are not uncommon in the Reading Comprehension section of the GMAT, but they are not all as easy as question I.15. The author of a passage does not always explicitly state his or her motive for selecting a particular supporting detail. Often, as in questions I.21 and II.13, you must infer the author's reason from the relationships between the supporting detail and the author's main idea.

I.20 The author's argument is directed against which of the following?

    I. The use of test-tube experimentation alone to establish the validity of scientific theories

    II. The exclusion of experimental facts from the formation of scientific theories

    II. The observation of certain cellular components in isolation

    (A) I only   (B) I and II only   (C) I and III only
    (D) II and III only   (E) I, II, and III

This is an example of a logical structure question that concerns the *purpose* of a logical argument. While reading any passage you should attempt to establish whether the author is attacking or supporting and what idea or situation is being attacked or supported. Thus, to answer this extremely difficult question, you must establish what the author's opinions are about how scientific experimentation *should* be carried out. In the third paragraph, the author states that the same ingredients undergo different reactions depending on whether they are mixed in a test tube or in a living cell. This statement indicates that information about the interactions of complex molecular processes cannot be based exclusively on test-tube experimentation; therefore, the author would almost certainly criticize the use of test-tube experimentation alone to verify a theory about cell chemistry. The idea expressed in I, then, must be part of the best answer, and D can be eliminated.

In the second paragraph, the author argues that experimental data contradict theoretical assumptions underlying the "central dogma," and suggests that those data call the "central dogma" into question. It can be inferred, then, that he would not favor the deliberate exclusion of experimental facts from the formation of scientific theories any more than he would favor overreliance on data that might not give the whole picture. The idea expressed in II, then, must also be part of the best answer, and choices A and C can be eliminated. To determine whether the idea expressed in III is part of the best answer, you must turn to the final paragraph, where the author asserts that "the unique properties of a complex system are not necessarily explicable solely by the properties that can be observed in its isolated parts." In the fourth paragraph the author explains a complex phenomenon from modern physics, and at the beginning of the final paragraph he draws an analogy between the properties of this complex system and the properties of the complex system of the living cell. His statement of this analogy in the final paragraph indicates that he would not approve of explaining the living cell by explaining how isolated cell components behave. Therefore, III must be part of the best answer, which is E.

I.25   The author presents his argument primarily by

    (A) contrasting two fields of science
    (B) providing experimental evidence against a point of view
    (C) criticizing proponents of other theories
    (D) stating a new theory and its important implications
    (E) comparing two theories of cellular structure

Question I.25 is a question that asks about the overall organization of a passage. You should approach it by asking yourself whether the passage is primarily an extended discussion of differences, a citation of evidence, a series of criticisms, a statement of a new theory, or an extended discussion of similarities. In the fourth paragraph, the author does discuss an example from physics. There is, however, no discussion of the differences between physics and biochemistry, and choice A can be eliminated. The author does criticize one theory, the "central dogma," but he does not criticize the scientists who subscribe to that theory, its "proponents." Nor would it be accurate to say that he criticizes "other theories," since he presents no theory of his own. Thus, choice C can be eliminated. Choices D and E can be eliminated because the author's argument is addressed to only one existing theory, which he criticizes without supplying a new theory to take its place. The author does question the assumptions behind the "central dogma," the one existing theory, by citing experimental data that challenge those assumptions. Hence, B is the best answer to this question of moderate difficulty.

II.7   Which of the following statements, if true, would most seriously undermine the author's arguments against expensive assistance programs?

    (A) People in developing countries have illnesses that are different from those that people in advanced countries have.
    (B) Advanced countries contribute to a more equal distribution of wealth when they donate medical facilities to other countries.
    (C) Expensive assistance programs provide useful technical knowledge for use in developing countries.
    (D) Expensive assistance programs train highly qualified doctors and technicians from both advanced and developing countries.
    (E) Expensive assistance programs improve all medical services available in developing countries.

Question II.7, like question I.25, is concerned with argumentation, but question II.7 is an evaluative one. Here, you are asked to recognize appropriate counterevidence that could be used to refute the argument made by the author. To answer such a question, you must carefully examine the basis for the author's contention that expensive assistance programs have adversely affected the development of health services in economically developing countries. In lines 10-19, the author charges that the "ill-adapted showpieces" transplanted from economically developed nations do not actually deliver primary health care to the people who need it, especially those in rural areas. If it were true that the presence of large hospitals improved all of the health services available throughout a country, then expensive assistance programs would have a beneficial rather than an adverse effect and the author's argument would be weakened. Choice E, then, is the best answer to this question of average difficulty. Choice A, if it were true, would strengthen rather than weaken the author's contention that outside assistance programs are inappropriate, since the author describes such programs as "ill-adapted" (line 12). Choices B and C are irrelevant to the argument; even if assistance programs did help to distribute wealth more evenly and did provide useful technical knowledge, as long as they failed to address basic public health needs the author's argument would still stand. Choice D neither strengthens nor weakens the argument; unless it were proved that the presence of highly qualified doctors and technicians improved the health care delivery system in a developing country, the argument against inappropriate, expensive outside assistance programs would not be undermined. Question II.19 is another example of this type of question.

III.24   The author's argument assumes an absolute dichotomy between

    (A) leisure time and working time
    (B) novelty and conservatism
    (C) art and mass culture
    (D) amusement and depersonalization
    (E) insight and disturbance

Question III.24 asks you to identify an important assumption underlying the author's central argument. In the first paragraph, the author argues that leisure time and working time must be, in essence, similar to one another in an industrial society, so choice A can be eliminated. Choice B is somewhat harder to eliminate because it requires that you use information from more than one part of the passage. In the fourth paragraph, the author describes a "quest for novelty" as an essential aspect of mass culture; then, in the final paragraph, he calls mass culture "conservative" because it is designed not to upset or disturb its passive audience. Thus, novelty and conservatism are compatible within the author's theory of mass culture, and choice B is incorrect. At the beginning of the fourth paragraph, the author states specifically that the "amusements" characteristic of mass culture are part of its depersonalizing effect, so choice D can be eliminated. In the third paragraph, the author says that mass culture "must provide amusement without insight and pleasure without disturbance—as distinct from art, which gives pleasure through disturbance." Here, insight and disturbance are equated as part of an argument the author is making that mass culture and art are polar opposites in the ways by which they give pleasure to an audience. Therefore, choice E is not the best answer. However, the author's argument in the third paragraph assumes that "pleasure through disturbance" and "pleasure without disturbance" are absolutely dichotomous, so C is the best answer to this difficult question.

Questions about logical structure tend to be very specific to the passages on which they are based. Each of the examples given above is virtually an isolated example within the sample tests, but the examples do represent kinds of logical reasoning questions that are often asked in the Reading Comprehension section of the GMAT.

QUESTIONS ABOUT STYLE AND TONE

I.8   The tone of the author's closing remarks can best be described as

**(A) humorous   (B) indifferent   (C) indecisive
(D) admonitory   (E) indignant**

To answer question I.8, which is typical of "tone" questions in the Reading Comprehension section, you must consider the language used by the author to present his closing remarks. In the last paragraph of the passage on which this question is based, the author is urging managers to reexamine their beliefs and assumptions about women in management so that any unjust differences in organizations' implicit expectations for men and for women can be identified and eradicated. Because the author ends by warning managers that they may well possess the biases revealed in the survey, the best answer to this comparatively easy question is D: "admonitory." The author is by no means indifferent to the importance of managerial discrimination toward women in the passage, nor uncertain about it, and so choices B and C can safely be eliminated. He treats the issue seriously, so choice A is not the answer, but he is neither angry nor outraged. The language of the passage is not the language of indignation: the verbs "might be" and "could represent" are speculative rather than accusatory, and the "discriminatory acts" mentioned in the last paragraph are labeled "unintentional," a word an indignant author would be unlikely to use. These verbal cues, coupled with the mildly reproachful phrase, "If managers are sincere . . . they ought to examine their own organizations' implicit expectations," establish the tone of the author's closing remarks as one of firm, but not harsh, admonition.

II.25 The author's attitude toward the pace of Western life can best be described as one of

**(A) anxiety   (B) apology   (C) resignation
(D) indignation   (E) unconcern**

Question II.25 is typical of questions that ask not about the tone of a passage but about the attitude of the author toward a particular topic as that attitude is revealed in the language of the passage. To determine the attitude of the author toward the pace of Western life, you must consider the first paragraph of the passage, in which the author describes that pace as "rapid" and states that it "gives no indication of slowing down." He goes on to say that "many people would not want it to slow down." Since the author attributes harmful effects such as high rates of hypertension and subsequent heart failure to the stress resulting from this rapid pace, he is not unconcerned about it; therefore, choice E is not correct. Choices B and D are slightly harder to eliminate, but the language of the passage is not really apologetic or indignant; phrases like "an inevitable result" and

"a permanent part of Western life" suggest resignation rather than anger or regret. These phrases indicate that, although the author would like the pace of Western life to be slower, he accepts its rapidity as a fact. Acceptance is not consistent with an attitude of indignation, which eliminates choice D, and choice B can be eliminated because the author offers no excuses for the dependence of Western life on such a dangerously rapid pace. Of the five choices, A and C are the most difficult to choose between. The fact that the author finds the pace of Western life fatal is certainly evidence that it has been a source of some concern to him. However, since he now sees that pace as inevitable—a fact that must be lived with—his dominant emotion as reflected in the fatalistic language of the passage is not active anxiety but disappointed acceptance. Therefore, the best answer to this question of above-average difficulty is C.

III.21 Which of the following best describes the tone of the passage?

**(A) Tentative and inquisitive
(B) Ambivalent and confused
(C) Critical and analytical
(D) Optimistic and whimsical
(E) Ill-tempered and harsh**

Question III.21, like question I.18, asks about the tone of a passage, but it asks about the tone of the passage as a whole. To answer it, you must consider the language and style of the entire passage. You must determine the author's overall attitude to mass culture from the words and phrases he uses to describe it. Choice A can be eliminated because the passage contains no questions—answered or unanswered—and because none of the assertions made in the passage is cautious. The author presents the material in a straightforward and firm manner, as a series of facts rather than as a theory. If he were confused or ambivalent about the issues, he would not use words like "certain" and "must," and so choice B is also incorrect. Choice D can be eliminated because the author's contrast of mass culture with art is unfavorable toward mass culture; the tone of the passage is not optimistic, and no humor is used, so it is not whimsical. Answering this question of average difficulty requires a choice between C and E. The author is decidedly critical of mass culture; he considers it inferior to art and calls it "the least troublesome solution" to the problem of what members of an industrial society should do with their leisure time. He labels it depersonalizing, describes its quest for novelty as "ceaseless and hectic," charges that it encourages "passivity and boredom," and, in the closing lines of the passage, condemns it as "safe." This language is undeniably severe, but it is not ill-tempered; the author's criticisms are intellectual rather than emotional. Therefore, choice E is not correct and the best answer to the question is C: "critical and analytical."

As you can see from examples discussed here, and from questions I.16 and II.17, all tone questions in the Reading Comprehension section of the GMAT are similar. To answer them, you must consider the language and style of a passage—both the literal meanings of the words the author uses and their implications and connotations. The tone of a passage may be elusive and difficult to grasp, but questions about tone are ordinarily quite straightforward. You can best approach them by looking among the answer choices for words that accurately express the attitude of the author toward his or her material.

VI Analysis of Situations

In Analysis of Situations questions you must classify on the basis of relative importance the facts and conditions that make up a management or business situation. Therefore, you should keep in mind six basic elements of the situations presented in the passages you will read. These six elements are the decision maker, the choices, the major objectives, the factors (major and minor), the major assumptions, and unimportant issues. Each of the six elements is explained below.

The decision maker is the person or group of persons in the business or management situation who must make the best choice for solving the problem.

The choices are the alternatives available to the decision maker for solving the problem. Each alternative will have both advantages and disadvantages; the decision maker wishes to pick the alternative that will best solve the problem.

The major objectives are the goals the decision maker is trying to achieve. Put another way, the major objectives are the conditions that will exist after the problem has been solved, that is, after the decision has been made and the choice implemented. For example, a decision maker might need a suitable location for a factory. The decision maker's problem is needing a new factory location. One of the decision maker's objectives is "a suitable location for the factory." The acquisition of such a location is one of the major objectives because it is an important condition that will exist after the decision maker has chosen from among the alternative locations and implemented that choice. In short, acquiring the location solves the problem.

It must be emphasized, however, that even though Analysis of Situations passages are generally developed in terms of one important decision to be made, the decision maker may have several important objectives. Analysis of Situations passages frequently have more than one objective. These objectives can be either concrete or abstract. In relocating a factory, the decision maker may wish to be nearer the market and may also wish to make a social contribution to the community at large. Other objectives may include, but are not limited to, such things as improved equipment, expanded production, compliance with laws, business reputation, or customer good will. You should keep in mind that although objectives are usually stated early in a passage, they may appear in any part of the passage. Sometimes information concerning objectives that appears in different parts of the passage may be synthesized in a question.

The factors are the financial, material, or time considerations that make up the business situation and that will influence, in varying degrees, the choice of an alternative. Factors can include a wide variety of concrete and abstract considerations. Factors may include, but are not limited to, such things as cost, available space, production schedules, compliance with laws, business reputation, or customer good will. There are two types of factors, major and minor.

■ Major factors are those aspects of the business situation that have direct and significant influence on the decision concerning which alternative to choose in order to solve a problem. Major factors are decisive in determining whether or not an objective can be reached. For example, the cost of equipment may be decisive in determining whether an objective of not significantly increasing a budget can be achieved. This kind of relationship to an objective gives a factor major importance.

Major factors may sometimes, but not always, be divided into smaller elements. For example, the final cost of a piece of equipment will include maintenance costs, shipping costs, and finance costs. Thus, depending on the passage, a question concerning the total cost of a piece of equipment might be a major factor whereas a question concerning shipping cost for the equipment would not. Major factors are always stated explicitly in the passage.

■ Minor factors are those aspects of the business situation that bear on and influence major factors. Minor factors may be more specific than major factors, and may frequently contribute to major factors. Minor factors are much more directly related to major factors than to objectives. Minor factors have only a tangential bearing on the achievement of an objective.

As stated above, if a decision maker's objective is to avoid significantly increasing a budget, the cost of a piece of equipment may be a major factor. The shipping cost of the equipment, or the distance to be shipped, depending on the situation, may be a minor factor. These minor factors bear directly on the major factor of cost of equipment, but have only a tangential or secondary bearing on the achievement of the objective; the overall cost of the equipment has a much more direct bearing on the accomplishment of the objective.

When stated in a question, a minor factor may take the form either of a secondary consideration that is relevant to only one of the choices or of a secondary consideration that is relevant to more than one of the choices. For example, a minor factor may be stated in a question as either "the shipping costs of bulldozer X" or "the shipping costs of all the bulldozers under consideration."

It is especially important to realize that whether an aspect of the business situation is a factor or an objective depends on the facts and conditions of the situation as stated and developed in the passage. For example, in one situation "compliance with laws" may be a factor. There may be, however, situations in which "compliance with laws" can be an objective. Since this is so, you must always evaluate each passage independently.

The major assumptions are the suppositions and projections made by the decision maker *before* he or she evaluates the factors. The assumptions establish a framework within which the decision maker works, and they are accepted by the decision maker as true without question or explanation. For example, if a seller assumes that the market for a product will increase, he or she then evaluates the factors involved in each of the alternatives and makes a decision accordingly. Assumptions often take the form of projections about future events. Sometimes the assumptions are suppositions about the quality of an entity. Assumptions may either be stated explicitly in a passage or remain unstated, yet logically inferrable.

You should keep in mind that, though assumptions are made before the factors are weighed, these assumptions do not necessarily precede, chronologically, the discussion or consideration of factors that occurs in a passage. It is true that often a decision maker will first set out his or her assumptions and then begin preliminary evaluation and discussion of the factors. On the other hand, sometimes suppositions are raised, as in real life, in the course of a discussion or a consideration. These suppositions are, however, brought up before any final evaluation of factors is made—before, in other words, a decision is reached. Thus, an assumption may be made "before the factors are weighed" in a strictly chronological sense as the Analysis of Situations passage develops, or an assumption may be made "before the factors are weighed" in the sense that the assumption precedes a final decision.

Unimportant issues are elements of the business situation that do not influence the choice of the best solution, do not bear on or influence a major factor in any appreciable way, and do not appear as part of the decision maker's assumptions about the business situation.

The questions that follow an Analysis of Situations passage are intended to determine how well you can classify the elements of the business situation into (A) major objectives, (B) major factors, (C) minor factors, (D) major assumptions, and (E) unimportant issues.

The following pages include test-taking strategies, sample tests, and detailed explanations of selected questions from the sample tests that further illustrate the way the elements explained above work in Analysis of Situations passages. The case studies appearing in these sample tests are not designed to present examples of either good or poor administrative practices.

TEST-TAKING STRATEGIES FOR ANALYSIS OF SITUATIONS

1. Become thoroughly familiar with the definitions of each element of Analysis of Situations passages as discussed above and as given in the directions for the Analysis of Situations section in the test itself.

2. Read the passages carefully. They will usually be about 850 words long. (The passages in the sample tests that follow below are somewhat longer.) Since this material establishes complex relationships among the elements of the business situation, it may be wise to analyze the passage closely the first time through.

3. While reading a passage, try to identify the basic elements.

   a. The decision maker and some of the objectives will usually be clearly stated early in the passage.

   b. A survey of the available choices will usually appear toward the beginning of the passage. Recognizing and isolating the choices will help you establish clearly the decision that is to be made.

   c. The greater part of the remainder of the passage will be a detailed discussion of the choices available to the decision maker and the factors and conditions involved in each choice. Read this material carefully.

   Note the arguments for and against each proposed solution, and note the factors that seem to determine the course of the discussion. Remember that the factors should be weighed with an awareness that the decision maker is working toward the best possible choice.

4. Read each of the questions carefully. Determine as precisely as possible the exact nature of the fact or concept involved in the question. Is it something that the decision maker wants? Is it something that will influence making the best choice? How significant is the fact in determining the best choice?

5. Keeping the entire business situation clearly and completely in mind, try to determine where the fact or concept fits into the process of making the best choice.

6. Select the answer that most nearly describes your evaluation of the fact or concept involved in the question.

   When you take the sample tests, use the answer spaces on the following page to mark your answers.

Answer Spaces for Sample Test I

1 Ⓐ Ⓑ Ⓒ Ⓓ Ⓔ   9 Ⓐ Ⓑ Ⓒ Ⓓ Ⓔ   17 Ⓐ Ⓑ Ⓒ Ⓓ Ⓔ   25 Ⓐ Ⓑ Ⓒ Ⓓ Ⓔ
2 Ⓐ Ⓑ Ⓒ Ⓓ Ⓔ   10 Ⓐ Ⓑ Ⓒ Ⓓ Ⓔ   18 Ⓐ Ⓑ Ⓒ Ⓓ Ⓔ   26 Ⓐ Ⓑ Ⓒ Ⓓ Ⓔ
3 Ⓐ Ⓑ Ⓒ Ⓓ Ⓔ   11 Ⓐ Ⓑ Ⓒ Ⓓ Ⓔ   19 Ⓐ Ⓑ Ⓒ Ⓓ Ⓔ   27 Ⓐ Ⓑ Ⓒ Ⓓ Ⓔ
4 Ⓐ Ⓑ Ⓒ Ⓓ Ⓔ   12 Ⓐ Ⓑ Ⓒ Ⓓ Ⓔ   20 Ⓐ Ⓑ Ⓒ Ⓓ Ⓔ   28 Ⓐ Ⓑ Ⓒ Ⓓ Ⓔ
5 Ⓐ Ⓑ Ⓒ Ⓓ Ⓔ   13 Ⓐ Ⓑ Ⓒ Ⓓ Ⓔ   21 Ⓐ Ⓑ Ⓒ Ⓓ Ⓔ   29 Ⓐ Ⓑ Ⓒ Ⓓ Ⓔ
6 Ⓐ Ⓑ Ⓒ Ⓓ Ⓔ   14 Ⓐ Ⓑ Ⓒ Ⓓ Ⓔ   22 Ⓐ Ⓑ Ⓒ Ⓓ Ⓔ   30 Ⓐ Ⓑ Ⓒ Ⓓ Ⓔ
7 Ⓐ Ⓑ Ⓒ Ⓓ Ⓔ   15 Ⓐ Ⓑ Ⓒ Ⓓ Ⓔ   23 Ⓐ Ⓑ Ⓒ Ⓓ Ⓔ   31 Ⓐ Ⓑ Ⓒ Ⓓ Ⓔ
8 Ⓐ Ⓑ Ⓒ Ⓓ Ⓔ   16 Ⓐ Ⓑ Ⓒ Ⓓ Ⓔ   24 Ⓐ Ⓑ Ⓒ Ⓓ Ⓔ   32 Ⓐ Ⓑ Ⓒ Ⓓ Ⓔ

Answer Spaces for Sample Test II

1 Ⓐ Ⓑ Ⓒ Ⓓ Ⓔ   9 Ⓐ Ⓑ Ⓒ Ⓓ Ⓔ   17 Ⓐ Ⓑ Ⓒ Ⓓ Ⓔ   25 Ⓐ Ⓑ Ⓒ Ⓓ Ⓔ
2 Ⓐ Ⓑ Ⓒ Ⓓ Ⓔ   10 Ⓐ Ⓑ Ⓒ Ⓓ Ⓔ   18 Ⓐ Ⓑ Ⓒ Ⓓ Ⓔ   26 Ⓐ Ⓑ Ⓒ Ⓓ Ⓔ
3 Ⓐ Ⓑ Ⓒ Ⓓ Ⓔ   11 Ⓐ Ⓑ Ⓒ Ⓓ Ⓔ   19 Ⓐ Ⓑ Ⓒ Ⓓ Ⓔ   27 Ⓐ Ⓑ Ⓒ Ⓓ Ⓔ
4 Ⓐ Ⓑ Ⓒ Ⓓ Ⓔ   12 Ⓐ Ⓑ Ⓒ Ⓓ Ⓔ   20 Ⓐ Ⓑ Ⓒ Ⓓ Ⓔ   28 Ⓐ Ⓑ Ⓒ Ⓓ Ⓔ
5 Ⓐ Ⓑ Ⓒ Ⓓ Ⓔ   13 Ⓐ Ⓑ Ⓒ Ⓓ Ⓔ   21 Ⓐ Ⓑ Ⓒ Ⓓ Ⓔ   29 Ⓐ Ⓑ Ⓒ Ⓓ Ⓔ
6 Ⓐ Ⓑ Ⓒ Ⓓ Ⓔ   14 Ⓐ Ⓑ Ⓒ Ⓓ Ⓔ   22 Ⓐ Ⓑ Ⓒ Ⓓ Ⓔ   30 Ⓐ Ⓑ Ⓒ Ⓓ Ⓔ
7 Ⓐ Ⓑ Ⓒ Ⓓ Ⓔ   15 Ⓐ Ⓑ Ⓒ Ⓓ Ⓔ   23 Ⓐ Ⓑ Ⓒ Ⓓ Ⓔ   31 Ⓐ Ⓑ Ⓒ Ⓓ Ⓔ
8 Ⓐ Ⓑ Ⓒ Ⓓ Ⓔ   16 Ⓐ Ⓑ Ⓒ Ⓓ Ⓔ   24 Ⓐ Ⓑ Ⓒ Ⓓ Ⓔ   32 Ⓐ Ⓑ Ⓒ Ⓓ Ⓔ

Answer Spaces for Sample Test III

1 Ⓐ Ⓑ Ⓒ Ⓓ Ⓔ   9 Ⓐ Ⓑ Ⓒ Ⓓ Ⓔ   17 Ⓐ Ⓑ Ⓒ Ⓓ Ⓔ   25 Ⓐ Ⓑ Ⓒ Ⓓ Ⓔ
2 Ⓐ Ⓑ Ⓒ Ⓓ Ⓔ   10 Ⓐ Ⓑ Ⓒ Ⓓ Ⓔ   18 Ⓐ Ⓑ Ⓒ Ⓓ Ⓔ   26 Ⓐ Ⓑ Ⓒ Ⓓ Ⓔ
3 Ⓐ Ⓑ Ⓒ Ⓓ Ⓔ   11 Ⓐ Ⓑ Ⓒ Ⓓ Ⓔ   19 Ⓐ Ⓑ Ⓒ Ⓓ Ⓔ   27 Ⓐ Ⓑ Ⓒ Ⓓ Ⓔ
4 Ⓐ Ⓑ Ⓒ Ⓓ Ⓔ   12 Ⓐ Ⓑ Ⓒ Ⓓ Ⓔ   20 Ⓐ Ⓑ Ⓒ Ⓓ Ⓔ   28 Ⓐ Ⓑ Ⓒ Ⓓ Ⓔ
5 Ⓐ Ⓑ Ⓒ Ⓓ Ⓔ   13 Ⓐ Ⓑ Ⓒ Ⓓ Ⓔ   21 Ⓐ Ⓑ Ⓒ Ⓓ Ⓔ   29 Ⓐ Ⓑ Ⓒ Ⓓ Ⓔ
6 Ⓐ Ⓑ Ⓒ Ⓓ Ⓔ   14 Ⓐ Ⓑ Ⓒ Ⓓ Ⓔ   22 Ⓐ Ⓑ Ⓒ Ⓓ Ⓔ   30 Ⓐ Ⓑ Ⓒ Ⓓ Ⓔ
7 Ⓐ Ⓑ Ⓒ Ⓓ Ⓔ   15 Ⓐ Ⓑ Ⓒ Ⓓ Ⓔ   23 Ⓐ Ⓑ Ⓒ Ⓓ Ⓔ   31 Ⓐ Ⓑ Ⓒ Ⓓ Ⓔ
8 Ⓐ Ⓑ Ⓒ Ⓓ Ⓔ   16 Ⓐ Ⓑ Ⓒ Ⓓ Ⓔ   24 Ⓐ Ⓑ Ⓒ Ⓓ Ⓔ   32 Ⓐ Ⓑ Ⓒ Ⓓ Ⓔ

ANALYSIS OF SITUATIONS SAMPLE TEST I

Time—40 minutes

32 Questions

Directions: Each passage in this section is followed by questions that require you to classify certain of the facts presented in the passage on the basis of their importance, as illustrated in the following example:

SAMPLE PASSAGE

Fred North, a prospering hardware dealer in Hillidale, Connecticut, felt that he needed more store space to accommodate a new line of farm equipment and repair parts that he intended to carry. A number of New York City commuters had recently purchased tracts of land in the environs of Hillidale and there had taken up farming on a small scale. Mr. North, foreseeing a potential increase in farming in that area, wanted to expand his business to cater to this market. North felt that the most feasible and appealing recourse open to him would be to purchase the adjoining store property owned by Mike Johnson, who used the premises for his small grocery store. Johnson's business had been on the decline for over a year since the advent of a large supermarket in the town. North felt that Johnson would be willing to sell the property at reasonable terms, and this was important since North, after the purchase of the new merchandise, would have little capital available to invest in the expansion of his store.

The following questions consist of items related to the passage above. Consider each item separately in terms of the passage and on the answer sheet blacken space

A if the item is a Major Objective in making the decision; that is, one of the outcomes or results sought by the decision-maker;

B if the item is a Major Factor in making the decision; that is, a consideration, explicitly mentioned in the passage, that is basic in determining the decision;

C if the item is a Minor Factor in making the decision; that is, a secondary consideration that affects the criteria tangentially, relating to a Major Factor rather than to an Objective;

D if the item is a Major Assumption in making the decision; that is, a supposition or projection made by the decision-maker before weighing the variables;

E if the item is an Unimportant Issue in making the decision; that is, a factor that is insignificant or not immediately relevant to the situation.

SAMPLE QUESTIONS

1. Increase in farming in the Hillidale area   Ⓐ Ⓑ Ⓒ ● Ⓔ

2. Acquisition of property for expanding store   ● Ⓑ Ⓒ Ⓓ Ⓔ

3. Cost of Johnson's property   Ⓐ ● Ⓒ Ⓓ Ⓔ

4. State of Johnson's grocery business   Ⓐ Ⓑ ● Ⓓ Ⓔ

5. Quality of the farm equipment North intends to sell   Ⓐ Ⓑ Ⓒ Ⓓ ●

GO ON TO THE NEXT PAGE.

The correct designation for number 1 is (D), a <u>Major Assumption</u>, since North bases his whole expansion project on his supposition that the new commuter-farmers in the Hillidale area are indicative of a trend in that direction. Number 2 is (A), a <u>Major Objective</u>, inasmuch as North's immediate purpose is to obtain room for expansion. (B), a <u>Major Factor</u>, is the correct answer for number 3 because North's present lack of capital renders cost a vital consideration. The best classification of number 4 is (C), a <u>Minor Factor</u>, because the depreciating value of Johnson's business influences his willingness to sell and also the price he will demand for his property; thus, this factor pertains to 3, the cost of Johnson's property, and is an indirect consideration in the case. Number 5, finally, is (E), an <u>Unimportant Issue</u>, for the quality of North's goods has no relevance to the situation at hand; i.e., the desire for room to expand his business.

NOW READ THE PASSAGES AND ANSWER THE QUESTIONS FOLLOWING THEM.

GO ON TO THE NEXT PAGE.

Empire Beauty, Inc. was a relatively modern, medium-sized women's beauty salon. Family-owned and family-operated, it had been doing business in the same urban location for almost eight years. Within three months, a new two-year lease was due to be signed. Instead of planning to sign it routinely, as they had done before, Mary and William Tracy, the owners, realized that some fundamental problems relating to the business had to be resolved.

For the past several years, Empire had been experiencing a steady decline in profits. Reasons for the decline were numerous. The growing popularity of inexpensive and easily cared-for wigs, along with the greater availability of easy-to-use hair-coloring and hair-treatment products for home use, had seriously decreased the number of "regular" beauty salon patrons. This decline in business was aggravated by the trend toward longer hair and simpler styling. Further, the increased expenses due to rising costs of labor and supplies could not be fully countered by increasing the prices to patrons, especially since several of the competing beauty salons in the neighborhood were offering cut-rate prices.

The Tracys realized that along with the decline of their own business, operated by more or less traditional standards, there was an upsurge in the business of beauty salons that had a more modern image. Over the past few years, they had thought of trying to change the image of Empire, but the store's cramped quarters had stopped them from taking any action. The Tracys knew that the situation was now serious and offered no promise of improvement unless important changes were made soon. Therefore, they investigated the options available to them.

They wanted to be able to retain as much of their old business as possible and to capture a new market. To do the former, it would be essential to retain their current employees. To do the latter, the Tracys realized that they would have to expand in several directions. They wanted to become a "unisex" salon, to do men's hairstyling as well as women's. They also would need new equipment in order to do henna treatments, protein treatments, and hair straightening, all very much in vogue. Further, they wanted to be able to sell products: small appliances such as blow dryers and electric hair curlers; wigs, special shampoos, conditioners, and other hair preparations; and, if possible, a prestigious line of makeup, handled by a special makeup consultant. The new and successful beauty parlors had expanded in these directions, and the Tracys knew that if Empire was to achieve a healthy profit margin, it too would have to change or else continue to decline.

The imminence of the decision about a new lease forced the Tracys to face the issues squarely. Of the options available to them, none was ideal, but the Tracys hoped to decide upon the one that would most nearly enable them to approach their goals. What they wanted was a store that offered ample space, convenient location, and good lease terms, without requiring an unreasonable outlay of cash for rent and for equipment and renovations.

The simplest and most obvious solution was to renew the lease at their current location, 416 Montgomery Street. This was appealing because Empire was already established there and also because the rental fee, at $450 a month, was relatively modest. The store was cramped, but one of the back rooms currently used for storage of supplies could be converted, at moderate cost, to a working area. This would, however, limit Empire to very little storage space and the Tracys' hopes of carrying additional products could not be fully realized. The cost of renovating the store and purchasing new equipment, about $6,000, would be low enough for them to afford comfortably. However the Tracys were extremely hesitant to make a major investment in a store that carried only a two-year lease without a clause for automatic renewal. They felt that they needed a longer lease to justify any renovations and the purchase of new equipment.

A second possibility was to retain their present quarters and expand by taking over the store next door, at 418 Montgomery Street. This store, formerly a carpet and rug store, was quite large and, combined with their present quarters, would give them more than enough space for both working and storage. Moreover, since the store had been vacant for several months at a considerable loss to the landlord, the landlord indicated that if the Tracys were to rent both stores, he would be willing to sign a five-year lease on both. The monthly rent at 418 Montgomery, however, was $550, which would require the Tracys to make a large cash outlay each month. Further, since 418 Montgomery had never been used as a beauty parlor, renovations would be expensive. Installing several new sinks, with the accompanying plumbing, and modernizing the electrical wiring to accommodate beauty equipment would represent a large investment. Renovations and equipment for the two Montgomery Street locations would cost about $12,000.

GO ON TO THE NEXT PAGE.

A third possibility, that of taking over a failing beauty parlor in Empire's neighborhood, attracted William Tracy. The store was relatively modern, so that the cost of renovations would be moderate; renovations and equipment would amount to approximately $5,000. The store was not quite as large as the Tracys would have liked, but it was large enough for them to be able to expand; and the monthly rent, at $675, was modest. Moreover, the store could be obtained with a six-year lease, with a clause for renewal. Mary Tracy, however, was hesitant because of the store's location. Although in the same neighborhood as Empire, which would allow Empire to retain its current workers and patrons, it was located on Archer Place, a small side street, unlike Montgomery Street, which was a main thoroughfare. Archer Place contained several small neighborhood stores and small houses but no apartment buildings. Therefore, Mary Tracy felt that Empire could not attract much new business in that location. Not many people lived on the street, those who did tended to be beyond middle age, and there were not many passersby at that location. New business, then, would be totally dependent on word-of-mouth, a situation she considered to be far too risky.

Mary Tracy, instead, was drawn to a different possibility. A small urban shopping center, York Mall, had recently opened about two miles away. At York Mall she found a store of sufficient size for both working and storage which could be rented for $750 a month and could be obtained with a ten-year lease. Here Empire could grow in a new business environment with numerous possibilities for new patrons. William Tracy pointed out that York Mall's distance from their current location, while not very great, might be great enough to lose them many, if not most, of their present patrons, especially since public transportation to the Mall was inadequate and difficult from the Montgomery Street area. He pointed out, too, that the peak business hours for most of the businesses already at York Mall did not accord with peak hours for beauty salons and that Mary's hopes of attracting new patrons were perhaps too optimistic.

Moreover, the mall store, being new, had no beauty equipment or sinks and would therefore require a considerable investment of about $14,000. William was worried about making a large investment in a store where they might lose many of their old patrons without being guaranteed much new business; Mary, though she understood and agreed with William's objections, was more willing to gamble on a new location even if it might mean sacrificing some of the old customers.

A final possibility then presented itself. On Stilton Boulevard, a busy street near Montgomery Street, was an old barbershop whose owner was ill and eager to retire. The store itself was not very large but there were three back rooms that the owner had used until recently for his living quarters. The total amount of space, which rented for $700 a month, would be adequate for the Tracys' plans. The lease was for four years and had a renewal clause. The store was old, however, and even though it contained adequate sinks, plumbing, electric wiring, and other basic necessities, it would require a substantial outlay of about $9,000 for renovations and equipment. It had the further disadvantage of having been a traditional men's barbershop, so that the Tracys would be "working backwards": instead of starting with a new store or with a women's salon that would be expanded to include men's hairstyling, the Tracys would have a men's shop that would have to expand to attract women. Both Mary and William were extremely concerned about this and were uncertain about just how much this would affect both their old patrons and potential new ones.

After preliminary explorations of the possibilities before them, Mary and William decided to give themselves a month to discuss them all thoroughly before making a final decision.

GO ON TO THE NEXT PAGE.

DATA EVALUATION QUESTIONS

Directions: The following questions consist of items related to the passage above. You may refer back to the passage and the directions. Consider each item separately in terms of the passage and on the answer sheet blacken space

    A if the item is a <u>Major Objective</u> in making the decision; that is, one of the outcomes or results sought by the decision-maker;

    B if the item is a <u>Major Factor</u> in making the decision; that is, a consideration, explicitly mentioned in the passage, <u>that is basic</u> in determining the decision;

    C if the item is a <u>Minor Factor</u> in making the decision; that is, a secondary consideration that affects the criteria tangentially, <u>relating</u> to a Major Factor rather than to an Objective;

    D if the item is a <u>Major Assumption</u> in making the decision; that is, a supposition or projection made by the decision-maker <u>before weighing</u> the variables;

    E if the item is an <u>Unimportant Issue</u> in making the decision; that is, a factor that is insignificant or not immediately <u>relevant to the situation</u>.

I. 1. Cost of rent and necessary renovations at the alternative locations

I. 2. Retaining old patrons

I. 3. Cost of sinks and plumbing for 418 Montgomery Street

I. 4. Cost of beauty supplies

I. 5. Appeal of beauty products and small appliances to patrons

I. 6. Ability of each location to attract new patrons

I. 7. Obtaining a sufficiently long lease to justify the costs of renovations and new equipment

I. 8. Capability of each location to keep old patrons

I. 9. Number of residents on Archer Place

I. 10. Cost of utilities at each location

I. 11. Continuation of cut-rate competition in the Montgomery Street area

I. 12. Size, including working and storage areas, of the locations under consideration

I. 13. Obtaining surficient space for working and storage

I. 14. Inadequacy of public transportation from Montgomery Street area to York Mall

I. 15. Competition from other beauty salons in each new location being considered

I. 16. Availability of capital for expansion

GO ON TO THE NEXT PAGE.

The Lopes Construction Company specializes in the construction of office buildings and electrical power plants. In January 1976, the company secured a contract to build an addition to a power plant in San Bernardino, California. In order to obtain the contract, the company had been forced to guarantee completion of the work within one year, and the contract specified a substantial financial penalty for failure to complete the work on time. David Lopes, president of the company, estimated that building the addition would require nearly a year.

The first six months of construction would involve excavation and the erection of structural steel by using a caterpillar crane with a 100-foot beam. To meet Mr. Lopes' schedule, his crane would be needed at the construction site by March 15. However, it had recently been severely damaged and Mr. Lopes feared that the crane could not be repaired in time. He decided to obtain a replacement for the damaged crane.

Mr. Lopes confined his search to the southern part of California because he felt that the time required to transport such a crane from a more distant location would be too great. Within a week he was able to locate five of the size required: three used cranes and two new ones. Lopes called a meeting of his company's executive board to discuss the alternatives.

Mr. Lopes: "In order to ensure that we complete the addition to the power plant on schedule, we must have a crane in good working order available at the construction site by March 15, four weeks from now. Failure to complete the work on schedule would result in a heavy loss because of the penalty clause in the contract. We want to find the most economical solution to this problem, and the equipment must be reliable. Any delays resulting from an inoperative crane will jeopardize the schedule. Obtaining a loan to pay for the replacement crane shouldn't be a problem."

Paul Webster, controller: "I think we should consider the used cranes first. Southwest Construction has a used crane for sale and is willing to make the repairs required to get it in working order at their own expense. On the other hand, they may not be able to obtain the necessary parts in time for the crane to be in working order by March 15."

Gina Gomez, treasurer: "What about the used crane that Tate Construction has for sale? It's the same model as our old crane, and we wouldn't have the expense of training our people to use a new machine."

Bob Harris, vice-president for operations: "That's true, and the cost of the Tate crane is fairly low. But it's so old that it can't be very reliable. There might be a real problem keeping it in operation. I don't think we should take that kind of risk. The other used crane, the one San Diego Construction is selling, is only 5 years old and should give another 7 years of relatively trouble-free operation."

Mr. Lopes: "But the San Diego Construction crane needs to be reconditioned and won't be ready for use until almost the end of March. That kind of a delay is very risky."

Tom Peoples, executive vice-president: "The Tate crane is available now. We could have it ready for use on March 15 and then switch over to the San Diego crane when it becomes available. I realize that this plan would be more expensive, but it would ensure that a replacement crane would be available for the remainder of the construction. That would certainly make it easier to stay on schedule, and the Tate crane could be sold at the end of the project."

Mr. Lopes: "There must be a cheaper solution. We would not only have to buy two cranes, but would also have to pay transportation costs for two cranes. Let's consider the new cranes. They are both available immediately."

Mr. Harris: "Maintenance costs for new equipment will certainly be lower than maintenance costs for used equipment. There would be no problem with reliability if we get a new crane, and the new cranes are faster and more efficient, too."

Ms. Gomez: "The crane sold by Los Angeles Manufacturing is the cheaper of the two new machines and the shipping charges are reasonable also. However, we have to look carefully at the operating expenses. The other new crane, the one for sale by Western Manufacturing, costs 20 per cent less per month to operate. We could make up the difference in initial costs in just two years."

Mr. Lopes: "We need to reach an immediate decision on this matter. Let's take a close look at the table Ms. Gomez has prepared to summarize the costs of each alternative."

GO ON TO THE NEXT PAGE.

COSTS ASSOCIATED WITH EACH CRANE

	Sale Price	Repairs	Shipping Costs	Monthly Operating Costs (labor, maintenance, etc.)
Southwest Construction's Crane	$30,000	$0	$3,000	$13,000
Tate Construction's Crane	$20,000	$2,500	$3,000	$14,000
San Diego Construction's Crane	$40,000	$2,500	$4,000	$13,000
Los Angeles Manufacturing's Crane	$75,000	$0	$3,000	$12,500
Western Manufacturing's Crane	$102,000	$0	$6,000	?

GO ON TO THE NEXT PAGE.

The correct designation for number 1 is (D), a <u>Major Assumption</u>, since North bases his whole expansion project on his supposition that the new commuter-farmers in the Hillidale area are indicative of a trend in that direction. Number 2 is (A), a <u>Major Objective</u>, inasmuch as North's immediate purpose is to obtain room for expansion. (B), a <u>Major Factor</u>, is the correct answer for number 3 because North's present lack of capital renders cost a vital consideration. The best classification of number 4 is (C), a <u>Minor Factor</u>, because the depreciating value of Johnson's business influences his willingness to sell and also the price he will demand for his property; thus, this factor pertains to 3, the cost of Johnson's property, and is an indirect consideration in the case. Number 5, finally, is (E), an <u>Unimportant Issue</u>, for the quality of North's goods has no relevance to the situation at hand; i.e., the desire for room to expand his business.

NOW READ THE PASSAGES AND ANSWER THE QUESTIONS FOLLOWING THEM.

GO ON TO THE NEXT PAGE.

Unisphere Productions, Inc., an independent and relatively new film company, was planning to launch a series of television movies especially designed to appeal to a young audience. The few movies that Unisphere had packaged in the last two years had not been successful and the company was in danger of bankruptcy. It was therefore particularly important that its next film, Summer Surf, be financially successful. The script had been written, a director with previous successful films to his credit had been hired, and roles had been discussed with several actors and actresses. The problem before Unisphere was the selection of a location for the filming of Summer Surf, which was scheduled for release in October 1979. In February of that year, George Andropolous, the president of Unisphere, called a meeting to discuss the shooting. Present at the meeting were Jeanette Forman, Executive Producer; Ted Shank, Production Manager; and Wilbur Goss, Director. Andropolous opened the meeting with some introductory remarks.

Andropolous: "Before I throw the meeting open, let me make a few things clear. Summer Surf must make money. If it doesn't, Unisphere will go under. We have a good script, we have good personnel, and we must make a good movie. It has to be appealing to the twelve-to-eighteen-year-olds, which means the lead characters must be both popular and believable. No matter what, the shooting must be completed by August 1—that is crucial. And needless to say, if we spend more, we make less, so it is equally important that we stay within our budget. The expenses to be incurred at any location we consider must be weighed. Where do we go from here?"

Goss: "I say we should shoot right here in Hollywood. The story is set near Los Angeles, and if the film is to have appeal, it must have the appearance of authenticity. We can use the local beaches for the beach scenes. And we can use real California kids."

Forman: "The real California kids are the problem. Summer Surf, to appear authentic, must have many teen-aged extras. Extras here cost us $100 each per day. We can't hire many extras at that rate. Our present financial status is too shaky. Equally important, if we shoot here, we're hemmed in by California's laws for children under eighteen years old. I needn't emphasize the trouble that involves—parents and child-welfare workers on the set, limited hours of work, and so on. It's bad enough when school is out—the kids can work six hours a day then. But we should start shooting by May, when school is still in session. That means only four hours of work each day for the kids. Shooting here will cost us a fortune and might even delay production. I say, let's go to New Jersey. Children under eighteen are not so restricted by the laws there, extras are far cheaper, and we will still be filming real beaches."

Shank: "New Jersey? That's almost 3,000 miles away. Do you realize what it would cost us to get the production crew and cast there? In addition, there would be enormous motel and other expenses for everyone. What we save on salaries for extras we'd spend on transportation and other costs, especially since we have a lot of equipment to ship as well. Besides, New Jersey is only semi-authentic—it doesn't look like Los Angeles."

Goss: "Another problem with New Jersey is the lead male role. We're all agreed that that role is crucial for the film's success, and we're all agreed that David Bellamy is our best bet for that role. He's dynamite with the young set! Bellamy has made it clear that he can't travel far from Hollywood to take the part. His father is very ill and his wife, who is expecting a baby in June, is having a difficult pregnancy. He has to be close to home."

Andropolous: "Well, how about using Mark Callender instead of Bellamy?"

Goss: "Callender is trouble. He's moody, temperamental, downright mean at times. I've worked with him before and I don't want to do it again. It's very important to keep staff relations smooth. Besides, one of our aims with Summer Surf is to launch a set of films. Callender is already getting a little too old to be a convincing young lead; soon he will be impossible for that kind of role. Callender's a bad choice all around."

Andropolous: "You're probably right. We should have a continuing star. Well, as for the location, there's always our old site in Colorado to consider. We've filmed there before. It's not too far away, which solves our problem with Bellamy; he can get back here quickly if he's needed. The cost of transporting cast, crew, and equipment to Colorado would be much lower than the cost of transportation to New Jersey. And we wouldn't have to worry about the laws covering children. Besides, extras are cheap there too. The college kids would be happy with the ten dollars a day we've given them before. And studio space for the indoor scenes is far cheaper there than it is here."

Forman: "What happens to our authenticity in Colorado? Do I have to remind you that Colorado has no ocean and no ocean beaches? The best we could do is to use a lake and create waves with a wave machine. It doesn't look very realistic, and besides, it would be impossible to have scenes with kids surfing."

Shank: "The wave machine is extremely difficult and expensive to transport. Besides, it breaks down too often. If we lose a few days of shooting because of

GO ON TO THE NEXT PAGE.

breakdowns, we're in trouble, both financially and in terms of our deadline. Another thing—I've had trouble with other kinds of equipment there. The last time I shot a film there, we were plagued by insufficient generators. The generators there don't have enough power to give us the amount of lighting we need and they also break down. We can't afford to take that risk."

Goss: "The only possible location we might use in Colorado is the one we've used before, and it's booked until the end of June. That would be too dangerous a delay. At least the indoor studio space in New Jersey is available when we need it, in May."

Shank: "I say let's stay here in Los Angeles. We can reduce costs by cutting the number of extras we hire. We can also hire many actors and actresses over eighteen to portray younger people. It's done all the time."

Goss: "How authentic would that be? No one of

even nineteen or twenty is going to look fourteen. Remember, we want this movie to be a success, not a foolish-looking flop."

Andropolous: "You're probably right about that. Well, why not combine sites, Hollywood and Colorado or Hollywood and New Jersey? We start in Hollywood. We use the real beaches for beach scenes and we shoot the scenes Bellamy is in. Then we move to Colorado and shoot around Bellamy."

Goss: "The Colorado site should be available to us then. But what do we do about the equipment problem in Colorado?"

Andropolous: "I don't know. Maybe we would move to New Jersey instead, but I shudder to think about the expense. Look, let's mull this over a bit more and meet again in two days to make a final decision."

GO ON TO THE NEXT PAGE.

DATA EVALUATION QUESTIONS

Directions: The following questions consist of items related to the passage above. You may refer back to the passage and the directions. Consider each item separately in terms of the passage and on the answer sheet blacken space

- A if the item is a Major Objective in making the decision; that is, one of the outcomes or results sought by the decision-maker;

- B if the item is a Major Factor in making the decision; that is, a consideration, explicitly mentioned in the passage, that is basic in determining the decision;

- C if the item is a Minor Factor in making the decision; that is, a secondary consideration that affects the criteria tangentially, relating to a Major Factor rather than to an Objective;

- D if the item is a Major Assumption in making the decision; that is, a supposition or projection made by the decision-maker before weighing the variables;

- E if the item is an Unimportant Issue in making the decision; that is, a factor that is insignificant or not immediately relevant to the situation.

II. 1. Producing a film that will attract an audience for a series of similar films

II. 2. Bellamy's willingness to appear in a series of films

II. 3. Cost of motel rooms in New Jersey for the cast and production crew

II. 4. Appearance of authenticity that can be achieved at each of the locations under consideration

II. 5. Availability of a sufficient number of motel rooms in Colorado or New Jersey

II. 6. Relative acting ability of the extras in the locations under consideration

II. 7. Willingness of the production crew to shoot outside Hollywood

II. 8. Avoiding costly delays in the filming of Summer Surf

II. 9. Continuance of Bellamy's appeal in films following Summer Surf

II. 10. Unisphere Productions' current financial status

II. 11. Cost of transporting a wave machine to Colorado

II. 12. Having a male star for Summer Surf who is attractive to young audiences

II. 13. Availability of a sufficient number of extras in Colorado or New Jersey

II. 14. Need for stunt actors in the surfing scenes of Summer Surf

II. 15. Net profits that Unisphere could expect given the expenses required at each location under consideration

II. 16. Producing a film that presents an appearance of authenticity

GO ON TO THE NEXT PAGE.

Barbara Lewis had spent several years on the administrative staff of World Oil Enterprises, a multinational oil company. When she was offered the position of budget controller in the company's Caracas office, she accepted it and moved to Venezuela with her two sons, selling her house and all of her furniture before leaving the United States. She was in Venezuela for three years and was then transferred back to the Woodhaven office as Administrative Director of the Research Division.

Ms. Lewis began looking for a place for her family to live. Her current income, after taxes, was $19,000 a year. She estimated that the family would spend about $5,000 a year on food, clothing, and entertainment. They could, of course, spend less, but she hoped to maintain the standard of living to which they were accustomed. Her elder son was entering his first year of high school and would be going to college in four years. Her younger son would be ready for college two years later. The colleges her sons wanted to attend were expensive, and Ms. Lewis realized that she had to be prepared to spend at least $5,000 a year for each of them for education. With only one of the boys in college, her regular income would cover the expenses, but for the two years when both sons would be in college, she would probably have to take out a loan to cover college expenses for one of them. She therefore did not want to burden herself with extra debts.

Although Ms. Lewis estimated that she could spend about $7,000 a year on housing, she did not have a large amount of money in reserve. Before the family had gone to Venezuela, Ms. Lewis' income had been just enough to support the family comfortably. Her total income in Venezuela had been quite high, but she and the boys had traveled extensively around South America and she had not been able to save any money. Therefore, all she had now was the $15,000 from the sale of the house and furniture. Since banks in Woodhaven would not approve mortgages for more than 75 per cent of the cost of a house, Ms. Lewis would have to make a sizable down payment. She also needed money to furnish the house. Even if she bought some of the furniture she needed secondhand, she estimated that the furniture would cost her at least $3,000. Therefore, her financial position with regard to buying a home was not very strong.

Because of her financial position, Ms. Lewis seriously considered renting a house. She found exactly the kind of house she wanted in the Barnton section of Woodhaven. The house was owned by a couple who had moved to Florida and used the income from renting the house to supplement their retirement income. The house was large and in good repair; and, although Barnton was very near the center of Woodhaven, it was nevertheless a very quiet part of town. Most of the residents of Barnton had lived there for a number of years and some families had been there for generations. Barnton, therefore, met one of Ms. Lewis' requirements, that is, that her new home provide a stable and secure environment for her family. This was especially important to her because her sons had had rather unsettled lives and

the younger one in particular seemed to need a secure home. She was, however, concerned about the fact that the owners of the house might decide that they did not want the responsibility of ownership any longer and might sell the house, possibly forcing her family to move again. The rent for the house was $450 a month and although major repairs were the responsibility of the landlord, the tenant was responsible for maintaining the grounds, paying for the heat and utilities, and doing minor repairs. Ms. Lewis estimated that all of this would amount to $80 a month. However, she felt that if she planned to stay in the area for any length of time, it would be wiser to buy a house than to rent one, largely because she could build up equity in a house by buying. Ms. Lewis assumed that she would be in Woodhaven for a long time because the only promotion she could foresee for quite a few years was within the Research Division.

Shortly after she saw the rental property, Ms. Lewis learned that another employee of World Oil Enterprises, Dr. Nelson, was retiring and selling his house in Barnton. The house, very much like the rental one, was on the market for $70,000. Monthly mortgage payments, including interest, would be $430 a month for a period of twenty-five years. Heat, utilities, and basic maintenance would be about the same as for the rented house, and taxes would be $100 a month. Therefore, Ms. Lewis felt that she could meet the routine expenses of running the house. Although emergency repairs and major maintenance such as painting were not figured in these expenses, Ms. Lewis decided that these costs could be covered by the $2,000 a year she had budgeted for emergencies. Since the money she had saved would not be enough to meet the down payment required for a mortgage, she would have to go into debt for some of that money. If she borrowed the money to cover part of the down payment and the furniture expenses, she was afraid that she would not be able to pay off that debt before she had to start paying college expenses for her elder son.

There was also a house for sale in the Maple Woods development just outside Woodhaven. Maple Woods was an attractive development, and the houses were well-built but small. Since most of the people who lived in Maple Woods were young people with small children, Maple Woods houses were usually first homes and people tended to move out in four or five years. This lack of stability concerned Ms. Lewis, but the financial aspects of buying a home in Maple Woods were attractive. The particular house she looked at was of ample size and was on the market for only $40,000. She could afford the $10,000 down payment and still have enough of her savings left to buy furniture. Total housing costs would be well within her budget since her monthly mortgage payments, including interest, would be $250 a month for a period of twenty-five years. Taxes would come to $65 a month and maintenance would be $50 a month.

While Ms. Lewis was considering whether to buy one of the two houses that she had looked at or rent the

GO ON TO THE NEXT PAGE.

house in Barnton, the Nelsons offered her their house under a land-contract agreement. The Nelsons were in a high tax bracket and knew that unless they managed to spread the income from the sale of their house over a number of years, their taxes on the profits from the sale would be high. If Ms. Lewis paid them $10,000 at the time they signed the land-contract agreement, the Nelsons would give her the right to legal possession of the property. She would keep that right for as long as she maintained the property in good repair and made monthly payments on the principal and interest (at the same rate charged by local banks) for the next twenty-five years. At any time that she did not meet these conditions, the Nelsons would have the right to fore-close, but even if they did foreclose Ms. Lewis would receive an equitable share in the value of the property. Upon the last payment, she would receive title to the property. Under this arrangement, the payment of principal and interest would be $490 a month. All other expenses in maintaining the house would be Ms. Lewis' and would be the same as if she had obtained an ordinary bank mortgage.

GO ON TO THE NEXT PAGE.

DATA EVALUATION QUESTIONS

Directions: The following questions consist of items related to the passage above. You may refer back to the passage and the directions. Consider each item separately in terms of the passage and on the answer sheet blacken space

    A if the item is a <u>Major Objective</u> in making the decision; that is, one of the outcomes or results sought by the decision-maker;

    B if the item is a <u>Major Factor</u> in making the decision; that is, a consideration, explicitly mentioned in the passage, <u>that is basic</u> in determining the decision;

    C if the item is a <u>Minor Factor</u> in making the decision; that is, a secondary consideration that affects the criteria tangentially, <u>relating</u> to a Major Factor rather than to an Objective;

    D if the item is a <u>Major Assumption</u> in making the decision; that is, a supposition or projection made by the decision-maker <u>before</u> weighing the variables;

    E if the item is an <u>Unimportant Issue</u> in making the decision; that is, a factor that is insignificant or not immediately relevant to the situation.

II. 17. Stability of the neighborhood

II. 18. Rate of interest Woodhaven banks charge on mortgages and other loans

II. 19. Keeping the initial cash outlay for housing and furniture no higher than $15,000

II. 20. Need to spend about $3,000 for furniture

II. 21. Amount that Ms. Lewis has budgeted annually for housing

II. 22. Avoiding borrowing money for a down payment or for furniture

II. 23. The probability that both sons will be in college at the same time

II. 24. Cost of major repairs on the house for rent in Barnton

II. 25. Enabling Ms. Lewis' sons to attend the colleges of their choice

II. 26. Cost of heat and utilities at each of the houses

II. 27. Keeping housing costs no higher than $7,000 yearly

II. 28. Likelihood that $2,000 yearly is sufficient to cover emergencies

II. 29. Average age of Maple Woods residents

II. 30. Economic advantage of buying rather than renting a home

II. 31. Unavailability of mortgage money outside Woodhaven

II. 32. Ms. Lewis' continued employment at World Oil Enterprises

END OF SAMPLE TEST II

ANALYSIS OF SITUATIONS SAMPLE TEST III

Time—40 minutes

32 Questions

<u>Directions</u>: Each passage in this section is followed by questions that require you to classify certain of the facts presented in the passage on the basis of their importance, as illustrated in the following example:

SAMPLE PASSAGE

Fred North, a prospering hardware dealer in Hillidale, Connecticut, felt that he needed more store space to accommodate a new line of farm equipment and repair parts that he intended to carry. A number of New York City commuters had recently purchased tracts of land in the environs of Hillidale and there had taken up farming on a small scale. Mr. North, foreseeing a potential increase in farming in that area, wanted to expand his business to cater to this market. North felt that the most feasible and appealing recourse open to him would be to purchase the adjoining store property owned by Mike Johnson, who used the premises for his small grocery store. Johnson's business had been on the decline for over a year since the advent of a large supermarket in the town. North felt that Johnson would be willing to sell the property at reasonable terms, and this was important since North, after the purchase of the new merchandise, would have little capital available to invest in the expansion of his store.

The following questions consist of items related to the passage above. Consider each item separately in terms of the passage and on the answer sheet blacken space

A if the item is a <u>Major Objective</u> in making the decision; that is, one of the outcomes or results sought by the decision-maker;

B if the item is a <u>Major Factor</u> in making the decision; that is, a consideration, explicitly mentioned in the passage, <u>that is basic</u> in determining the decision;

C if the item is a <u>Minor Factor</u> in making the decision; that is, a secondary consideration that affects the criteria tangentially, <u>relating</u> to a Major Factor rather than to an Objective;

D if the item is a <u>Major Assumption</u> in making the decision; that is, a supposition or projection made by the decision-maker before weighing the variables;

E if the item is an <u>Unimportant Issue</u> in making the decision; that is, a factor that is insignificant or not immediately relevant to the situation.

SAMPLE QUESTIONS

1. Increase in farming in the Hillidale area   Ⓐ Ⓑ Ⓒ ● Ⓔ

2. Acquisition of property for expanding store   ● Ⓑ Ⓒ Ⓓ Ⓔ

3. Cost of Johnson's property   Ⓐ ● Ⓒ Ⓓ Ⓔ

4. State of Johnson's grocery business   Ⓐ Ⓑ ● Ⓓ Ⓔ

5. Quality of the farm equipment North intends to sell   Ⓐ Ⓑ Ⓒ Ⓓ ●

GO ON TO THE NEXT PAGE.

The correct designation for number 1 is (D), a <u>Major Assumption</u>, since North bases his whole expansion project on his supposition that the new commuter-farmers in the Hillidale area are indicative of a trend in that direction. Number 2 is (A), a <u>Major Objective</u>, inasmuch as North's immediate purpose is to obtain room for expansion. (B), a <u>Major Factor</u>, is the correct answer for number 3 because North's present lack of capital renders cost a vital consideration. The best classification of number 4 is (C), a <u>Minor Factor</u>, because the depreciating value of Johnson's business influences his willingness to sell and also the price he will demand for his property; thus, this factor pertains to 3, the cost of Johnson's property, and is an indirect consideration in the case. Number 5, finally, is (E), an <u>Unimportant Issue</u>, for the quality of North's goods has no relevance to the situation at hand; i.e., the desire for room to expand his business.

NOW READ THE PASSAGES AND ANSWER THE QUESTIONS FOLLOWING THEM.

GO ON TO THE NEXT PAGE.

On October 8, 1974, Samuel Echington, president of the Northern Folding Paper Box Company of Chicago, was considering a proposal to bid for a major contract with King Foods Corporation, one of the largest packaged food marketers in the United States. If the bid was accepted, the job would be the biggest to come along for Northern in the past two years, which had been marked by declining sales and depressed prices. The job required production of custom-folding paper cartons for twelve of King's dessert items; the total volume was estimated to be $550,000, or more than 10 per cent of Northern's present annual sales volume of $5.2 million.

Mr. Echington was primarily interested in reversing Northern's two-year financial slump, a situation resulting largely from shrinking markets for two of Northern's largest customers in the past—soaps and dry foods. He hoped that a contract with King Foods would provide the needed stimulus. Northern's board of directors had been urging the company to develop more fully its potential for using local markets as a first step in reducing overhead costs. Shipping costs, for example, were a major problem because the company's major customers were located long distances from Chicago. Echington also was anxious to begin using a new package design developed by his company. King's representatives had judged the design superior in quality and attractiveness to the competing designs, so Echington hoped it could be more fully developed under the King Foods contract.

Echington, however, saw major problems in the proposed contract. First, J. B. Seller, Northern's sales representative, reported that Northern's bid of $10.03 per 1,000 cartons was 11 per cent higher than the lowest bid King Foods had received for the job. According to Mr. Seller, King Foods would give one year's business to Northern if it would meet the lowest competitive bid of $8.90 per 1,000. Second, the job would require Northern to use a third shift on certain equipment. Northern's production manager had resisted third-shift operations in the past because of the additional costs in labor and equipment maintenance. Therefore, Echington was not sure whether to take the job at the lower price. He decided to hold a meeting of Northern's upper-level managers and others whose technical advice might be needed.

The meeting began with several brief comments:

Mr. Echington: "This is a vital decision for Northern. Of course we're concerned with profits, but there are other concerns as well. If we lower our price to $8.90 per 1,000, we will probably lose about $20,000 in the first year because of the initial costs involved. But in the long run, the King Foods job provides us with a substantial guaranteed market, one that is expanding, not contracting as the soap and dry foods markets have been doing."

Jimmy Farley, production manager: "Our new design approach has great sales potential. We want to get maximum use and profits from it. This is the perfect sort of job for further research and development."

Cal Williams, sales manager: "Also King Foods is right here in Chicago. Pickering Paper Box Company, a San Francisco outfit, now supplies them with packaging materials. If we had the business right here in our own backyard, we could provide King with more efficient service and at the same time stimulate more local markets and generate more customers for ourselves. We've never done business with King, but I think now is the time to start."

Cost figures were then discussed. Cost estimates made by Northern's controller are summarized in the following table:

TABLE I

Item	Quantity	
	Per 1,000 Cartons	Per 60 Million Cartons (annual output)
Material	$4.95	$297,000
Labor	1.73	103,800
Freight and Warehousing	0.63	37,800
Plant Operation	1.93	115,800
	$9.24	$554,400

J. B. Seller: "We can take the job at a low rate per thousand and then work the price up later."

Vern Symington, cost analyst: "Here is a list of all bids that have been made to King Foods:

TABLE II

Pickering Paper Box	$10.10
Northern	10.03
Davidson Paper Co.	8.99
Texas Container	8.90

"A small company, Boxer Brothers, indicated informally that it was willing to price the job at $8.70 per 1,000, with no minimum quantity or time limit on the agreement. I think we all agree, however, that $8.90 is as low as we can possibly go and still do quality work. There are, and will be, other costs. Up to this point, we have invested approximately $4,500 in the development of our new package, the one that would go into the King Foods job. Although King's managers like the design better than any of the others they've seen, they're unwilling to reimburse us for that expense. They say that the design work is the price we pay to become King Foods' supplier."

Bob Smith, area sales representative: "The figures we've seen are incomplete. The new design will require a modified packaging system, to be installed at the King Foods plant, costing $70,000. How do we pay for that?"

GO ON TO THE NEXT PAGE.

Mr. Symington: "We would finance the machinery investment for King. They would repay us a total of $85,000 over an initial four-year period. Thereafter, King would pay an additional 3 per cent per year delayed interest for four more years. This interest would be based on the initial cost of $70,000."

Sam Farmer, cost analyst: "Finished artwork, engravings, and color proofs would have to be produced under the direction of Northern Folding Paper Box; the estimated cost of these items, $24,000, would be charged to King Foods as an extra cost item. The boxboard required for this contract is not of the type which our paperboard supplier, Pennsylvania Paper, can provide; therefore it would have to be purchased outside at market prices."

Mr. Smith: "Although King Foods expressed its willingness to sign a one-year contract for the cartons 'at the right price,' it insisted upon reserving the right to select another supplier later on, if it were to King Foods' advantage to do so. However, they have assured us that we will be given the opportunity to match any competing bid that King Foods receives."

Jane Russel, plant manager: "King Foods requires its carton suppliers to store the packaging for slow-moving items for up to one year, at no extra cost, and has obtained this concession from Northern's competitors on the dessert carton. However, King Foods agreed to a maximum inventory of these packages of $150,000 at any one time during the year. They anticipate that finished goods inventory through the year will average $100,000. Northern's in-plant warehousing facilities would be unable to handle this additional volume, but ample space could be obtained in the old Kirkland warehouse at a monthly cost of seventy-five cents per one hundred pounds. The Kirkland warehouse is probably all right."

GO ON TO THE NEXT PAGE.

DATA EVALUATION QUESTIONS

Directions: The following questions consist of items related to the passage above. You may refer back to the passage and the directions. Consider each item separately in terms of the passage and on the answer sheet blacken space

A   if the item is a Major Objective in making the decision; that is, one of the outcomes or results sought by the decision-maker;

B   if the item is a Major Factor in making the decision; that is, a consideration, explicitly mentioned in the passage, that is basic in determining the decision;

C   if the item is a Minor Factor in making the decision; that is, a secondary consideration that affects the criteria tangentially, relating to a Major Factor rather than to an Objective;

D   if the item is a Major Assumption in making the decision; that is, a supposition or projection made by the decision-maker before weighing the variables;

E   if the item is an Unimportant Issue in making the decision; that is, a factor that is insignificant or not immediately relevant to the situation.

III. 1. Development of local markets for Northern's products

III. 2. Continuation of decline in the demand for soap and dry-foods products

III. 3. Low bid made by Boxer Brothers

III. 4. Sales potential of Northern's new package design

III. 5. Size of the King Foods contract

III. 6. Inability of Pennsylvania Paper to supply the box-board needed for the King Foods contract

III. 7. Effect of the King Foods contract on Northern's sales volume

III. 8. Additional costs associated with third shifts

III. 9. Increase in Northern's sales volume

III. 10. Quality of Northern's cost-estimating procedures

III. 11. Likelihood that Northern could compete effectively for the King Foods job after the one-year contract was up

III. 12. Availability to Northern of warehouse facilities to accommodate the added volume produced by the King Foods contract

III. 13. Long-range advantages for Northern of the contract with King Foods

III. 14. Prospects of introducing a second new design into Northern's proposal for the King Foods contract

III. 15. King Foods' requirement that Northern store packaging for slow-moving items

III. 16. Length of present union contract between Northern and its machine operators

GO ON TO THE NEXT PAGE.

Ms. Bella Speranza, who owned the Shop-In supermarket in the summer resort of Yorkville, had become quite uneasy about recent changes in the Foodfill supermarket, her rival and neighbor. The owners of Foodfill had just completed major renovations which transformed their crowded and dimly lit store into a bright, spacious market with computerized registers and scales to weigh produce at each checkout counter. The Foodfill managers were now staging a grand reopening; the store was attracting eager customers who arrived with handfuls of discount coupons.

Ms. Speranza had become convinced that it was time to make the changes at Shop-In that she had long hoped to make and for which she had been saving for several years. Too many of her customers had been attracted by her neighbor's renovations, and Speranza could not afford to lose her old clientele permanently. Over the years, Shop-In and Foodfill had maintained a healthy competition, and Speranza was intent on successfully maintaining Shop-In's competitive position as well as increasing its profits. Each year, Yorkville was becoming more popular; its close proximity to major urban areas, combined with its reputation as a quiet and clean resort, made it a favorite vacation spot for families from the city. Speranza was anxious to give Shop-In a new dimension that would make it more attractive to these vacationers. She wanted to undertake some major store-wide renovations, since she felt that the store was now too dark and cramped. However, structural changes would have to be minimal since it was crucial to interfere as little as possible with the daily operation of the store and to complete the work in time for the tourist season.

Speranza had already asked her three assistant managers to investigate three of what she considered to be the four most practical ways of improving the store. Speranza herself had investigated the possibility of expanding packaged food lines in order to offer customers more choices among high-quality items. Leonard Lubrano had begun researching the possibility of adding a housewares department to Shop-In, while Mary Fran Saretsky was investigating the feasibility of expanding the delicatessen department in order to offer more cheeses and a new line of breads. Jonna Boronson had been considering the possibility of saving space by consolidating frozen foods into new stand-up freezers and displaying an expanded stock of local fresh produce under awnings in front of the store. In addition, Speranza and her assistants were seriously considering renovating Shop-In to give it the appearance of a country general store.

An enlarged delicatessen area, a specialty-food section, or a new housewares department could be incorporated by constructing a small addition at the side of the store. Setting up a fruit and vegetable section in front of the store would simply require the purchase of large awnings and extra weighing equipment. The basic question before the managers involved determining which combination of renovations would involve the least risk and expense and would best ensure a strong economic future for Shop-In. A discussion of the alternatives for Shop-In followed.

Speranza: If we expand our food product lines, our initial expenses could be kept to a minimum through careful ordering. Our distributors all carry specialty items and we could easily expand, for example, our stock of frozen products and soups. The main problem is that these items tend to be expensive.

Lubrano: Adding onto the building just to stock more packaged food doesn't seem worth the expense. It seems to me that we need to consider offering more than just new food products. Although our initial expenses would be higher, I'm convinced that adding a section of basic housewares would be a better risk; all we need to do is determine which items are most needed by people renting vacation cottages. The cost of building the addition in either case would be the same, and I've learned from the managers of other stores that have undertaken similar expansion programs that housewares are very popular. It's been found that shoppers prefer to eliminate a trip to another store, and I'm sure that vacationers are especially interested in minimizing shopping time.

Speranza: The only drawback I see in your housewares plan, Leonard, is time. I'm not sure we could complete all the necessary research, make the orders, receive the merchandise, inventory and stock it, and have everything ready for the tourist season. We'll also need to order new display equipment since food-item shelving won't be appropriate for all housewares. But I'm still wondering whether we'll have enough space in our store for implementing either of these plans, even with some expansion.

Lubrano: The addition we'd construct would be big enough to house two aisles of merchandise—one for a new line of products and one for items we already stock. By carefully redistributing other goods, we could easily gain extra space and be able to widen our aisles.

Saretsky: Since time is so important and since we know we can add onto the side of the store quite easily, I think an expanded delicatessen would be a better risk. A bakery may seem to be too expensive an undertaking, but we can get a good price on used equipment from the bakery that went out of business in Bridgetown. I've also found out that one of the bakers from that firm is still looking for work and might be interested in this kind of limited undertaking.

GO ON TO THE NEXT PAGE.

124

Speranza: We're not only talking about potentially very expensive items; we're talking about a potential spoilage problem if the baked goods don't move fast. Baked goods have to be very carefully selected and planned. I'll say one good thing about the bakery idea: an array of homemade breads would certainly go along well with a general store atmosphere.

Saretsky: I've determined that maintenance costs on the baking equipment would be minimal, so that our major expenses would be supplies and the baker's salary. We'll have to plan on hiring at least one new staff member no matter what kind of addition we choose to make, and although the salary for a baker would be higher than that for a clerk, it could be easily offset by making the bakery a special Sunday morning attraction. There is no real competition in Yorkville, since no one else can offer bakery goods, the Sunday paper, and a large stock of grocery items.

Lubrano: There's a risk here, though, since we have no way of knowing just how popular the deli-bakery will be on a daily basis—especially since baked goods are fairly expensive. If we keep the rest of the week's baking limited to various kinds of breads, we should be able to offset the extra expenses of offering special baked goods on Sunday.

Boronson: Since our neighbors have just completed a major modernization, I think we should seriously consider the "general store" alternative and really take advantage of our reputation as an old and respected business.

Speranza: But we should also make the store look and feel more spacious; we've been too cramped and too dark for several years now.

Boronson: I'm not saying we should leave the store dark and cramped, but that while providing more light and room, we should also make Shop-In appear more old-fashioned. Simulated gas lamps and barn board will cost about the same as fluorescents and paint, and I really think the general store atmosphere will appeal to vacationers from the city. I'm sure that our customers would appreciate a store that's out of the ordinary.

Speranza: The country store look would be enhanced if we put an expanded display of produce outside in front of the store. We should be able to purchase produce at a low price from local farmers and at the same time eliminate the need for our customers to stop at both the supermarket and a vegetable stand.

GO ON TO THE NEXT PAGE.

DATA EVALUATION QUESTIONS

Directions: The following questions consist of items related to the passage above. You may refer back to the passage and the directions. Consider each item separately in terms of the passage and on the answer sheet blacken space

A   if the item is a <u>Major Objective</u> in making the decision; that is, one of the outcomes or results sought by the decision-maker;

B   if the item is a <u>Major Factor</u> in making the decision; that is, a consideration, explicitly mentioned in the passage, <u>that is basic</u> in determining the decision;

C   if the item is a <u>Minor Factor</u> in making the decision; that is, a secondary consideration that affects the criteria tangentially, relating to a Major Factor rather than to an Objective;

D   if the item is a <u>Major Assumption</u> in making the decision; that is, a supposition or projection made by the decision-maker before weighing the variables;

E   if the item is an <u>Unimportant Issue</u> in making the decision; that is, a factor that is insignificant or not immediately relevant to the situation.

III. 17.   Time required to complete alterations at Shop-In

III. 18.   Existence of adequate funds to cover costs of renovations

III. 19.   Shop-In's long record of satisfying Yorkville customers

III. 20.   Floor space to be gained by purchasing new freezer units

III. 21.   Attractiveness to customers of a store with wide aisles and good lighting

III. 22.   Foodfill's special reopening discount coupons

III. 23.   Minimal interruption of Shop-In's business hours

III. 24.   Attractiveness to customers of each proposed renovation

III. 25.   Foodfill's closing for renovations

III. 26.   Previous success of housewares departments in other supermarkets

III. 27.   Initial expense of ordering new specialty food items

III. 28.   Continued attractiveness to area shoppers of Foodfill's newly renovated store

III. 29.   Causing Shop-In to have a special attraction

III. 30.   Ability of Shop-In's bakery to attract Sunday morning business

III. 31.   Capacity of each remodeling plan to provide additional space in Shop-In's present store

III. 32.   Completing store alterations by the opening of the tourist season

END OF SAMPLE TEST III

ANSWER KEYS FOR SAMPLE TESTS

Answers preceded by asterisks indicate questions discussed in detail in the explanatory material. This discussion is designed to provide you with the best preparation for Analysis of Situations questions in the GMAT. Therefore, it is less important that you focus on the individual explanation of a particular answer than that you study the discussion as a whole in order to grasp the underlying principles for answering Analysis of Situations questions.

ANALYSIS OF SITUATIONS

Sample Test I

I.1	B	*I.9	C	I.17	B	I.25	C
I.2	A	I.10	E	*I.18	A	I.26	D
I.3	C	I.11	D	I.19	D	I.27	E
*I.4	E	*I.12	B	*I.20	C	I.28	A
I.5	D	I.13	A	*I.21	B	I.29	B
I.6	B	I.14	C	*I.22	E	*I.30	D
*I.7	A	I.15	E	I.23	A	I.31	C
I.8	B	*I.16	D	I.24	D	I.32	E

Sample Test II

II.1	A	II.9	D	II.17	B	*II.25	A
II.2	D	II.10	B	II.18	C	*II.26	C
*II.3	C	II.11	C	II.19	A	II.27	A
II.4	B	II.12	A	II.20	D	II.28	D
II.5	D	II.13	D	II.21	B	II.29	C
II.6	E	*II.14	E	II.22	A	*II.30	B
*II.7	D	*II.15	B	II.23	D	*II.31	E
II.8	A	*II.16	A	II.24	E	*II.32	D

Sample Test III

III.1	A	*III.9	A	*III.17	B	III.25	E
*III.2	D	III.10	E	III.18	D	*III.26	C
*III.3	E	III.11	D	III.19	E	III.27	C
III.4	D	III.12	C	III.20	C	III.28	D
*III.5	B	III.13	B	*III.21	D	III.29	A
III.6	C	III.14	E	*III.22	E	III.30	D
III.7	B	III.15	C	*III.23	A	III.31	B
*III.8	C	III.16	E	III.24	B	III.32	A

EXPLANATORY MATERIAL: ANALYSIS OF SITUATIONS

The following discussion is intended to familiarize you with the most efficient and effective approaches to the kinds of problems common to Analysis of Situations. The particular examples taken from the sample tests in this chapter are generally represent-ative of the kinds of questions you will encounter in this section of the GMAT. Remember that it is the problem-solving strategy that is important, not the specific details of a particular question.

References in the explanatory material to questions from the sample tests are indicated by the Roman numeral of a particular sample test followed by the Arabic numeral of the particular question.

A. MAJOR OBJECTIVES

I.7 Obtaining a sufficiently long lease to justify the costs of renovations and new equipment

The Tracys are hesitant about doing major remodeling at their current location because a renewed lease there will run only two years. The passage states directly that the Tracys "felt that they needed a longer lease to justify any renovations and the purchase of new equipment." Faced with this problem or need, one of the Tracys' objectives is obtaining a lease of sufficient duration to justify the costs of expansion; the best answer to this difficult question is therefore A. Another way to approach this question is to recall the explanatory material describing a major objective. Such an objective is the condition that the de-cision maker wishes to exist after a decision has been imple-mented. For the Tracys, this would mean that, after picking a location from the available alternatives, they would eventually have a salon with a lease long enough to justify the costs of renovations and new equipment.

Question I.7 is difficult for several reasons. First, the question paraphrases rather than states verbatim an objective; the "longer lease," which in the passage means a lease longer than two years, becomes in this question a "sufficiently long lease." Also, the objective is stated near the middle of the passage rather than, as is often the case, near the beginning. You should re-member from the explanatory material for Analysis of Situations, however, that objectives need not always appear early in a pas-sage. You should also keep in mind that objectives can be par-aphrased when stated in questions. Probably the most impor-tant reason for the difficulty of this question is that it can be easily mistaken for a factor. It is not a factor because acquiring a long lease is not used by the Tracys to help them decide which alternative to choose to reach their objective. You need to distinguish in this passage between *obtaining* a long lease and *the length of* the lease at any of the locations. The former is one of the things the Tracys want, while the latter is a con-sideration that would bear directly on their decision about which location to choose. By the definition given in the explanatory material, the latter is a major factor. You need to be especially careful not to be misled by the word "costs" in question I.7. This question is concerned not with costs in themselves but with obtaining a lease of sufficient duration to justify certain costs. Question I.1, on the other hand, is directly concerned with costs, specifically the costs of rent and necessary renovations at the alternative locations. The answer to that question is B, or a major factor, because such costs would bear directly on one of the Tracys' objectives, that of acquiring a store that does not require "an unreasonable outlay of cash."

I.18 Acquisition of a reliable replacement for Lopes Con-struction's damaged crane

A, the correct answer to this easy question, is determined through a careful reading of paragraphs two and four of the passage. These paragraphs state that Lopes "decided to obtain a re-placement for his damaged crane," and that he wanted the replacement to be "reliable." In other words, after making a decision and implementing it, Lopes and his board want to have acquired a reliable replacement crane; they will then have achieved one of their objectives and thus will have solved their problem of needing a reliable replacement crane. Note that this question, like question I.7, states a concrete objective, in this case obtaining a piece of reliable construction equipment. (If the passage were worded differently, however, a possible goal might be something more abstract, such as the retention of Lopes Construction's reputation for honest workmanship.) The reason the decision makers want a reliable crane can be traced to information given in the first paragraph of the passage, which states that the company faces a financial penalty if the addition to the power plant is not completed within a year. Such a time limit would be threatened by a crane that might break down. The reliability of each of the cranes under consideration would be of major importance to the decision makers, then, as the discussion of question I.21 below will indicate.

Note, finally, that the objective stated in question I.18 is composed of information from two parts of the passage, paragraphs two and four. You should remember that objectives will sometimes be synthesized in this way. (An even greater synthesis is explained in question II.25 below.) On other occasions, as in question II.16 below, you will find objectives restated explicitly from one part of the passage.

II.16 Producing a film that presents an appearance of authenticity

It is important to remember that though the decision makers in an Analysis of Situations passage may have only one decision to make, they may have several objectives. In this passage you are told that Unisphere needs to decide on a location for the filming of *Summer Surf*. The location, however, must accomplish several objectives for Andropolous and his colleagues. Some of these objectives are concrete: producing a profitable film and maintaining a reasonable budget. A careful reading of the passage indicates another objective, one slightly more abstract or less tangible than the two just mentioned. Wilbur Goss states that "if the film is to have appeal it must have the appearance of authenticity." Thus, producing a film that seems authentic is an objective of the decision makers and A is the answer to this moderately difficult question. As in question I.7, you must distinguish between an objective and a factor. The authenticity resulting from filming in Hollywood, Colorado, or New Jersey—a consideration raised in question II.4—is a major factor because it is fundamental in determining whether of an authentic-seeming location can be achieved. Question II.16, however, does not refer to something the decision makers would weigh before picking a location, but rather restates—rather than paraphrases—an outcome that the decision makers wish to achieve.

II.25 Enabling Ms. Lewis' sons to attend the colleges of their choice

From reading a number of Analysis of Situations passages you may have noticed that objectives in a passage are often introduced by phrases such as the decision makers "were interested in" something, or the decision makers "wanted" something, or the decision makers knew that "they must have" something. The objectives explained in the preceding discussions were introduced, in their respective passages, by some form of one of these phrases. The passage describing Ms. Lewis' situation, on the other hand, does not state explicitly that Ms. Lewis wanted

her sons to be able to attend the college of their choice. That Ms. Lewis' objectives, however, include enabling her sons to attend their desired colleges—along with those objectives stated in questions II.19, II.22, and II.27—can legitimately be inferred from a reading of the second paragraph of the passage. There you learn that, in making her decision about which home to buy or rent, Ms. Lewis "did not want to burden herself with extra debts." She does not want to do this because she knows she might eventually "have to take out a loan to cover college expenses" for that son whose expenses would not be covered by her income. A close reading of the second paragraph indicates, in short, that Ms. Lewis is already making plans to enable her sons to attend the colleges of their choice: she is considering a college loan and she does not want to make that loan more burdensome by incurring extra debts in choosing a home. Thus, enabling her sons to attend college is one of Ms. Lewis' objectives, one that can logically be inferred from reading and synthesizing the information in the second paragraph; the question is a moderately difficult one because you must make an inference.

Note that this question cannot be classified as a factor because enabling her sons to attend college does not make any of the alternative homes more or less attractive. On the other hand, the expenses incurred in purchasing or renting any of these homes would be a factor in the decision, since these expenses would bear directly on Ms. Lewis' objective of being financially able to have her sons attend their desired colleges.

III.9 Increase in Northern's sales volume

This is an easy question. It restates fairly directly a concrete objective that is mentioned early in the passage. The second paragraph of the passage states that Mr. Echington is "primarily interested in reversing Northern's two-year financial slump." Put another way, he is interested in—a phrase that often precedes an objective in a passage—increasing his company's sales volume. Such an increase is therefore one of his objectives, objectives that also include developing local markets for his company's products (see also question III.1).

III.23 Minimal interruption of Shop-In's business hours

In choosing a way to renovate her store, Ms. Speranza has several concrete objectives, some of which appear together at the end of the second paragraph of the passage. One of these, completing alterations by the opening of the tourist season, is restated almost verbatim in question III.32. Another, stated in the passage as "it was crucial to interfere as little as possible with the daily operation of the store," is paraphrased in question III.23. Note that the phrase "it was crucial to" is a substitute in this case for the more common phrases, such as "he wanted" or "she needed," that often precede objectives. The most compelling reason, however, that question III.23 is classified as an objective is that it corresponds to the definition of a major objective as stated in the explanatory material: question III.23 states a condition that the decision makers want to exist after the decision has been implemented. After Ms. Speranza has decided on a renovation plan and begun work, she wants that work to be completed with little interruption in daily operations, operations that would include the maintenance of business hours. Notice that, though several of Ms. Speranza's objectives are stated in the second paragraph of the passage, other objectives, including giving Shop-In the appearance of a country store, are stated in other parts of the passage. (You can notice the same dispersion of objectives in the Unisphere Productions passage in Sample Test II. In that passage the objective of launching a set of films is not mentioned until late in the passage, well after other objectives are set forward.) To return to question III.23, you need to notice that while an objective is stated here, a factor would be stated in a question about the amount of interruption of business hours caused by each renovation. How much interruption would result from implementing any of the alternatives is a factor that would bear directly on the decision about which alternative to choose; minimally interrupting business hours, however, is one of Ms. Speranza's objectives in picking a renovation project. Question III.23 is a difficult one because you must see the distinction between objective and factor.

B. MAJOR FACTORS

I.12 Size, including working and storage areas, of the locations under consideration

One of the Tracys' objectives is "a store that offered ample space." The passage later indicates that such space would include areas for working and storage. The Tracys want, in short, a store large enough for ample work and storage areas. Question I.12, in fact, tests your ability to see that obtaining sufficient space is an objective. It is logical, then, that the size, including work and storage areas, of each of the locations under consideration would be a major factor because the size of the locations will bear directly on the decision. (Remember that a major factor, as defined in the explanatory material, is a consideration that has a direct and significant influence on the decision.) The size of any of the potential locations directly influences the decision because the size will determine how well or how poorly a location will meet the Tracys' objective of ample space. The best answer, then, to this easy question is B. The size of the locations, along with such issues as the cost of rent and necessary renovations at the locations (question I.1), and the ability of the locations to attract new patrons and retain old ones (questions I.6 and I.8), are all major considerations that will bear directly on the Tracys' decision.

Note that the directions to Analysis of Situations state that a major factor is a "consideration, explicitly mentioned in the passage, that is basic in determining the decision." It might be argued that the formulation given in question I.12 is not explicitly stated in the passage. While it is true that this precise formulation is never directly stated, the elements of that formulation—"size," "work and storage areas"—are explicitly stated. Moreover, these elements are mentioned in the passage only because they are potential considerations for each of the alternatives being weighed. Thus, the information given in this question is, in a different form, explicitly mentioned in the passage.

Question I.12 must be read carefully in order to avoid classifying it as a major objective. Although the Tracys want to *have* ample space after making their decision, the size of each of the possible locations is a major factor in making that decision since the size will determine how well the objective of ample space can be met.

I.21 Reliability of the cranes under consideration

As noted earlier, in the discussion of question I.18, one of the decision makers' objectives is the acquisition of a reliable replacement crane. Lopes has decided "to obtain a replacement for the damaged crane"; he also wants the replacement crane he will choose to be "reliable" because a dependable crane will permit the power plant project to be completed in a year, as stipulated by the contract. The reliability, then, of each of the alternative replacements is a major factor since it is a consideration that is directly related to the achievement of an objective. Put another way, the reliability of each of the alternatives is a basic consideration in the decision concerning the most suitable crane to pick. The best answer to this easy question is B. To test whether you fully understand why this question is an example of a major factor, consider why the question cannot be classified as a minor factor. Remember that the directions for Analysis of Situations state that a minor factor is a consideration more related to a major factor than to an objective. The reliability of the cranes would not be a minor factor because this reliability is directly related to the objective of finding a reliable crane. If, on the other hand, the question concerned the age of the cranes—as does question I.25—the answer would be C, a minor factor, because the consideration of age relates to and bears on a major factor, the reliability of the cranes. A moment's thought suggests the connection between age and reliability: part of what determines whether a crane is dependable is its age or how long it has been in operation. The distinctions between major and minor factors suggested by these examples are crucial in an Analysis of Situations passage.

II.15 Net profits that Unisphere could expect given the expenses required at each location under consideration

Perhaps the most basic objective of the decision makers in this passage is articulated by Andropolous: " 'Summer Surf must make money.' " Given this requirement, the profits that the film company could expect to make at each location—profits affected by the necessary expenses of each location—would have a direct influence on the decision makers. How much money Unisphere could make after expenses at each location is, in other words, a major factor, because it directly determines whether the objective of making money will be met. For this reason, the best answer to this moderately difficult question is B. Note that as in question I.12, the exact words in question II.15 do not appear explicitly in the passage. Once again, however, the individual elements in the question do appear in the passage. Unisphere's need to have *Summer Surf* " 'make money' " appears in this question as "net profits"; "the expenses incurred at any location" is almost directly quoted in the question. Putting these elements together, and keeping in mind how the information in the question will bear directly on one of the objectives, you can logically conclude that the question is a major factor.

In answering the question, you should keep clearly in mind the distinction between an objective and a factor. Making a net profit on the movie, staying within budget, reducing costs—these are all outcomes desired by the decision makers. The net profits to be gained by filming at each location, the opportunities for staying within budget or for reducing costs at each location, however, are major factors because they are directly related to how well each location will satisfy the objectives.

II.30 Economic advantage of buying rather than renting a home

One of Ms. Lewis' objectives is to spend "about $7,000 a year on housing." She also does "not have a large amount of money in reserve." In short, Ms. Lewis wants to select a home that permits her to stay within a strict budget. The economic advantage of buying a home—or, conversely, the economic disadvantage of renting a home—would bear directly on the achievement of this objective. Put another way, the economic benefits in buying or the economic liabilities in renting would directly determine whether Ms. Lewis will have a home that matches her budgetary requirements and ultimately whether she will buy or rent a home. B, or a major factor, is therefore the best answer to this question.

For several reasons question II.30 is moderately difficult. You must see, for example, that "Economic advantage of buying rather than renting a home" is a legitimate paraphrase of the information in the passage that "it would be wiser to buy a house than to rent one, largely because [one] could build up equity in a house by buying." You must recognize, in other words, that question II.30 is a consideration that is—in different terms—explicitly mentioned in the passage. In addition, you must recognize why this question is *not* a minor factor or an assumption. It is not the former because it bears so directly on the achievement of an objective, that of staying within a budget. Neither is the question an assumption, because the relative economic advantage of buying versus renting is not a supposition made by Ms. Lewis before she begins weighing the alternatives. Rather, the issue of economic advantage is a consideration that makes the Nelson house and the Maple Woods house more attractive than the rental property. Economic advantage is thus a factor and one that will directly influence Ms. Lewis' decision.

III.5 Size of the King Foods contract

As explained in the discussion of question III.9, Echington and his colleagues have as one of their objectives increasing Northern's sales volume. The size of the King Foods contract is a major factor for the Northern executives because it would directly determine how well or how poorly the King Foods contract meets a key objective; the size of the contract has a direct influence on the decision to accept or reject the contract. B is the best answer, therefore, to this easy question. The question is easy, in part, because you do not have to see, as you do in question II.30, that the information in the question is a summary and a paraphrase of explicit information in the passage. The size of the contract is mentioned, in monetary terms, explicitly in the passage.

III.17 Time required to complete alterations at Shop-In

As explained in the discussion of question III.23, one of Ms. Speranza's objectives is to pick a renovation plan that interferes as little as possible with her store's business hours. At the same time, she wants the work on whatever renovation plan she picks to be completed "in time for the tourist season." This objective is stated in question III.32. The time required to complete alterations at Shop-In, whatever these alterations will eventually be, is a major factor because it is a consideration that directly determines how well or how poorly each plan will meet the objective of completing work in time for the tourist season. Note that

although the formulation given in question III.17 is not explicitly stated in the passage, the elements of that formulation—"time," "complete alteration"—are explicitly stated. Question III.17 is an easy question.

C. MINOR FACTORS

I.9 Number of residents on Archer Place

This moderately difficult question must be approached with some caution. Although the correct answer is C, a minor factor, some readers might at first believe that the number of people living on Archer Place is irrelevant to the decision. Careful analysis, however, proves otherwise. In answering the question, you must realize, first, that one of the Tracys' objectives, in addition to those mentioned in the discussion of question I.7, is "to capture a new market." Next, you must understand that the number of new customers any of the locations would provide is a major factor because it bears directly on the achievement of this objective. Put another way, because the Tracys' decision concerning which location to choose will be directly and significantly affected by the number of new customers each location, including Archer Place, might provide, this number is a major factor. Having reasoned to this point, you are in a position to see why the number of residents on Archer Place is a minor factor in the decision. Common sense suggests that the number of people living on Archer Place would bear, in part, on the total number of new customers the location might provide. If few people live on Archer Place, as the passage in fact indicates, then probably that location will not furnish much new local business for the Tracys' shop. At this point it is important to recall that minor factors are defined in the explanatory material as "those aspects of the business situation that bear on or influence major factors." Because the number of residents on Archer Place bears on the major factor of how many new customers that location might provide, the number of residents is, therefore, a minor factor.

You should remember that in any Analysis of Situations passage it is important to distinguish between major and minor factors. In the business situation presented in this passage you should note that the number of residents on Archer Place is *not* itself a major factor because the number of people living there is only one of several facts about that location that would have an effect on the number of new customers the location might provide. The lack of apartment buildings on Archer Place and the small number of passersby also contribute to the overall number of new customers that the location might furnish. Were the lack of such buildings or the number of such passersby raised in a question, these facts would also be classified as minor factors.

Another way to approach the classification of question I.9—or the classification of questions about a lack of apartment buildings or passersby—is to recall the description of a minor factor in the directions. There you are told that a minor factor is "a secondary consideration" of the decision maker. Such a characterization accurately describes the number of residents on Archer Place. It is relevant to the decision but has a less direct and significant influence on that decision than does the issue of how many new customers the location might provide or, as you have seen in the discussion of question I.12, the issue of the size of each location. Finally, note that although this question raises a secondary consideration about one of the alternatives, minor factors can also be secondary considerations that are relevant to all the alternatives under consideration. Question II.26 is an example of such a minor factor.

I.20 Higher maintenance costs for used cranes

In addition to the objective discussed in question I.18, a careful reading of the fourth paragraph of the passage indicates that the decision makers also have as an objective the "most economical" crane. The overall cost of any of the cranes under consideration has a direct influence on the decision: if the decision makers want to obtain the most economical crane, the overall cost of any of the alternatives will be crucial in determining which crane will be selected. The overall cost of any of the alternatives is, therefore, a major factor in the decision. (Note that this major factor is stated in question I.17.) Because the high maintenance costs for used cranes contribute, in part, to the overall cost of these cranes (because, in other words, high maintenance costs for used cranes bear on a major factor), the best answer to this question of moderate difficulty is C, a minor factor. It is important to note that the maintenance costs are only part of the overall cost of these cranes; if you look at the chart that accompanies the discussion you will see that other costs contributing to the overall cost are such things as sale price and shipping costs. Both of these costs would also be minor factors. Because maintenance costs—or sale price or shipping costs—are only part of the overall cost, and because such costs have a much more significant bearing on a major factor than on the achievement of an objective, such costs should not be considered a major factor.

Note also that question I.20 is not an assumption made by the decision makers since "higher maintenance costs for used cranes" is not a supposition or a projection made by the decision makers *before* they evaluate factors; rather, such costs are raised as a factor in the course of the decision process. Finally, note that this question, unlike question I.9, states a secondary consideration that is relevant to more than one of the alternatives (there are three used cranes under consideration).

II.3   Cost of motel rooms in New Jersey for the cast and production crew

It is often helpful in trying to decide whether a question states a minor factor to have first identified some of the objectives and major factors in a passage. You can then decide whether the question bears more significantly on an objective or on a major factor; if a question does the former, it will be a major factor, and if it does the latter, it will be a minor factor. In the Unisphere Productions passage, one of the objectives of the decision makers is to stay within their budget. Given this objective, the total expense to be incurred at each of the locations under consideration is a major factor in the decision since such costs are decisive in determining whether the budgetary objective can be achieved. Indeed, immediately after emphasizing the importance of maintaining the budget, Andropolous states explicitly that the "expenses to be incurred at any location we consider must be weighed." When you have identified this major factor and the budgetary objective, you can see that the cost of motel rooms in New Jersey is a minor factor because it directly contributes to a major factor rather than to an objective: the cost of motel rooms contributes, in part, to the total expenses incurred at the New Jersey location. Other costs that contribute to these expenses include salaries and transportation costs. Because the cost of motel rooms is only part of the overall cost of shooting the film in New Jersey, question II.3 is not a major factor. It is also not a major factor because it has a much more tangential or secondary relationship to the budgetary objective than do the overall expenses at the New Jersey location. These overall expenses directly bear on the objective, while the cost of motel rooms bears only secondarily on the objective. Question II.3 is a difficult question.

II.26 Cost of heat and utilities at each of the houses

As mentioned in the discussion of question II.30, Ms. Lewis wants to select a home that will allow her to stay within a strict budget. It is logical, therefore, that the costs associated with each of the homes she is considering would be a major factor in her decision since the magnitude of these costs will determine whether she will be able to achieve her budgetary objective. Several costs contribute to the overall cost; these include rent or mortgage payments, maintenance costs, and heat and utility costs, the costs stated in question II.26. Each of these is a minor factor in the decision because each bears in part on the major factor of overall cost. None of these individual costs, including heat and utility costs, is a major factor because, though relevant to the decision, none significantly contributes in and of itself to an objective. Each of these individual costs is a secondary rather than a major consideration for Ms. Lewis. You should also note that question II.26 is concerned with a secondary consideration that applies to all the alternatives; questions I.9 and II.3, on the other hand, are concerned with secondary considerations that apply to only one alternative.

III.8   Additional costs associated with third shifts

As noted in the discussion of III.9, Echington wants to reverse Northern's "financial slump." He wants, in other words, to increase his company's sales volume and its profits. The magnitude of the costs that Northern would incur by taking on the King Foods contract would be a major factor in Echington's decision because it will directly determine whether he will achieve his objective of making Northern more profitable. If the costs of accepting the contract are too large, Northern will not make money; such costs will have an important bearing on whether Northern takes on the contract. The "additional costs associated with third shifts" is a minor factor because it directly contributes, in part, to a major factor, the overall cost of doing business with King Foods. If you consult Table I, you will see that warehouse and freight costs and the costs of materials and plant operations also have a bearing on overall cost. Each of these is also a minor factor. Note that costs of third shifts should not be classified as a major factor because of their relation to the objective of making profits. Echington would consider such costs when making a decision, but they would be less decisive in determining whether the objective can be achieved than would the overall cost of the King Foods contract. Because of this relation to an objective and because of a much more direct relation to a major factor, costs associated with third shifts constitute a minor factor. This is a moderately difficult question.

III.26 Previous success of housewares departments in other supermarkets

One of Ms. Speranza's objectives is to make her market "more attractive"; she wants to spark the interest of potential customers and so make her market more popular. It follows that the potential attractiveness to customers of each proposed renovation (question III.24)—i.e., the potential popularity of each renovation—would be a major factor because it bears so directly on Ms. Speranza's objective. If you consider what would contribute to the popularity of any of the alternatives, including the alternative of a housewares department, you must logically conclude that the previous success of such a department with customers would be a contributing factor. A market owner who is considering how popular a particular product might be is very likely to take account of, among other things, the previous popularity of that product when it was introduced in other supermarkets. (The passage suggests that Ms. Speranza, when considering the potential popularity of housewares, would also weigh the desire of customers to minimize their shopping time.) Because the past success is a consideration that directly contributes to a major factor and is only tangentially related to an objective, question III.26 is a minor factor.

This is a difficult question partly because it is tempting to see past success with housewares as a major assumption of the decision makers. It is not such an assumption because the previous success of housewares departments is a consideration that concerns events in the past rather than a projection of what will happen in the future. Previous success is also not an assumption because, unlike an assumption, previous success does not establish a framework for the decision; it does not fundamentally determine what objectives the decision maker will have. (On the other hand, as the discussion of question III.21 in the Assumptions section of the explanations indicates, the "attractiveness to customers of a store with wide aisles and good lighting" *is* one of Ms. Speranza's assumptions because it provides just this framework: because she assumes that a well-lit, spacious store is attractive to customers, Ms. Speranza has made this kind of store one of her objectives.)

D. MAJOR ASSUMPTIONS

I.16 Availability of capital for expansion

As the discussion of question I.7 indicates, the Tracys need a new location for their business; they are eager to expand their salon. The Tracys would be unlikely to have decided on expansion—the accomplishment of which will require some outlay of capital—if they did not already suppose that the necessary capital were available. It is logical to believe, in other words, that the Tracys assumed or supposed the availability of capital for expansion before they even began to discuss and weigh the factors. Remember the definition of a major assumption: a projection or supposition made by the decision makers before they evaluate the factors. Using this definition, you can determine that the availability of capital is a major assumption of the decision makers; the best answer to this difficult question is, therefore, D. As in all Analysis of Situations questions, you need to be able to identify the exact nature of the fact or concept involved in the question. It is important to recognize that the availability of capital does not make any of the alternatives more or less attractive to the decision makers—does not, in other words, bear on the choice of a location. The decision makers do not discuss, for example, whether financing one location will be easier or more difficult than financing another. For this reason the availability of capital for expansion is not a factor in the decision but is a supposition that is accepted by the Tracys as a given before they start weighing the factors. Note, finally, that this supposition is not stated explicitly in the passage. However, because common sense argues that the Tracys would suppose the availability of expansion capital since they have already begun making plans and evaluating the locations, you are justified in inferring that such availability is one of the Tracys' assumptions.

I.30 Possibility of obtaining suitable equipment in time to meet contractual obligations

As both the discussion of question I.16 and the explanatory material indicate, you must rely on common sense and logical reasoning to answer Analysis of Situations questions. In question I.30 you must use your common sense to perceive that the possibility of obtaining suitable equipment in time to meet contractual obligations is a logical supposition that Lopes and the board would make before beginning to evaluate the alternatives. Put negatively, it makes little sense to believe that the decision makers would discuss replacing the damaged crane by March 15 so that work could be finished within one year as stipulated by contract if they did not suppose that meeting such objectives was a real possibility. D, then, is the best answer to this difficult question. The question is difficult in part because it calls upon your ability to make a clear distinction between assumptions on the one hand and objectives and factors on the other. Question I.30 must not be classified as an objective because the decision makers are not trying to achieve the possibility of obtaining suitable cranes in time to meet their obligations; they are trying to obtain such equipment, but they assume before they begin their discussion that the possibility of such acquisition already exists. Note also that the question should not be classified as a factor because the possibility of obtaining replacement equipment does not make any one of the alternatives more or less attractive to Lopes and the board. Question I.30 is also difficult because, like question I.16, it is an unstated, though logically inferrable, assumption made by the decision makers. Note, however, that another of Lopes' assumptions, the availability of credit to purchase a crane (question I.26), is in fact explicitly stated in the passage (" 'Obtaining a loan to pay for the replacement crane shouldn't be a problem.' "). In short, assumptions can either be stated or unstated; indeed, the assumption of availability of credit or capital can in one passage be stated outright and in another, such as the Empire Beauty passage, remain unstated.

II.7 Willingness of the production crew to shoot outside Hollywood

According to the explanatory material, a major assumption is a supposition made by the decision maker that establishes a framework within which the decision process takes place. In the Unisphere Productions passage, the willingness of the production crew to shoot outside Hollywood is such a supposition: it sets a framework in that its acceptance as true by the decision makers makes possible a meaningful discussion of New Jersey and Colorado as potential shooting locations. Put negatively, if Andropolous and his colleagues did not already assume that the crew would be willing in the future to shoot outside Hollywood, they could never seriously discuss the pros and cons of a non-Hollywood location. It is because this unstated yet logically inferrable assumption has such a bearing on the decision-making process that it would be incorrect to classify this difficult question as an unimportant issue. Finally, it is important to remember that the willingness of the crew to shoot outside Hollywood is not a factor because such willingness does not make either of the non-Hollywood alternatives more or less attractive. Were the passage to indicate that some crew members were not willing to travel more than 1,500 miles, the crew's willingness to travel only a certain distance from Hollywood would be a factor in the decision since it would make New Jersey less attractive than Colorado. As the passage is presently written, however, no such information about the crew's unwillingness appears.

II.32 Ms. Lewis' continued employment at World Oil Enterprises

There is explicit evidence in the passage that Ms. Lewis assumes she will continue to work for World Oil Enterprises: at the end of the fourth paragraph, you are told that "Ms. Lewis assumed that she would be in Woodhaven for a long time because the only promotion she could foresee for quite a few years was within the Research Division" of World Oil. If Ms. Lewis has thought about being in Woodhaven "for a long time" because the Research Division, her new division, is located there, and if she has thought ahead about having her position at World Oil over a period of "quite a few years," she must suppose she will continue to work for World Oil in the future. Indeed, it is because she assumes she will continue to work for World Oil, in particular for World Oil in Woodhaven, that she wants a home in or near that community. Her assumption of continued employment for World Oil sets a framework for her decision, then, in that it determines that she will look for a home in the Woodhaven area. Since question II.32 provides this framework (and so is not irrelevant to the decision), the question should be classified as an assumption.

Note that although the exact wording of the assumption given in question II.32 does not appear in the passage, the question does paraphrase an assumption that is explicitly stated in the passage ("Ms. Lewis assumed that she would be in Woodhaven . . ."). Question II.32 differs from questions I.16 and I.30 in that the assumption given in question II.32 is a rewording of an assumption explicitly stated in the passage, whereas the assumptions stated in I.16 and I.30 do not appear in the passage. You should especially note where in the passage this assumption occurs. Unlike the assumption explained in question III.21 below, the assumption in question II.32 is raised in the course of a consideration by the decision maker of the factors, rather than before a consideration begins. You should recall, however, that though an assumption is a supposition that is made before the factors are weighed and evaluated, that supposition can occur in a passage either before the preliminary consideration of the factors or in the course of the consideration, but before the final evaluation or decision is made. In the case of question II.32, the assumption of continued employment is raised after Ms. Lewis has begun to evaluate the factors associated with the rental property, but before any final evaluation or decision is made. Question II.32 is moderately difficult.

III.2 Continuation of decline in the demand for soap and dry-foods products

Before Echington and his managers meet to discuss the King Foods contract, you are told that Northern's sales are down because of "shrinking markets for two of Northern's largest customers in the past—soaps and dry foods." There has been, in other words, a decline in the demand for these two products. That Echington assumes this decline will continue in the future is logically inferrable from the sentence that follows the quotation above: "He hoped that a contract with King Foods would provide the needed stimulus" for his company's sales. Echington most probably would not want King Foods to be the stimulus for his company's business if he did not already assume that the markets of his soap and dry foods customers would continue to decline. In other words, if Echington did not assume a continuation of the decline in the demand for soap and dry foods— a decline that will affect Northern's sales—he would probably expect those products to be, as they have been in the past, the stimulus for Northern's sales. Because he expects such a continuation, he is looking for a new stimulus. Though unstated in the passage, the continued decline in the demand for soap and dry foods is a logically inferrable assumption made by the decision maker, a projection of a future trend that is made before the alternatives are weighed. Note that question III.2 should not be classified as a major factor because the continuation of a decline in demand does not bear on the achievement of any of Northern's objectives. Question III.2 is a very difficult question.

III.21 Attractiveness to customers of a store with wide aisles and good lighting

There is explicit information in the passage to indicate that this is one of Ms. Speranza's assumptions. Foodfill has just completed renovations "which transformed their crowded and dimly lit store into a bright, spacious market." Foodfill has, in other words, widened its aisles and improved its lighting. Ms. Speranza believes that "many of her customers had been attracted by her neighbor's renovations," and this belief has led her to plan a similar renovation project in her own market. In short, she is planning the renovation of her market based on the assumption that spaciousness and good lighting are attractive in a store. The attractiveness of a spacious and well-lit store provides a framework for Ms. Speranza's decision in that her supposition of this attractiveness leads her to conclude that she must renovate her store so it will have a similar attractiveness. One of the ways she will evaluate each renovation plan is according to how well it accomplishes this attractiveness. Because it provides such a framework before the decision process begins, the attractiveness to customers of a brightly lit, spacious store is a major assumption. Note that this assumption is in the form of a supposition about a quality of an entity (attractiveness of a store), rather than in the form of a projection about a trend in the future, as in question III.2.

Question III.21 is difficult because, to classify it correctly, you must realize the distinctions among assumptions, objectives, and factors. The question should not be classified as an objective. Ms. Speranza wants the store to *be* attractive, but she assumes that certain characteristics (wide aisles and good lighting) are attractive to customers. She is seeking an attractive store; she makes assumptions about what is attractive. Neither is the question a major factor, because it does not make any of the proposed renovations more or less acceptable. The attractiveness of each of the proposed renovations (question III.24) *is* a major factor because the degree to which each renovation is attractive would be weighed by the decision maker in her efforts to pick the best renovation plan. The attractiveness of each renovation bears on Ms. Speranza's objective of having an attractive store. However, any notion about what is attractive in a store is an assumption made by Ms. Speranza.

E. UNIMPORTANT ISSUES

I.4   Cost of beauty supplies

When you are answering Analysis of Situations questions, remember that your point of reference should always be the decision that must be made. The factors influence the decision in varying degrees; the objectives are the conditions the decision maker wants to have achieved after the decision has been made and implemented; and the assumptions are suppositions made by the decision maker in establishing a framework within which to make the decision. The final components of an Analysis of Situations passage are the unimportant issues—those facts and conditions that are irrelevant to the decision. With respect to question I.4, there is no mention in the passage that the cost of beauty supplies is something the Tracys plan to consider in making a decision about which location to choose. The best answer to this easy question, then, is E because the cost of beauty supplies is not immediately relevant to the decision makers. The issue raised in this question is a good example of why it is important to read the passage carefully. Near the beginning of the passage there is an indication that the Tracys are concerned about the rising cost of supplies, but the cost of these supplies is not a factor in the Tracys' decision about which of the alternative locations to choose. Cost of beauty supplies is never mentioned when the Tracys consider each location, and the cost of such supplies makes none of the locations more or less attractive.

It is possible, of course, to imagine the present passage altered in such a way that the cost of beauty supplies would be relevant. For example, if a location were closer to or farther away from a supplier, thereby making a significant difference in the cost of transporting supplies, and if one of the Tracys' objectives were to keep down the cost of expansion, then the cost of obtaining beauty supplies would probably become a factor in the Tracys' decision. Since, however, the present passage does not contain these facts, the cost of beauty supplies remains irrelevant to the decision.

I.22   Versatility of each of the cranes considered

In answering this question, you need to ask yourself whether the versatility of the cranes has a bearing upon the choice to be made by Lopes and his executive board. The lack of any mention of versatility in the passage is an indication that Lopes and the board are not interested in how versatile the alternative cranes are and consequently will not consider versatility in making their decision. Thus, the best answer to this moderately difficult question is E. You should note that it is necessary in this business situation to distinguish between the versatility of the cranes and their reliability; only the latter is a factor in the decision process. You can refer to the discussion of question I.21 above for an explanation of why reliability is a factor. Note that it is possible to imagine altering the present passage to include information to the effect that some of the cranes under consideration perform several different tasks—are, in other words, particularly versatile. This versatility would permit construction work to be done rapidly. Because such versatility would probably bear on the objectives of completing the project economically and within a year, the decision makers would be likely, in this hypothetical passage, to consider versatility as a factor in picking a crane. Since, however, the actual passage does not mention versatility, it is irrelevant to the decision.

II.14   Need for stunt actors in the surfing scenes of *Summer Surf*

A close reading of the passage indicates that nowhere do Andropolous and his colleagues express any need to obtain stunt actors for surfing scenes (although they do mention that they need "extras"). Nor would it be logical for you to infer that a need for stunt actors is an assumption of the decision makers since there is no indication that the actors in the film are incapable of surfing. In addition, the need for stunt actors has no influence on the decision about which of the three locations to choose; none of the alternatives is made more or less attractive by the need for stunt actors or by their availability at any of the alternative sites. Question II.14, an easy question, should be classified, therefore, as an irrelevant issue. In a passage worded differently, it is possible to imagine that an issue such as the need for stunt actors at each of the locations might be a factor. If, for example, the water at the New Jersey location were rougher than the water at the other locations, then perhaps stunt actors would be needed at the New Jersey location. The need for stunt actors—another expense—would probably be a minor factor that would bear on the major factor of overall cost. In the present passage, however, there is no discussion of rough water or of stunt actors.

II.31   Unavailability of mortgage money outside Woodhaven

There is no indication in the passage that mortgage money is unavailable outside Woodhaven. Nor is it logical to infer that Ms. Lewis assumes such unavailability. She is considering buying a home in Maple Woods, an area outside Woodhaven, with mortgage payments of $250 a month, payments "well within her budget." If anything, she would be likely to assume that mortgage money would be available outside Woodhaven since she is already calculating mortgage payments. If the passage had stated that mortgage money were unavailable outside Woodhaven and also stated that banks in Woodhaven would not grant mortgages on homes outside Woodhaven, then question II.31 could probably be classified as a factor in Ms. Lewis' decision since it would make the Maple Woods house less attractive. Since, however, Ms. Lewis never even considers the possibility that mortgage money would be unavailable, this question must be classified as an issue irrelevant to her decision.

III.3 Low bid made by Boxer Brothers

Although the low bid made by Boxer Brothers is explicitly mentioned in the passage, this bid has no bearing on the decision at hand. That decision concerns whether to take on the King Foods contract at a price ($8.90 per 1,000 cartons) lower than the price originally bid ($10.03 per 1,000). On first glance, it might seem that Boxer Brothers' bid of $8.70 per 1,000 would influence Echington and his managers to offer a bid on the King Foods contract even lower than $8.90 per 1,000; presumably, they would want to match the low Boxer bid of $8.70. However, a close reading of the passage indicates that the decision makers will not weigh the Boxer Brothers' bid in making their decision about what bid to make for the King Foods contract. When Vern Symington says that " 'I think we all agree, however, that $8.90 is as low as we can possibly go'," he is making it clear that Northern's decision will not be affected by a bid from Boxer Brothers. Thus that bid, which might seem to a careless reader a factor in the decision, is actually an unimportant issue. Question III.3 is a moderately difficult question because you must read very carefully to decide on the relevance of Boxer Brothers' bid.

III.22 Foodfill's special reopening discount coupons

As the discussion of question III.21 indicates, Foodfill's renovations, including its new spacious aisles and bright lighting, have so attracted customers that Ms. Speranza is considering a renovation plan that will make her store less cramped and brighter. Besides making renovations, Foodfill is described in the passage as offering discount coupons for its grand reopening. However, these coupons, unlike the new aisles and lighting, have no bearing on Ms. Speranza's actions. The passage gives no indication that Ms. Speranza has as one of her goals the offering of similar discount coupons, nor does the passage offer any evidence that Ms. Speranza will consider Foodfill's coupons as a factor when she evaluates the alternative renovation plans for her own store. The coupons are an irrelevant issue in Ms. Speranza's decision about which plan to pick. This is an easy question.

VII Writing Ability

Two types of Writing Ability questions, Usage and Sentence Correction, have appeared in past editions of the GMAT. As stated in Chapter I, in editions of the GMAT appearing in June 1982 and thereafter, Writing Ability questions will appear in the Sentence Correction format only. In the sample tests that follow, however, you will see Writing Ability questions in the Usage format. The answers to these questions appear after the two sample tests. The explanatory material discusses both kinds of Writing Ability questions, Usage and Sentence Correction. The discussion of Writing Ability is organized according to common types of problems you might encounter in Writing Ability questions.

Because actual test material in the Sentence Correction format is not available, there is no Sentence Correction sample test. Nevertheless, Sentence Correction questions appear with Usage questions as illustrative examples in each section of the explanatory material. Questions from the sample tests illustrative of each type of problem are listed at the end of each section of the explanatory material. Both Usage and Sentence Correction questions address similar grammatical and syntactical problems, and thus practice in both will help prepare you for the Writing Ability section of the GMAT. You should, however, be especially familiar with the directions and strategies for Sentence Correction questions (see Chapter I).

TEST-TAKING STRATEGIES FOR SENTENCE CORRECTION

1. Read the entire sentence carefully. Try to understand the specific idea or relationship that the sentence should express.

2. Since the part of the sentence that *may* be incorrect is underlined, concentrate on evaluating the underlined part for errors and possible corrections.

3. Before reading the choices, try to identify the exact nature of the error or errors in the sentence.

4. Read each choice carefully. Choice A always repeats the underlined portion of the original sentence. Choose A if you think that the sentence is correct as it stands, but only after examining all of the other choices.

5. Try to determine how well each choice corrects whatever you consider to be wrong with the sentence.

6. Make sure that you evaluate the sentence and the choices in terms of general clarity, economy of language, and appropriateness of diction.

7. Read the whole sentence, substituting the choice that you prefer for the underlined part. A choice may be wrong because it does not fit grammatically or structurally with the rest of the sentence. Remember that some sentences will require no corrections. The answer to such sentences should be A.

For your convenience, following are some suggestions for working through the Usage sample tests.

TEST-TAKING STRATEGIES FOR USAGE

1. One way to gain familiarity with the basic conventions of standard written English is to read material that reflects standard usage. Suitable material will usually be found in good magazines and nonfiction books, editorials in outstanding newspapers, and the collections of essays used by many college and university writing courses.

2. A general review of basic rules of grammar and practice with writing exercises are also ways of studying for the Writing Ability section. If you have papers that have been carefully evaluated for grammatical errors, it may be helpful to review the comments and corrections.

3. During the test, read carefully through the entire sentence and then evaluate each of the underlined parts. Remember that you are looking for the *one* part that must be corrected to make the sentence acceptable; there is either a single error or no error in each of the sentences. Never assume that you have found the error until you have evaluated all of the underlined parts.

When you take the sample tests, use the answer spaces on the following page to mark your answers.

Answer Spaces for Sample Test I

1 Ⓐ Ⓑ Ⓒ Ⓓ Ⓔ   6 Ⓐ Ⓑ Ⓒ Ⓓ Ⓔ   11 Ⓐ Ⓑ Ⓒ Ⓓ Ⓔ   16 Ⓐ Ⓑ Ⓒ Ⓓ Ⓔ   21 Ⓐ Ⓑ Ⓒ Ⓓ Ⓔ
2 Ⓐ Ⓑ Ⓒ Ⓓ Ⓔ   7 Ⓐ Ⓑ Ⓒ Ⓓ Ⓔ   12 Ⓐ Ⓑ Ⓒ Ⓓ Ⓔ   17 Ⓐ Ⓑ Ⓒ Ⓓ Ⓔ   22 Ⓐ Ⓑ Ⓒ Ⓓ Ⓔ
3 Ⓐ Ⓑ Ⓒ Ⓓ Ⓔ   8 Ⓐ Ⓑ Ⓒ Ⓓ Ⓔ   13 Ⓐ Ⓑ Ⓒ Ⓓ Ⓔ   18 Ⓐ Ⓑ Ⓒ Ⓓ Ⓔ   23 Ⓐ Ⓑ Ⓒ Ⓓ Ⓔ
4 Ⓐ Ⓑ Ⓒ Ⓓ Ⓔ   9 Ⓐ Ⓑ Ⓒ Ⓓ Ⓔ   14 Ⓐ Ⓑ Ⓒ Ⓓ Ⓔ   19 Ⓐ Ⓑ Ⓒ Ⓓ Ⓔ   24 Ⓐ Ⓑ Ⓒ Ⓓ Ⓔ
5 Ⓐ Ⓑ Ⓒ Ⓓ Ⓔ   10 Ⓐ Ⓑ Ⓒ Ⓓ Ⓔ   15 Ⓐ Ⓑ Ⓒ Ⓓ Ⓔ   20 Ⓐ Ⓑ Ⓒ Ⓓ Ⓔ   25 Ⓐ Ⓑ Ⓒ Ⓓ Ⓔ

Answer Spaces for Sample Test II

1 Ⓐ Ⓑ Ⓒ Ⓓ Ⓔ   6 Ⓐ Ⓑ Ⓒ Ⓓ Ⓔ   11 Ⓐ Ⓑ Ⓒ Ⓓ Ⓔ   16 Ⓐ Ⓑ Ⓒ Ⓓ Ⓔ   21 Ⓐ Ⓑ Ⓒ Ⓓ Ⓔ
2 Ⓐ Ⓑ Ⓒ Ⓓ Ⓔ   7 Ⓐ Ⓑ Ⓒ Ⓓ Ⓔ   12 Ⓐ Ⓑ Ⓒ Ⓓ Ⓔ   17 Ⓐ Ⓑ Ⓒ Ⓓ Ⓔ   22 Ⓐ Ⓑ Ⓒ Ⓓ Ⓔ
3 Ⓐ Ⓑ Ⓒ Ⓓ Ⓔ   8 Ⓐ Ⓑ Ⓒ Ⓓ Ⓔ   13 Ⓐ Ⓑ Ⓒ Ⓓ Ⓔ   18 Ⓐ Ⓑ Ⓒ Ⓓ Ⓔ   23 Ⓐ Ⓑ Ⓒ Ⓓ Ⓔ
4 Ⓐ Ⓑ Ⓒ Ⓓ Ⓔ   9 Ⓐ Ⓑ Ⓒ Ⓓ Ⓔ   14 Ⓐ Ⓑ Ⓒ Ⓓ Ⓔ   19 Ⓐ Ⓑ Ⓒ Ⓓ Ⓔ   24 Ⓐ Ⓑ Ⓒ Ⓓ Ⓔ
5 Ⓐ Ⓑ Ⓒ Ⓓ Ⓔ   10 Ⓐ Ⓑ Ⓒ Ⓓ Ⓔ   15 Ⓐ Ⓑ Ⓒ Ⓓ Ⓔ   20 Ⓐ Ⓑ Ⓒ Ⓓ Ⓔ   25 Ⓐ Ⓑ Ⓒ Ⓓ Ⓔ

USAGE SAMPLE TEST I

Time—15 minutes

25 Questions

<u>Directions:</u> The following sentences contain problems in grammar, usage, diction (choice of words), and idiom.

Some sentences are correct.
No sentence contains more than one error.

You will find that the error, if there is one, is underlined and lettered. Assume that all other elements of the sentence are correct and cannot be changed. In choosing answers, follow the requirements of standard written English.

If there is an error, select the <u>one underlined part</u> that must be changed in order to best correct the sentence, and blacken the corresponding space on the answer sheet.

If there is no error, mark answer space E.

EXAMPLES:

SAMPLE ANSWERS

I. <u>Between</u> 1960 and 1964, Switzerland's
   A

annual industrial-growth rate <u>were</u> eight
               B

percent—a figure <u>surpassed only</u>
          C

by Japan's. <u>No error</u>
  D   E

I. Ⓐ ● Ⓒ Ⓓ Ⓔ

II. Plants are <u>important to</u> human existence
         A

because of <u>their unique</u> ability <u>to transform</u>
       B   C

the energy of sunlight <u>into</u> the food that
            D

sustains all life. <u>No error</u>
        E

II. Ⓐ Ⓑ Ⓒ Ⓓ ●

I.1. <u>It should be remembered</u> that, <u>as a general rule,</u>
     A   B

the quantity of advertising, not the quality of the

paper, <u>determine</u> the <u>profit margin of a magazine.</u>
     C   D

<u>No error</u>
 E

I.2. The virus that caused <u>several hundred cases of</u>
           A

flu at Fort Dix is <u>similar with</u> <u>one that causes</u>
        B   C

a flu-like illness <u>in swine.</u> <u>No error</u>
       D   E

I.3. <u>Like</u> Europe, the United States cycle of inflation
   A

and recession <u>no longer</u> <u>responds to</u> the traditional
       B   C

means <u>once used</u> to deal with the problem.
     D

<u>No error</u>
 E

I.4. Because automobiles provide us with mobility,

<u>a choice of routes,</u> and <u>freedom from</u> the
   A   B

schedules of public transportation, we are
        C

<u>enslaved by it.</u> <u>No error</u>
   D   E

GO ON TO THE NEXT PAGE.

I. 5. The classic Barcelona chair with its handsewn
welts <u>joining the forty leather panels</u> and a frame
                  A
of polished stainless steel is <u>priced at</u> $1,680, but
                                    B
a machine-sewn version on a chromeplate frame
<u>costs</u> <u>only half that amount</u>. <u>No error</u>
  C   D   E

I. 6. <u>Had it finally become law</u>, the bill would ban
          A
<u>the owning of handguns</u> by private citizens
          B
who do not already <u>have permits for them</u>.
  C   D
<u>No error</u>
  E

I. 7. <u>Unlike some other</u> very wealthy families, the
          A
Rockefellers and Kennedys, <u>for example</u>, the
                              B
<u>Mellons are not active in politics</u>. <u>No error</u>
          C   D   E

I. 8. <u>In many areas of the state</u>, legal titles to large
          A
tracts of land <u>are</u> <u>so uncertain that</u> thousands of
                  B   C
acres are <u>virtuously</u> a no-man's-land. <u>No error</u>
              D   E

I. 9. To vote for a candidate <u>who promises both</u>
                                    A
<u>an increase</u> in public services and a decrease
  (A)
in taxes <u>is voting for</u> <u>someone who</u>
              B   C
<u>is unlikely to keep</u> his promises. <u>No error</u>
          D   E

I. 10. Blacks constituted 19.3 per cent of the United States
census in 1790, <u>but only 11.1 per cent in 1970,</u>
                      A
<u>a phenomenon</u> reflecting the massive immigration
          B
<u>of whites</u> <u>from Europe during the last century.</u>
    C   D
<u>No error</u>
    E

I. 11. The rate increase for electricity <u>will add about</u>
                                              A
twenty-three cents <u>to the monthly bill</u> of
                          B
<u>a typically residential customer</u>, who uses
              C
about 250 kilowatt hours <u>per month</u>. <u>No error</u>
                              D   E

I. 12. The prime minister <u>insisted that</u> his country
                                A
<u>has not and will not be</u> a <u>base for aggression</u>
          B   C
<u>against neighboring countries</u>. <u>No error</u>
              D   E

I. 13. <u>Once eaten</u>, the campers worried that the mush-
          A
rooms <u>were poisonous</u>, but, <u>fortunately</u>, a nearby
          B   C
ranger <u>was able to reassure</u> them. <u>No error</u>
                  D   E

I. 14. <u>In dismissing the army and returning</u>,
                          A
<u>like the Roman general</u> Cincinnatus, to the life
              B
of a gentleman farmer, Washington honored
<u>one of the principles that</u> had sparked the
              C
revolution—hostility <u>to a standing army</u> in
                              D
peacetime. <u>No error</u>
              E

I. 15. <u>Within reach</u> of the invalid <u>was</u> a camera, the
          A   B
violin <u>he had learned to play</u> <u>as a child</u>, and a
              C   D
religious medal. <u>No error</u>
                      E

GO ON TO THE NEXT PAGE.

I. 16. Your picture taken by daguerreotypy in 1850
       <u>   A   </u>
       required <u>sitting patiently</u> <u>for nearly</u> half a minute
                      B   C
       without <u>either breathing or blinking.</u>   <u>No error</u>
                              D   E

I. 17. <u>Until recently</u>, most developmental psychologists
              A
       believed that a child's future intelligence,

       social competence, and general ability

       <u>were, for the most part,</u> <u>determined during</u> the
                    B   C
       first year or two of <u>their lives.</u>   <u>No error</u>
                                 D   E

I. 18. <u>Half the fun of</u> gardening lies in the
              A
       special <u>relationship with nature</u> that
                          B
       <u>comes from the observing</u> how plants
                    C
       grow and <u>take different shapes.</u>   <u>No error</u>
                         D   E

I. 19. The "Bhagavad-Gita," <u>written about</u> twenty-five
                                   A
       hundred <u>years ago</u>, is <u>part of</u> the "Mahabharata,"
                    B   C
       one of India's two great epics, <u>another</u> being the
                                              D
       "Ramayana."   <u>No error</u>
                         E

I. 20. At a time <u>when many firms</u> are
           A   B
       struggling to remain solvent, the question
                             C
       of federal subsidies <u>are of great importance.</u>
                                        D
       <u>No error</u>
           E

I. 21. A generous donor <u>who wishes to remain anonymous</u>
                                        A
       <u>has made possible</u> the new exhibition and its
                  B
       catalogue, which, <u>like</u> the American Bicentennial
                              C
       Wing, <u>pay</u> tribute to the accomplishments of the
                  D
       early settlers.   <u>No error</u>
                              E

I. 22. Most of the land <u>now owned by</u> Indian tribes is
                                A
       neither scenic <u>or</u> productive; the Oglala Sioux,
                           B
       for example, <u>were ousted</u> from the Black Hills
                            C
       and <u>ordered back to</u> a reservation of semiarid
                    D
       grazing land.   <u>No error</u>
                            E

I. 23. <u>Certain that the treasurer would rebel</u>
                         A
       <u>if asked to resign</u>, the team of lawyers
                B
       set in motion a series of events <u>that led him</u>
                                               C
       to reach the decision <u>on his own.</u>   <u>No error</u>
                                    D   E

I. 24. During the building boom <u>in the decade after</u> the
                                         A
       Second World War, <u>much of</u> the <u>moderately priced</u>
                              B   C
       homes <u>were built with asbestos shingle siding.</u>
                              D
       <u>No error</u>
           E

I. 25. The client <u>who comes into</u> a lawyer's office is a
                          A
       troubled person, and <u>what surfaces as</u> a legal
                                   B
       problem <u>very often usually</u> has <u>its roots in</u> deep-
                        C   D
       seated social problems.   <u>No error</u>
                                      E

END OF SAMPLE TEST I

USAGE SAMPLE TEST II

Time—15 minutes

25 Questions

Directions: The following sentences contain problems in grammar, usage, diction (choice of words), and idiom.

Some sentences are correct.
No sentence contains more than one error.

You will find that the error, if there is one, is underlined and lettered. Assume that all other elements of the sentence are correct and cannot be changed. In choosing answers, follow the requirements of standard written English.

If there is an error, select the one underlined part that must be changed in order to best correct the sentence, and blacken the corresponding space on the answer sheet.

If there is no error, mark answer space E.

EXAMPLES: SAMPLE ANSWERS

I. Between 1960 and 1964, Switzerland's   I. Ⓐ ● Ⓒ Ⓓ Ⓔ
     A

   annual industrial-growth rate were eight
                                     B

   percent—a figure surpassed only
                           C

   by Japan's. No error
        D   E

II. Plants are important to human existence   II. Ⓐ Ⓑ Ⓒ Ⓓ ●
                    A

   because of their unique ability to transform
               B   C

   the energy of sunlight into the food that
                            D

   sustains all life. No error
                         E

II. 1. The car manufacturers plan offering a series of
                                A   B
     demonstrations designed to help automobile
                              C
     mechanics improve their skills. No error
                   D   E

II. 2. Illness as a metaphor for political disorder
               A   B
     is one of the oldest notions of political philosophy.
           C   D
     No error
       E

II. 3. With the advance north of modern
                          A
     technological civilization, the Eskimos

     have been losing the hunting and fishing skills
            B   C
     that once made him self-reliant. No error
               D   E

GO ON TO THE NEXT PAGE.

II. 4. As headquarters for the European Economic
          A
Community, Brussels acts not only as

a center for Continental businessmen,
          B
and as a source of information
          C
about trends, markets, and opportunities.
                              D
No error
   E

II. 5. In 1975 the Dutch Ministry of Education

proposed that all prospective medical students,
                A
irregardless of their grades, participate in a lottery
          B   C
to determine whether they would be admitted to
                    D
medical school.   No error
                     E

II. 6. The human body's immunological system,

its primary defense mechanism,
        A
is capable of identifying, attacking, killing,
    B
and disposing of such complex structures

like bacteria, parasites, and malignant growths;
                        C
but pollutants bypass the protective

walls of the skin and mucosae

as well as the detoxification mechanisms of
                              D
the liver and kidneys.   No error
                           E

II. 7. Starting seeds indoors in the winter months
          A
so that seedlings are ready to be set outdoors in
   B   C
the spring is an annual ritual each year for many
                        D
gardeners.   No error
              E

II. 8. The disparate individuals who formed the group of

musicians known as Les Six were held together
          A   B
by very tenuous bonds, and they soon went their
        C
six separate, but significant, way.   No error
                              D   E

II. 9. Many of the old plantation gardens around
       A   B
Charleston were planted a century or more ago

and had been carefully tended and improved ever
        C   D
since.   No error
            E

II.10. In search of the Noble Savage and the Northwest
       A
Passage, Chateaubriand visited America in 1791,

blissfully unaware of the Rockies and of
          B   C
other obstacles to his enterprise.   No error
                D   E

II. 11. Psychoanalysis portrays the unconscious to be a
                                              A
residue of impulsive, forbidden wishes; therapy

attempts to bring these often unacceptable
                    B
unconscious motives to light by showing
                        C
how they affect the patient's personality.
                    D
No error
   E

II. 12. Neither Wright's nor Corbusier's ideal city

was ever actually built, but both men's plans
        A
were precursors of the urban patterns that

economical, political, and technological forces
                    B
have brought to realization all over the world.
    C   D
No error
   E

GO ON TO THE NEXT PAGE.

II. 13. The British flight <u>from Crete in 1941 was a</u>
                               A

shambles <u>as harrowing as</u> the retreat of Sir John
              B

Moore's army to La Coruña in 1809

<u>or Wellington's to Portugal after</u> his
                C

failure to take Burgos in 1812. No error
           D   E

II. 14. <u>During the recent period of growth</u> in higher
                A

education, colleges and universities helped to keep

the unemployment rate <u>lower than it</u> would
                  B

<u>otherwise have been</u> by enrolling large numbers of
      C

students who <u>may not normally</u> have matriculated.
            D

<u>No error</u>
  E

II. 15. The medieval <u>perception of</u> the plague
             A

<u>was firmly tied to</u> notions of moral pollution,
     B

and people <u>inherently looked for</u> a scapegoat
            C

<u>external to the stricken community.</u> No error
        D   E

II. 16. Professor Harris, an anthropologist at

Columbia University, <u>suggests that</u> warfare
             A

in tribal societies <u>results from</u> the interaction
           B

<u>between protein supply</u> with <u>population density.</u>
      C   D

<u>No error</u>
  E

II. 17. The <u>recent reissues of</u> jazz records of the
       A

twenties <u>have restored</u> the Bessie Smiths that
         B

<u>had become rare and expensive</u> and corrected
     C

the taciturnity of the original labels, which

offered <u>only the names of the featured performer</u>
              D

and the composer of the song. <u>No error</u>
                   E

II. 18. Life insurance <u>can often be</u> purchased
           A

<u>relatively cheaper</u> <u>when a person</u>
    B   C

<u>is young and in good health.</u> <u>No error</u>
      D   E

II. 19. The proposed legislation <u>would aid the woman</u> who
                     A

<u>through divorce</u>, death of the spouse,
    B

<u>or other loss of</u> traditional family income find
     C

themselves in the labor market <u>without the necessary</u>
                   D

skills to find work. <u>No error</u>
             E

II. 20. Dickens <u>was probably the most popular writer who</u>
                A

<u>ever lived</u>: his works aroused such a frenzy of
 (A)

admiration <u>that there were near riots</u> on the New
           B

York docks <u>as the ships bearing the final installment</u>
            C

of "The Old Curiosity Shop" <u>approached shore.</u>
                   D

<u>No error</u>
  E

II. 21. The new books by Clark and Fiedler

<u>have the same purpose</u>, to examine the lasting
     A

<u>fascination of men and women with</u> other living
        B

beings (animals and freaks) who <u>are both</u> like
                 C

and unlike them, but Fiedler's style, <u>unlike Clark,</u>
                    D

is one given to overstatement, exaggeration, and

hyperbole. <u>No error</u>
         E

GO ON TO THE NEXT PAGE.

II. 22. The Secretary of State <u>can and has been</u> a
                                    A
mediator in certain international disputes, but the
role of arbiter, <u>appraising the legitimacy of claims</u>
                              B
<u>which have historical as well as moral bases</u>, is a
                              C
responsibility <u>he should not assume.</u>   <u>No error</u>
                        D   E

II. 23. Rock salt, a chunky, less pure form of the seasoning
<u>almost everyone sprinkles on salads and steaks</u>,
                              A
has <u>become important</u> <u>to winter travel</u> <u>in much of</u>
          B   C   D
the United States as the roads themselves.

    <u>No error</u>
        E

II. 24. <u>To join</u> the travel club, <u>you need only</u> fill out an
          A   B
application, <u>to pay a</u> small initiation fee, and
                  C
indicate <u>when and where</u> you wish to go on your
                    D
vacation. <u>No error</u>
                  E

II. 25. <u>Threatening the wildlife refuge</u>, a group of
                        A
ecologists <u>lobbied to prevent</u> a new jetport
                      B
<u>from being constructed</u> <u>near the wetlands.</u>
            C   D
<u>No error</u>
    E

END OF SAMPLE TEST II

ANSWER KEYS FOR SAMPLE TESTS

USAGE

Sample Test I

I. 1. C	I. 10. E	I. 18. C
I. 2. B	I. 11. C	I. 19. D
I. 3. A	I. 12. B	I. 20. D
I. 4. D	I. 13. A	I. 21. E
I. 5. E	I. 14. E	I. 22. B
I. 6. A	I. 15. B	I. 23. E
I. 7. E	I. 16. A	I. 24. B
I. 8. D	I. 17. D	I. 25. C
I. 9. B		

Sample Test II

II. 1. A	II. 10. E	II. 18. B
II. 2. E	II. 11. A	II. 19. A
II. 3. D	II. 12. B	II. 20. E
II. 4. C	II. 13. E	II. 21. D
II. 5. B	II. 14. D	II. 22. A
II. 6. C	II. 15. C	II. 23. B
II. 7. D	II. 16. C	II. 24. C
II. 8. D	II. 17. E	II. 25. A
II. 9. C		

EXPLANATORY MATERIAL: SENTENCE CORRECTION

The following explanations present and discuss types of grammatical and syntactical problems you will find in the Writing Ability section of the GMAT. Further examples of each type of problem from the two sample tests are noted at the end of each section of explanation.

I. NOUN NUMBER

1. **The Anasazis, the ancestors of the modern Pueblo peoples, have been the subject of scholarly inquiry for more than a century, but there is no consensus among archaeologists for what caused them to leave their homeland.**

   (A) among archaeologists for what caused them to leave
   (B) between archaeologists about why they were caused to leave
   (C) among archaeologists as to what caused them to leave
   (D) between archaeologists of what was the cause of their leaving
   (E) among archaeologists concerning for what cause they left

To correct this sentence you must find the choice with the phrase that can follow *consensus: consensus . . . for what* in A, *consensus . . . about why* in B, *consensus . . . of what*

in D, and *consensus . . . concerning for what* in E are all unidiomatic. These word combinations are not customary or acceptable in English. C is the best answer since *consensus . . . as to what* is idiomatic. Additionally, choices B and D are incorrect because they use *between* rather than *among*; *among* is proper here since the consensus discussed involves many archaeologists. If there were only two archaeologists, or if the archaeologists were being considered individually, *between* would be correct. The best choice for this easy question is C.

2. **The high beef prices of the last few years may be a**
                    A
   symptom of an irreversible beef shortage that will per-
         B   C
   manently affect the eating habits of many of the world's
         (C)   D
   population. No error
                  E

The error in this sentence is at choice D because "much" should be used to modify *the world's population*; *many* is used to modify plural nouns—that is, to describe things that can be counted. One could say, for example, "many segments of the world's population." This is a difficult question.

3. **Like a human chess player, computers are given only a**
                              A   B
   limited amount of time (about 120 minutes for 40 moves
         (B)   C
   in tournament play) in which to select its moves. No
   (C)   D   E
   error
   (E)

The error in this sentence is at choice A: *computers,* which is plural here, should agree in number with *player,* the singular noun to which it is compared. The sentence can be corrected by changing choice A to read "a computer is." This is a difficult question.

(For further practice with Noun Number also see Sample Test I, questions 19, 24; Sample Test II, question 8.)

II. NOUN AND PRONOUN

1. **The villainous characterizations of the wolf in numerous**
                                                    A
   folk-tales have ignored that part of their nature that is
   (A)   B   C   D
   friendly and gregarious. No error.
   (D)   E

The error in this sentence is at choice C, where *their,* a plural pronoun, refers to the singular noun *wolf.* The plural nouns *characterizations* and *folktales* may make it difficult at first to see that *their* is incorrect, but a pronoun must agree in number with the noun to which it refers. This error in agreement can be corrected if the singular pronoun "its" is substituted for the plural pronoun *their.* This is a difficult question.

2. **Contestants in many sports <u>prepare for competition by eating pasta as</u> part of a ''carbohydrate-loading'' regimen that is supposed to provide quick energy.**

(A) prepare for competition by eating pasta as
(B) prepare for competition and eat pasta, which is
(C) prepare for competition by eating pasta because this is
(D) eat pasta to prepare for competing, which is
(E) eat pasta to prepare for competing as

Choice A is the best answer. In choice B, *which* is ambiguous: it is not clear whether *which* refers only to *pasta,* the nearest noun, or to the whole preceding clause. In other words, it is not clear exactly what is part of the ''carbohydrate-loading'' regimen—the pasta itself or the act of eating pasta to prepare for competition. Moreover, *and* is incorrect here: the use of *and* suggests that the contestants eat pasta in addition to preparing themselves for competition, not that they eat pasta as a means of preparing themselves. In C, the phrase *because this is* implies wrongly that contestants eat pasta more because it is part of a regimen than because it helps them prepare for competition. The word *this* may refer to *pasta* or to the act of eating pasta as part of preparation. In D, as in B, *which* is ambiguous. The phrase *for competition* is preferable to *for competing* because *competition* is clearly a noun, whereas *competing* may be mistaken for a part of a verb. When combined with the rest of the sentence, choice E seems to say that those who eat pasta are competing not as athletes but as part of a ''carbohydrate-loading'' regimen. Word order is important here; *as* links what stands immediately before it with what comes immediately after it, so the proper sentence must say *eating pasta as part of.* A, then, is the best answer for this moderately easy question.

3. **The percentage of the labor force that is unemployed has dropped sharply this month, <u>even though it may be only temporarily.</u>**

(A) even though it may be only temporarily
(B) but it may be temporary only
(C) but the drop may be only temporary
(D) even though the drop may only be temporary
(E) but such a drop may only be a temporary one

The pronoun *it* in choice A cannot refer logically to any noun in the sentence, and so *it* must be replaced by a noun such as *drop.* The noun that replaces the pronoun *it* should be modified by an adjective (*temporary*), not an adverb (*temporarily*), because adverbs modify verbs, not nouns. Also, the words *even though* do not correctly express the relationship between the ideas in the two clauses: *even though* suggests that unemployment dropped sharply despite the fact that the drop may be temporary. The conjunction *but* would suggest nothing more than a contrast between the ideas. Again, in choice B, *it* has no referent, and *only* should immediately precede the adjective it modifies. In choice D, *even though* is incorrect and *only* is out of position. The phrase *such a drop* in choice E wrongly implies that this drop is but one example of a whole class of similar events being dis-

cussed, and *only* is misplaced once again. The best answer for this difficult question is C.

(For further practice with Noun and Pronoun also see Sample Test I, questions 4, 17; Sample Test II, question 19.)

III. NOUN AND VERB

1. **The practice of building higher and higher smokestacks to relieve local pollution <u>have turned what are typically local problems into regional ones.</u>**

(A) have turned what are typically local problems into regional ones
(B) have turned what is typically a local problem into regional ones
(C) have typically turned local problems into a regional one
(D) has typically turned a local problem into regional ones
(E) has turned what is typically a local problem into a regional one

Choice A is incorrect because the plural verb form *have* does not agree with *practice,* the singular subject of the sentence: *have* should be *has.* The plural auxiliary verb *have* also makes B and C wrong. Note, too, the lack of agreement in noun and pronoun number in these choices: *problem* is used with *ones* in choice B and *problems* with *one* in choice C. Choice C can also be faulted because the adverb *typically* has been moved so as to distort the meaning of the sentence: the statement now indicates that local problems typically turn into regional ones, not that local pollution is typically a local problem. The adverb is misplaced again in choice D; also, *problem* does not agree with *ones.* The best answer for this easy question is E.

2. **The Chanel collection, <u>consisting of</u> about forty suits**
    A

    and dresses and forty-four pieces of costume jewelry designed by Chanel between 1954 and 1971, together with some three dozen accessories <u>such as handbags</u>
    B

    <u>and scarves,</u> <u>were assembled by</u> Mme. Lilian Grumbach,
    (B)   C

    the designer's closest colleague during the <u>last fourteen</u>
    D

    <u>years</u> of her life. <u>No error</u>
    (D)   E

The error in this sentence is at choice C; the plural verb *were* must be changed to ''was'' in order to agree with *collection,* the singular subject. The various plural nouns that follow *collection* merely describe the collection; they are not part of the subject and do not determine the number of the verb. This is a question of average difficulty.

3. The quality of both spaghetti and espresso coffee depends as much on the softness and purity of the water
with which they are made as on the characteristics of
the coffee beans and pasta dough used.

(A) of both spaghetti and espresso coffee depends as
much
(B) of both spaghetti and espresso coffee depend equally
(C) both of spaghetti and espresso coffee depends
equally
(D) both of spaghetti and espresso coffee depend as
much
(E) both of spaghetti and espresso coffee depend just
as much

Choice A is the best answer. In B, the plural verb *depend*
does not agree with *quality,* the singular subject of the sentence. Also, *equally* is wrong here because it produces an
unidiomatic construction: *equally on . . . as on.* The phrase
following *depends* must read *as much on . . . as on,* as in
the best answer, A. In choice C, *equally* is incorrect and the
phrase *both of spaghetti and espresso coffee* does not describe the two quantities that follow *both* in grammatically
identical ways; the preposition *of* appears before *spaghetti*
but not before *espresso coffee.* In other words, the phrase
lacks parallel structure. The parallel phrase *both spaghetti
and espresso coffee* is preferable to the nonparallel *both of
spaghetti and espresso coffee.* Choices D and E lack sub-
ject-verb agreement and parallel phrasing. A, then, is the
best choice. The question is a little harder than average.

(For further practice with Noun and Verb also see Sample
Test I, questions 1, 15, 20; Sample Test II, question 19.)

IV. VERB FORMS

1. To adopt a new name whose associations one finds attractive is, in a sense, attempting to assert control over
your identity.

(A) To adopt a new name whose associations one finds
(B) To adopt a new name whose associations you find
(C) To adopt a new name the associations of which one
finds
(D) Adopting a new name whose associations you find
(E) Adopting a new name the associations of which one
finds

Choice A is flawed because *To adopt* is not parallel with
attempting; the correct equation should be *Adopting . . . is
. . . attempting. . . .* Also, the use of *one* (third person) in the
underlined part of the sentence constitutes a shift in person
from *your* (second person) at the end of the sentence. Choice
B corrects this shift in person but not the lack of parallelism.
To adopt and *one* are wrong again in choice C, and *the
associations of which* is an awkward phrase here and in
choice E. This awkward phrase and the third person *one*
make choice E faulty. The best answer for this question of
average difficulty is D.

2. The Aztecs did not arrive in the Valley of Mexico until
the thirteenth century A.D., centuries after Teotihuacán
had been abandoned and was fallen into ruin.

(A) had been abandoned and was fallen
(B) had been abandoned and had fallen
(C) had been abandoned, having fallen
(D) was abandoned and was falling
(E) was abandoned and was fallen

The correct sentence requires the past perfect verb tense
(that is, "had" plus the "-ed" form of the verb) to describe
an event, the ruin of Teotihuacán, that was completed before
the occurrence of another past event, the arrival of the Aztecs in the Valley of Mexico. Choice A is incorrect because
only half of the compound verb is in the past perfect: *was*
should be *had.* In choice C, *having fallen* distorts the meaning of the sentence by suggesting that the city had been
abandoned after, and perhaps because, it had fallen into
ruin. Choices D and E do not have verbs in the past perfect.
The best answer is B. The second *had* is necessary because
had been abandoned and fallen would mean *had been
abandoned and (had been) fallen;* this predicate is wrong in
that *fallen* cannot be in the passive voice, as *abandoned* is
here. This is a fairly easy question.

3. As bacteria develop <u>resistance to</u> the traditional anti-
                        A
biotics, an <u>increased</u> use of new products <u>became nec-</u>
         B   C   D
essary. <u>No error</u>
(D)   E

The error in this sentence is at choice C; the past tense verb
became must be "becomes" in order to agree with the present
tense verb *develop.* This question is a little easier than the
average.

4. <u>Theoretically,</u> a good screwdriver should last a lifetime,
   A
but it <u>rarely has,</u> usually because it is used <u>at one time</u>
       B   C
or another as a substitute for some other tool. <u>No error.</u>
(C)   D   E

There is an error at choice B because *has* cannot substitute
for the verb *last.* Choice B should read "rarely does." This
part of the sentence says, in effect, "but it rarely does (last),"
with the verb *last* being omitted as understood. This is an
easy question.

5. Historians have in the past and do at this moment differ
widely in their estimates of Charles II, both as a king and
as a man.

(A) in the past and do at this moment differ widely
(B) in the past and at the moment do differ widely
(C) differed widely both in the past and at this moment
(D) always differed widely
(E) always widely differ

This sentence needs a verb in the present perfect tense (that
is, "have" or "has" plus the "-ed" form of the verb) to indicate

that an action or situation begun in the past has continued into the present. Choice A is incorrect because the past participle *differed* must follow the present tense auxiliary verb *have* in order to form the present perfect tense of the verb: *differ* at the end of the underlined construction cannot join with *have*. In choice B, the minor change in word order and the switch from *this* to *the* do nothing to correct the tense problem. The present perfect tense appears in choice C, but it cannot properly describe actions that are limited either to *the past* or to *this moment*. In choice E, *differ* cannot join with *have*, and the adverb *widely* is out of place. In the best answer, D, the present perfect verb (*have . . . differed*) allows the sentence to make a statement that holds at once for the past and the present. This is a question of average difficulty.

6. <u>All over</u> North America people <u>dimmed their</u> house lights
    A   B
and <u>drove fewer miles</u> in an effort <u>for conserving</u> energy.
         C   D
<u>No error</u>
  E

The error in this sentence is at choice D. The phrase that begins with *in an effort* should be completed with the infinitive "to conserve" following the noun *effort*. An equivalent phrase is "in order to conserve," where again the infinitive is idiomatic. This is an easy question.

(For further practice with Verb Forms also see Sample Test I, questions 9, 12, 16; Sample Test II, questions 1, 9, 14, 22, 24.)

V. ADJECTIVES AND ADVERBS

1. <u>According to the head of</u> the lecture bureau, a Shirley
             A
Chisholm or a Dick Gregory—people who speak to the
<u>social</u> or politically significant—<u>could be booked</u> <u>365 days</u>
 B   C   D
<u>a year.</u> <u>No error</u>
 (D)   E

In this sentence the error occurs at choice B: *social* should be changed to "socially" in order to modify *significant*. In the corrected sentence, *socially* and *politically* would then be parallel modifiers of *significant*. This is an easy question.

2. Of the three species of North American weasels, the long-tailed weasel is <u>larger and it destroys the most</u> livestock.

  (A) larger and it destroys the most
  (B) the largest and most destructive to
  (C) larger and most destructive of
  (D) largest and more destructive to
  (E) the larger, and it destroys the most

In choice A, *larger* is incorrect because the sentence is discussing which of three species of weasels exhibits some characteristics to the highest degree. The adjective should be *largest*; *larger* would be correct only if a comparison were being made between two species. Choice C is faulty because *larger* is wrong and because the preposition following *de-*

structive should be *to*, not *of*. In choice D, *more* should be *most*. Choice E can be discounted because of the comparative form *larger*. The best answer is B; *the* is advisable here because *the largest* is understood to mean "the largest species." This is a fairly easy question.

(For further practice with Adjectives and Adverbs also see Sample Test I, question 11; Sample Test II, question 12.)

VI. COMPARISONS

1. Amerigo Vespucci, <u>as Columbus</u>, believed that he <u>had</u>
                 A   B
<u>reached</u> the shores of Asia, and his letters home <u>seemed</u>
 (B)   C
<u>to confirm</u> Mandeville's fantastic <u>accounts of the mar-</u>
 (C)   D
<u>vels of the East.</u> <u>No error</u>
 (D)   E

The error in this sentence is at choice A, which should read "like Columbus." In stated comparisons, "like" is a preposition and "as" is a conjunction. That is, "like" compares nouns (such as *Vespucci* and *Columbus*), and "as" combines clauses: "Vespucci mistook America for Asia, as Columbus did." With choice A unchanged, the sentence suggests that Vespucci was pretending to be Columbus when he reached the shores of America. This is a question of medium difficulty.

2. Like <u>Byrne's position, Meyner was in opposition against mandatory wage</u> and price controls; he believed in voluntary guidelines and supported the President's economic program.

  (A) Byrne's position, Meyner was in opposition against mandatory wage
  (B) the position of Byrne, Meyner was in opposition against mandatory wages
  (C) Byrne, Meyner was in opposition to mandatory wages
  (D) Byrne, Meyner was opposed against mandatory wage
  (E) Byrne, Meyner was opposed to mandatory wage

Choice A wrongly compares Byrne's position to Meyner: the comparison should be between Byrne and Meyner or Byrne's position and Meyner's position. The phrase *was in opposition against* is unnecessarily wordy, and the preposition here should be *to* rather than *against*. The comparison in choice B is more wordy but no more logical than that in choice A. Also, because *wages* and *controls* are both plural, choice B suggests that Meyner was opposed to mandatory wages as well as to price controls; in the best choice, *wage* and *price* will both be singular modifiers of *controls*. In choice C the comparison and the preposition are correct, but the phrasing is still wordy and *wages* is still wrong. The use of *against* for *to* makes choice D faulty. The best answer for this easy question is choice E.

3. <u>Like those of other ancient cities</u>, Athens did not have
          A

a systematic method <u>of naming streets and numbering</u>
                             B

houses; in documents <u>concerned with the disposal of</u>
 (B)   C

house property, <u>the site is usually defined by reference</u>
                      D

to its neighbors. <u>No error</u>
              E

The error in this sentence is at choice A. There is no plural noun to which *those* can refer: the sentence intends to compare Athens to other ancient cities, not to *those of other ancient cities*. The sentence will read correctly if the words *those of* are deleted. This is a moderately difficult question.

4. Early colonists had homes that <u>were</u> <u>better planned and</u>
                          A   B

more solidly <u>built</u> <u>than people today.</u> <u>No error</u>
          C   D   E

This sentence wrongly compares colonists' homes to *people today;* it should compare homes to homes. The sentence can be corrected if choice D is made to read "than those erected by people today," or something similar. This question is somewhat easier than average.

5. The names of the women who sang the blues <u>are often not as well known as those of</u> the musicians who accompanied them.

(A) are often not as well known as those of
(B) are often not so well known as
(C) have not often been as well known as
(D) have often not been as well known as have those of
(E) are often not known so well as are those of

Choice A is the best answer because it compares names to names. Choice B wrongly compares *names* to *musicians;* a correct comparison must include *those of* to match the names of *women* with the names of *musicians.* Choice C also compares *names* to *musicians,* and the verb tense is questionable here: the simple present tense in choice A indicates that the situation described in the sentence continues to be the case, whereas the present perfect (have . . . been) indicates that the situation has been the case only to the present moment. The present perfect tense reappears in choice D, and the second *have* is unnecessary in any case. In E, the second *are* is unnecessary. Choice A is the best answer for this question, which is a little more difficult than average.

(For further practice with Comparisons also see Sample Test I, question 3; Sample Test II, questions 6, 21.)

VII. LOGICAL MODIFICATION

1. <u>Although partially destroyed, the archaeologists were able to infer</u> from what remained of the inscription that the priest Zonainos was buried in the crypt.

(A) Although partially destroyed, the archaeologists were able to infer
(B) Although partially destroyed, the archaeologists had inferred
(C) Although it had been partially destroyed, the archaeologists were able to infer
(D) Partially destroyed though it had been, the archaeologists had been able to infer
(E) Destroyed partially, the archaeologists were able to infer

Choice A illustrates a grammatical problem known as "the dangling modifier." The phrase *Although partially destroyed* "dangles" because it can fit nowhere in the sentence and make logical sense. Coming first, it modifies *archaeologists,* the nearest noun and the subject of the sentence; in other words, choice A says that the archaeologists were partially destroyed. They fare no better in choice B, where the change in verb form (to *had inferred*) cannot save them. The opening phrase of choice D is needlessly awkward, but the modification is logical. *Partially destroyed* describes *it,* which refers to *inscription.* The verb tense in the latter half of choice D is wrong, though, because it fails to indicate that the archaeologists made their inference sometime after the inscription had been partially destroyed: the simple past *were* in place of the past perfect *had been* will convey this idea. In choice E, the verb form is correct, but the dangling modifier again asserts that the archaeologists were partially destroyed. The best answer is C. This is a question of average difficulty.

2. <u>After being held</u> <u>for ten days</u>, the government of Kurda
         A   B

released the wounded Marine and <u>formally apologized</u>
                                     C

to the representative <u>who was to</u> accompany the soldier
(C)   D

home. <u>No error</u>
      E

The error in this sentence, which occurs at choice A, provides another example of a dangling modifier. The phrase *After being held* can fit nowhere in the sentence so as to modify *the wounded Marine.* When the phrase comes first, as it does here, the sentence says that the government of Kurda was held for ten days. The sentence can be corrected if choice A is revised to "After holding him." This is a very difficult question.

3. **Once the main artery of commerce between Philadelphia and New York, the Great Depression forced the closing of the Delaware and Raritan Canal.**

  (A) Once the main artery of commerce between Philadelphia and New York, the Great Depression forced the closing of the Delaware and Raritan Canal.
  (B) Once the main artery of commerce between Philadelphia and New York, the Delaware and Raritan Canal's closing was forced because of the Great Depression.
  (C) The Great Depression forced the closing of the Delaware and Raritan Canal, once the main artery of commerce between Philadelphia and New York.
  (D) Forced to close because of the Great Depression, the Delaware and Raritan Canal was the main artery of commerce at one time between Philadelphia and New York.
  (E) The Delaware and Raritan Canal, the main artery of commerce between Philadelphia and New York once, was forced to close by the Great Depression.

Choice A provides an example of a misplaced modifier. The initial phrase modifies the subject of the sentence; in other words, the sentence says that the Great Depression was once the main artery of commerce between Philadelphia and New York. The modifying phrase is called "misplaced" rather than "dangling" because it can properly modify *Canal* if it is placed near that noun. In choice B, the phrase illogically modifies the *Canal's closing*. The modification in choice D is logical, but the sentence has some unnecessary words: *at one time* replaces *once* and should in any case appear immediately after *was*, the verb it modifies, not after *commerce*. Choice E is awkward. The modifier *once* should appear before *the main*, not after *New York*. Logical and compact, C is the best answer. The question is somewhat more difficult than average.

4. **If a single strain of plant is used for a given crop over a wide area, a practice fostered by modern seed-marketing methods, it increases the likelihood that the impact of a single crop disease or pest will be disastrous.**

  (A) If a single strain of plant is used for a given crop over a wide area, a practice fostered by modern seed-marketing methods, it
  (B) If a single strain of plant is used for a given crop over a wide area, as is fostered by modern seed-marketing methods, it
  (C) A practice fostered by modern seed-marketing methods, a single strain of plant used for a given crop over a wide area
  (D) A single strain of plant used for a given crop over a wide area, a practice fostered by modern seed-marketing methods,
  (E) The use of a single strain of plant for a given crop over a wide area, a practice fostered by modern seed-marketing methods,

Choice A is faulty because the subject of the sentence, the pronoun *it*, has no noun to which it can refer; neither does the noun appositive *a practice*. (A noun appositive explains or characterizes another noun, as in "*Jones, the farmer.*") In choice B, *as is* and *it* again have no specific referent. Choice C entails a false appositive: the sentence here says not that the *use* of a single strain of plant is a practice fostered by modern seed-marketing methods, but rather that the *strain* itself is such a method. Choice D reverses the order of the construction, but the appositive is just as illogical as that in choice C. Choice E is the best answer: *use* is a logical subject for the verb *increases* and a logical governing noun for the appositive *practice*. This is a question of average difficulty.

(For further practice with Logical Modification also see Sample Test I, question 13; Sample Test II, question 25.)

VIII. RELATIVE CLAUSES

1. One reason for the uncertainty in national energy policy may be **because policymakers are lacking in the information to enable** them to choose rational objectives.

  (A) because policymakers are lacking in the information to enable
  (B) that policymakers lack the information that would enable
  (C) because of policymakers' lacking the information to enable
  (D) the lack of information that makers of policy have that would enable
  (E) due to the lack of information makers of policy have enabling

In choice A, *because* should be changed to *that* in order to form a relative clause (a clause that is linked to the noun *reason* by a relative pronoun such as *that*). Phrases such as "the reason is because" and "the reason is due to" are not generally acceptable in standard written English. There is no need to prefer the present progressive verb form *are lacking* to the simple present verb *lack;* the simple present is the verb form typically used to represent a situation as general, customary, or characteristic. Also, *information* should be modified by a relative clause rather than an infinitive: in other words, *that would enable* specifically describes the information that is needed and should replace *to enable,* which makes a confusing parallel with *to choose.* In choice C, *because* and *to enable* are faulty, and *of policymakers' lacking* is an awkward complication of *policymakers lack.* In choice D, the phrase *that would enable* is ambiguous: because *lack* is a noun here, *that* could grammatically refer to *information,* which is the object of a preposition, or to *lack,* which completes the verb. According to the latter reading, a lack of information would enable policymakers to choose rational objectives. The syntax of choice E is awkward and confusing. *One reason . . . may be due to the lack* is a poor phrase: the reason does not result from the lack—the reason is the lack. And one cannot really *have* a *lack of information.* The verb form *enabling* is wrong here: it tends to modify *lack,* not *information,* and the use of a present participle ("-ing" form of a verb) suggests, contrary to the sense of the sentence, that policymakers are currently able to choose rational objectives. The phrase *that would enable* should clearly modify *information.* Choice B is the best answer for this fairly easy question.

2. **The proposed regulations require private pension plans,**
   ‾‾‾‾‾‾‾‾   **‾‾‾‾‾‾‾‾‾‾‾‾‾‾‾‾‾‾‾‾‾‾‾**
       A   B

   including those covering many college faculty members,
   provide not only for equal contributions by men and
   women performing similar jobs in the same organiza-
          ‾‾‾‾‾‾‾‾‾‾‾‾‾‾‾‾‾‾‾‾‾‾‾‾‾‾
                   C

   tion, but also for equal periodic benefits for members of
      ‾‾‾‾‾‾‾‾‾‾‾‾‾‾‾‾‾‾‾‾‾‾‾‾‾‾‾‾‾‾‾
                D

   both sexes. No error
           ‾‾‾‾‾‾‾‾
             E

The error in this sentence is at choice B: *that* must appear after *require* to show that *plans* is not the direct object of the verb *require* but rather the subject of a relative clause in which the verb is *provide.* In choice D, *but also for* idiomatically completes the construction that begins *not only for.* Essentially, the sentence says, "The regulations require that plans provide not only for contributions but also for benefits." This is a difficult question.

(For examples of relative clauses used correctly see Sample Test I, questions 8, 12, 14, 23; Sample Test II, questions 3, 16, 20.)

IX. OTHER PROBLEMS

1. **Like F. A. Hayek, Sowell views the concern for social justice to be nothing more but a pretext to enhance government power at the expense of individual freedom.**

   (A) to be nothing more but a pretext to enhance
   (B) to be nothing more than a pretext to enhance
   (C) as nothing more but a pretext for enhancing
   (D) as nothing more than a pretext for enhancing
   (E) as nothing more but a pretext to enhance

Choice A contains several errors. The idiom is "views X as Y," not "views X to be Y," and *nothing more but* should be *nothing more than.* Also, it is customary and acceptable in English to say *pretext for enhancing,* but it is not idiomatic to say *pretext to enhance.* Only choice D is correct, for each of the other choices contains at least one of these errors. This is a question of average difficulty.

2. **Ordinary techniques of chemical analysis do not distin-**
     ‾‾‾‾‾‾‾‾‾‾‾‾‾‾‾‾ **‾‾‾‾‾‾‾‾‾‾‾‾‾‾‾‾‾**
         A   B

   guish between one tautomeric form of a molecule from
        ‾‾‾‾‾‾‾‾‾‾‾‾
           C

   another. No error
   ‾‾‾‾‾‾‾ **‾‾‾‾‾‾‾‾**
     D   E

The phrase *distinguish between one . . . from another* is not acceptable in standard written English. The sentence can be corrected if *between* is deleted from choice C. This is a question of average difficulty.

(For further practice with Other Problems also see Sample Test I, question 22; Sample Test II, questions 4, 16, 23.)

VIII An Authentic Graduate Management Admission Test

The test that follows is a Graduate Management Admission Test that has been slightly modified. The actual test book contains eight sections, two of which consist of trial questions that are not counted in the scoring. Those trial questions have been omitted from this test. Also, the total testing time for this test is three hours; the actual test takes four hours.

Taking this test will help you become acquainted with testing procedures and requirements and thereby approach the real test with more assurance. Therefore, you should try to take this test under conditions similar to those in an actual test administration, observing the time limitations, and thinking about each question seriously.

The facsimile of the response portion of a GMAT answer sheet below may be used to mark your answers to the test. After you have taken the test, compare your answers with the correct ones on page 184 and determine your score using the information that follows the answer key.

SECTION 1	SECTION 2	SECTION 3	SECTION 4	SECTION 5	SECTION 6
1 Ⓐ Ⓑ Ⓒ Ⓓ Ⓔ	1 Ⓐ Ⓑ Ⓒ Ⓓ Ⓔ	1 Ⓐ Ⓑ Ⓒ Ⓓ Ⓔ	1 Ⓐ Ⓑ Ⓒ Ⓓ Ⓔ	1 Ⓐ Ⓑ Ⓒ Ⓓ Ⓔ	1 Ⓐ Ⓑ Ⓒ Ⓓ Ⓔ
2 Ⓐ Ⓑ Ⓒ Ⓓ Ⓔ	2 Ⓐ Ⓑ Ⓒ Ⓓ Ⓔ	2 Ⓐ Ⓑ Ⓒ Ⓓ Ⓔ	2 Ⓐ Ⓑ Ⓒ Ⓓ Ⓔ	2 Ⓐ Ⓑ Ⓒ Ⓓ Ⓔ	2 Ⓐ Ⓑ Ⓒ Ⓓ Ⓔ
3 Ⓐ Ⓑ Ⓒ Ⓓ Ⓔ	3 Ⓐ Ⓑ Ⓒ Ⓓ Ⓔ	3 Ⓐ Ⓑ Ⓒ Ⓓ Ⓔ	3 Ⓐ Ⓑ Ⓒ Ⓓ Ⓔ	3 Ⓐ Ⓑ Ⓒ Ⓓ Ⓔ	3 Ⓐ Ⓑ Ⓒ Ⓓ Ⓔ
4 Ⓐ Ⓑ Ⓒ Ⓓ Ⓔ	4 Ⓐ Ⓑ Ⓒ Ⓓ Ⓔ	4 Ⓐ Ⓑ Ⓒ Ⓓ Ⓔ	4 Ⓐ Ⓑ Ⓒ Ⓓ Ⓔ	4 Ⓐ Ⓑ Ⓒ Ⓓ Ⓔ	4 Ⓐ Ⓑ Ⓒ Ⓓ Ⓔ
5 Ⓐ Ⓑ Ⓒ Ⓓ Ⓔ	5 Ⓐ Ⓑ Ⓒ Ⓓ Ⓔ	5 Ⓐ Ⓑ Ⓒ Ⓓ Ⓔ	5 Ⓐ Ⓑ Ⓒ Ⓓ Ⓔ	5 Ⓐ Ⓑ Ⓒ Ⓓ Ⓔ	5 Ⓐ Ⓑ Ⓒ Ⓓ Ⓔ
6 Ⓐ Ⓑ Ⓒ Ⓓ Ⓔ	6 Ⓐ Ⓑ Ⓒ Ⓓ Ⓔ	6 Ⓐ Ⓑ Ⓒ Ⓓ Ⓔ	6 Ⓐ Ⓑ Ⓒ Ⓓ Ⓔ	6 Ⓐ Ⓑ Ⓒ Ⓓ Ⓔ	6 Ⓐ Ⓑ Ⓒ Ⓓ Ⓔ
7 Ⓐ Ⓑ Ⓒ Ⓓ Ⓔ	7 Ⓐ Ⓑ Ⓒ Ⓓ Ⓔ	7 Ⓐ Ⓑ Ⓒ Ⓓ Ⓔ	7 Ⓐ Ⓑ Ⓒ Ⓓ Ⓔ	7 Ⓐ Ⓑ Ⓒ Ⓓ Ⓔ	7 Ⓐ Ⓑ Ⓒ Ⓓ Ⓔ
8 Ⓐ Ⓑ Ⓒ Ⓓ Ⓔ	8 Ⓐ Ⓑ Ⓒ Ⓓ Ⓔ	8 Ⓐ Ⓑ Ⓒ Ⓓ Ⓔ	8 Ⓐ Ⓑ Ⓒ Ⓓ Ⓔ	8 Ⓐ Ⓑ Ⓒ Ⓓ Ⓔ	8 Ⓐ Ⓑ Ⓒ Ⓓ Ⓔ
9 Ⓐ Ⓑ Ⓒ Ⓓ Ⓔ	9 Ⓐ Ⓑ Ⓒ Ⓓ Ⓔ	9 Ⓐ Ⓑ Ⓒ Ⓓ Ⓔ	9 Ⓐ Ⓑ Ⓒ Ⓓ Ⓔ	9 Ⓐ Ⓑ Ⓒ Ⓓ Ⓔ	9 Ⓐ Ⓑ Ⓒ Ⓓ Ⓔ
10 Ⓐ Ⓑ Ⓒ Ⓓ Ⓔ	10 Ⓐ Ⓑ Ⓒ Ⓓ Ⓔ	10 Ⓐ Ⓑ Ⓒ Ⓓ Ⓔ	10 Ⓐ Ⓑ Ⓒ Ⓓ Ⓔ	10 Ⓐ Ⓑ Ⓒ Ⓓ Ⓔ	10 Ⓐ Ⓑ Ⓒ Ⓓ Ⓔ
11 Ⓐ Ⓑ Ⓒ Ⓓ Ⓔ	11 Ⓐ Ⓑ Ⓒ Ⓓ Ⓔ	11 Ⓐ Ⓑ Ⓒ Ⓓ Ⓔ	11 Ⓐ Ⓑ Ⓒ Ⓓ Ⓔ	11 Ⓐ Ⓑ Ⓒ Ⓓ Ⓔ	11 Ⓐ Ⓑ Ⓒ Ⓓ Ⓔ
12 Ⓐ Ⓑ Ⓒ Ⓓ Ⓔ	12 Ⓐ Ⓑ Ⓒ Ⓓ Ⓔ	12 Ⓐ Ⓑ Ⓒ Ⓓ Ⓔ	12 Ⓐ Ⓑ Ⓒ Ⓓ Ⓔ	12 Ⓐ Ⓑ Ⓒ Ⓓ Ⓔ	12 Ⓐ Ⓑ Ⓒ Ⓓ Ⓔ
13 Ⓐ Ⓑ Ⓒ Ⓓ Ⓔ	13 Ⓐ Ⓑ Ⓒ Ⓓ Ⓔ	13 Ⓐ Ⓑ Ⓒ Ⓓ Ⓔ	13 Ⓐ Ⓑ Ⓒ Ⓓ Ⓔ	13 Ⓐ Ⓑ Ⓒ Ⓓ Ⓔ	13 Ⓐ Ⓑ Ⓒ Ⓓ Ⓔ
14 Ⓐ Ⓑ Ⓒ Ⓓ Ⓔ	14 Ⓐ Ⓑ Ⓒ Ⓓ Ⓔ	14 Ⓐ Ⓑ Ⓒ Ⓓ Ⓔ	14 Ⓐ Ⓑ Ⓒ Ⓓ Ⓔ	14 Ⓐ Ⓑ Ⓒ Ⓓ Ⓔ	14 Ⓐ Ⓑ Ⓒ Ⓓ Ⓔ
15 Ⓐ Ⓑ Ⓒ Ⓓ Ⓔ	15 Ⓐ Ⓑ Ⓒ Ⓓ Ⓔ	15 Ⓐ Ⓑ Ⓒ Ⓓ Ⓔ	15 Ⓐ Ⓑ Ⓒ Ⓓ Ⓔ	15 Ⓐ Ⓑ Ⓒ Ⓓ Ⓔ	15 Ⓐ Ⓑ Ⓒ Ⓓ Ⓔ
16 Ⓐ Ⓑ Ⓒ Ⓓ Ⓔ	16 Ⓐ Ⓑ Ⓒ Ⓓ Ⓔ	16 Ⓐ Ⓑ Ⓒ Ⓓ Ⓔ	16 Ⓐ Ⓑ Ⓒ Ⓓ Ⓔ	16 Ⓐ Ⓑ Ⓒ Ⓓ Ⓔ	16 Ⓐ Ⓑ Ⓒ Ⓓ Ⓔ
17 Ⓐ Ⓑ Ⓒ Ⓓ Ⓔ	17 Ⓐ Ⓑ Ⓒ Ⓓ Ⓔ	17 Ⓐ Ⓑ Ⓒ Ⓓ Ⓔ	17 Ⓐ Ⓑ Ⓒ Ⓓ Ⓔ	17 Ⓐ Ⓑ Ⓒ Ⓓ Ⓔ	17 Ⓐ Ⓑ Ⓒ Ⓓ Ⓔ
18 Ⓐ Ⓑ Ⓒ Ⓓ Ⓔ	18 Ⓐ Ⓑ Ⓒ Ⓓ Ⓔ	18 Ⓐ Ⓑ Ⓒ Ⓓ Ⓔ	18 Ⓐ Ⓑ Ⓒ Ⓓ Ⓔ	18 Ⓐ Ⓑ Ⓒ Ⓓ Ⓔ	18 Ⓐ Ⓑ Ⓒ Ⓓ Ⓔ
19 Ⓐ Ⓑ Ⓒ Ⓓ Ⓔ	19 Ⓐ Ⓑ Ⓒ Ⓓ Ⓔ	19 Ⓐ Ⓑ Ⓒ Ⓓ Ⓔ	19 Ⓐ Ⓑ Ⓒ Ⓓ Ⓔ	19 Ⓐ Ⓑ Ⓒ Ⓓ Ⓔ	19 Ⓐ Ⓑ Ⓒ Ⓓ Ⓔ
20 Ⓐ Ⓑ Ⓒ Ⓓ Ⓔ	20 Ⓐ Ⓑ Ⓒ Ⓓ Ⓔ	20 Ⓐ Ⓑ Ⓒ Ⓓ Ⓔ	20 Ⓐ Ⓑ Ⓒ Ⓓ Ⓔ	20 Ⓐ Ⓑ Ⓒ Ⓓ Ⓔ	20 Ⓐ Ⓑ Ⓒ Ⓓ Ⓔ
21 Ⓐ Ⓑ Ⓒ Ⓓ Ⓔ	21 Ⓐ Ⓑ Ⓒ Ⓓ Ⓔ	21 Ⓐ Ⓑ Ⓒ Ⓓ Ⓔ	21 Ⓐ Ⓑ Ⓒ Ⓓ Ⓔ	21 Ⓐ Ⓑ Ⓒ Ⓓ Ⓔ	21 Ⓐ Ⓑ Ⓒ Ⓓ Ⓔ
22 Ⓐ Ⓑ Ⓒ Ⓓ Ⓔ	22 Ⓐ Ⓑ Ⓒ Ⓓ Ⓔ	22 Ⓐ Ⓑ Ⓒ Ⓓ Ⓔ	22 Ⓐ Ⓑ Ⓒ Ⓓ Ⓔ	22 Ⓐ Ⓑ Ⓒ Ⓓ Ⓔ	22 Ⓐ Ⓑ Ⓒ Ⓓ Ⓔ
23 Ⓐ Ⓑ Ⓒ Ⓓ Ⓔ	23 Ⓐ Ⓑ Ⓒ Ⓓ Ⓔ	23 Ⓐ Ⓑ Ⓒ Ⓓ Ⓔ	23 Ⓐ Ⓑ Ⓒ Ⓓ Ⓔ	23 Ⓐ Ⓑ Ⓒ Ⓓ Ⓔ	23 Ⓐ Ⓑ Ⓒ Ⓓ Ⓔ
24 Ⓐ Ⓑ Ⓒ Ⓓ Ⓔ	24 Ⓐ Ⓑ Ⓒ Ⓓ Ⓔ	24 Ⓐ Ⓑ Ⓒ Ⓓ Ⓔ	24 Ⓐ Ⓑ Ⓒ Ⓓ Ⓔ	24 Ⓐ Ⓑ Ⓒ Ⓓ Ⓔ	24 Ⓐ Ⓑ Ⓒ Ⓓ Ⓔ
25 Ⓐ Ⓑ Ⓒ Ⓓ Ⓔ	25 Ⓐ Ⓑ Ⓒ Ⓓ Ⓔ	25 Ⓐ Ⓑ Ⓒ Ⓓ Ⓔ	25 Ⓐ Ⓑ Ⓒ Ⓓ Ⓔ	25 Ⓐ Ⓑ Ⓒ Ⓓ Ⓔ	25 Ⓐ Ⓑ Ⓒ Ⓓ Ⓔ
26 Ⓐ Ⓑ Ⓒ Ⓓ Ⓔ	26 Ⓐ Ⓑ Ⓒ Ⓓ Ⓔ	26 Ⓐ Ⓑ Ⓒ Ⓓ Ⓔ	26 Ⓐ Ⓑ Ⓒ Ⓓ Ⓔ	26 Ⓐ Ⓑ Ⓒ Ⓓ Ⓔ	26 Ⓐ Ⓑ Ⓒ Ⓓ Ⓔ
27 Ⓐ Ⓑ Ⓒ Ⓓ Ⓔ	27 Ⓐ Ⓑ Ⓒ Ⓓ Ⓔ	27 Ⓐ Ⓑ Ⓒ Ⓓ Ⓔ	27 Ⓐ Ⓑ Ⓒ Ⓓ Ⓔ	27 Ⓐ Ⓑ Ⓒ Ⓓ Ⓔ	27 Ⓐ Ⓑ Ⓒ Ⓓ Ⓔ
28 Ⓐ Ⓑ Ⓒ Ⓓ Ⓔ	28 Ⓐ Ⓑ Ⓒ Ⓓ Ⓔ	28 Ⓐ Ⓑ Ⓒ Ⓓ Ⓔ	28 Ⓐ Ⓑ Ⓒ Ⓓ Ⓔ	28 Ⓐ Ⓑ Ⓒ Ⓓ Ⓔ	28 Ⓐ Ⓑ Ⓒ Ⓓ Ⓔ
29 Ⓐ Ⓑ Ⓒ Ⓓ Ⓔ	29 Ⓐ Ⓑ Ⓒ Ⓓ Ⓔ	29 Ⓐ Ⓑ Ⓒ Ⓓ Ⓔ	29 Ⓐ Ⓑ Ⓒ Ⓓ Ⓔ	29 Ⓐ Ⓑ Ⓒ Ⓓ Ⓔ	29 Ⓐ Ⓑ Ⓒ Ⓓ Ⓔ
30 Ⓐ Ⓑ Ⓒ Ⓓ Ⓔ	30 Ⓐ Ⓑ Ⓒ Ⓓ Ⓔ	30 Ⓐ Ⓑ Ⓒ Ⓓ Ⓔ	30 Ⓐ Ⓑ Ⓒ Ⓓ Ⓔ	30 Ⓐ Ⓑ Ⓒ Ⓓ Ⓔ	30 Ⓐ Ⓑ Ⓒ Ⓓ Ⓔ
31 Ⓐ Ⓑ Ⓒ Ⓓ Ⓔ	31 Ⓐ Ⓑ Ⓒ Ⓓ Ⓔ	31 Ⓐ Ⓑ Ⓒ Ⓓ Ⓔ	31 Ⓐ Ⓑ Ⓒ Ⓓ Ⓔ	31 Ⓐ Ⓑ Ⓒ Ⓓ Ⓔ	31 Ⓐ Ⓑ Ⓒ Ⓓ Ⓔ
32 Ⓐ Ⓑ Ⓒ Ⓓ Ⓔ	32 Ⓐ Ⓑ Ⓒ Ⓓ Ⓔ	32 Ⓐ Ⓑ Ⓒ Ⓓ Ⓔ	32 Ⓐ Ⓑ Ⓒ Ⓓ Ⓔ	32 Ⓐ Ⓑ Ⓒ Ⓓ Ⓔ	32 Ⓐ Ⓑ Ⓒ Ⓓ Ⓔ
33 Ⓐ Ⓑ Ⓒ Ⓓ Ⓔ	33 Ⓐ Ⓑ Ⓒ Ⓓ Ⓔ	33 Ⓐ Ⓑ Ⓒ Ⓓ Ⓔ	33 Ⓐ Ⓑ Ⓒ Ⓓ Ⓔ	33 Ⓐ Ⓑ Ⓒ Ⓓ Ⓔ	33 Ⓐ Ⓑ Ⓒ Ⓓ Ⓔ
34 Ⓐ Ⓑ Ⓒ Ⓓ Ⓔ	34 Ⓐ Ⓑ Ⓒ Ⓓ Ⓔ	34 Ⓐ Ⓑ Ⓒ Ⓓ Ⓔ	34 Ⓐ Ⓑ Ⓒ Ⓓ Ⓔ	34 Ⓐ Ⓑ Ⓒ Ⓓ Ⓔ	34 Ⓐ Ⓑ Ⓒ Ⓓ Ⓔ
35 Ⓐ Ⓑ Ⓒ Ⓓ Ⓔ	35 Ⓐ Ⓑ Ⓒ Ⓓ Ⓔ	35 Ⓐ Ⓑ Ⓒ Ⓓ Ⓔ	35 Ⓐ Ⓑ Ⓒ Ⓓ Ⓔ	35 Ⓐ Ⓑ Ⓒ Ⓓ Ⓔ	35 Ⓐ Ⓑ Ⓒ Ⓓ Ⓔ
36 Ⓐ Ⓑ Ⓒ Ⓓ Ⓔ	36 Ⓐ Ⓑ Ⓒ Ⓓ Ⓔ	36 Ⓐ Ⓑ Ⓒ Ⓓ Ⓔ	36 Ⓐ Ⓑ Ⓒ Ⓓ Ⓔ	36 Ⓐ Ⓑ Ⓒ Ⓓ Ⓔ	36 Ⓐ Ⓑ Ⓒ Ⓓ Ⓔ
37 Ⓐ Ⓑ Ⓒ Ⓓ Ⓔ	37 Ⓐ Ⓑ Ⓒ Ⓓ Ⓔ	37 Ⓐ Ⓑ Ⓒ Ⓓ Ⓔ	37 Ⓐ Ⓑ Ⓒ Ⓓ Ⓔ	37 Ⓐ Ⓑ Ⓒ Ⓓ Ⓔ	37 Ⓐ Ⓑ Ⓒ Ⓓ Ⓔ
38 Ⓐ Ⓑ Ⓒ Ⓓ Ⓔ	38 Ⓐ Ⓑ Ⓒ Ⓓ Ⓔ	38 Ⓐ Ⓑ Ⓒ Ⓓ Ⓔ	38 Ⓐ Ⓑ Ⓒ Ⓓ Ⓔ	38 Ⓐ Ⓑ Ⓒ Ⓓ Ⓔ	38 Ⓐ Ⓑ Ⓒ Ⓓ Ⓔ
39 Ⓐ Ⓑ Ⓒ Ⓓ Ⓔ	39 Ⓐ Ⓑ Ⓒ Ⓓ Ⓔ	39 Ⓐ Ⓑ Ⓒ Ⓓ Ⓔ	39 Ⓐ Ⓑ Ⓒ Ⓓ Ⓔ	39 Ⓐ Ⓑ Ⓒ Ⓓ Ⓔ	39 Ⓐ Ⓑ Ⓒ Ⓓ Ⓔ
40 Ⓐ Ⓑ Ⓒ Ⓓ Ⓔ	40 Ⓐ Ⓑ Ⓒ Ⓓ Ⓔ	40 Ⓐ Ⓑ Ⓒ Ⓓ Ⓔ	40 Ⓐ Ⓑ Ⓒ Ⓓ Ⓔ	40 Ⓐ Ⓑ Ⓒ Ⓓ Ⓔ	40 Ⓐ Ⓑ Ⓒ Ⓓ Ⓔ

SECTION I

Time—30 minutes

25 Questions

Each passage in this group is followed by questions based on its content. After reading a passage, choose the best answer to each question and blacken the corresponding space on the answer sheet. Answer all questions following a passage on the basis of what is stated or implied in that passage.

In the past decade or so, some scientists have come to believe that many particles long thought to be elementary, including such familiar ones as the proton and the neutron, are not elementary at all.
(5) Instead they appear to be composite structures made up of the more fundamental entities named quarks, in much the same way that atoms are considered to be made up of protons, neutrons, and electrons.
(10)   The quark model amounts to an impressive simplification of nature. In the initial formulation of the theory there were supposed to be just three species of quark, and those three were enough to account for the properties of an entire class of
(15) particles with several dozen members. Every known member of that class could be understood as a combination of quarks; moreover, every allowed combination of the quarks gave rise to a known particle. The correspondence between
(20) theory and observation seemed too close to be coincidental, and experiments were undertaken with the aim of detecting the quarks themselves.
        If the quarks are real particles, it seems reasonable that we should be able to see them.
(25) We know that the atom consists of a nucleus and a surrounding cloud of electrons because we can take the atom apart and study its constituents in isolation. We know that the nucleus in turn consists of protons and neutrons because the
(30) nucleus can be split into fragments and the constituent particles identified. It is easy to imagine a similar experiment in which particles thought to be made of quarks, such as protons, are violently decomposed. When that is attempted,
(35) however, the debris consists only of more protons and other familiar particles. No objects with the properties attributed to quarks are seen. Physicists have searched extensively, but free quarks have not been found.
(40)   It is possible, of course, that no experiment has yet looked in the right place or with the right instruments, but that now seems unlikely. It is also possible that the quarks simply do not exist, but physicists are reluctant to abandon a theory
(45) that carries such explanatory force. The successes of the theory represent compelling evidence that quarks exist inside particles such as the proton; on the other hand, the repeated failure of experimental searches to discover a free quark argues
(50) that the quarks do not exist independently. This paradox can be resolved, but only by making

further theoretical assumptions about the quarks and the forces that bind them together. It must be demonstrated that quarks exist, but that for some
(55) reason they do not show themselves in the open. Theorists, who invented the quarks in the first place, are now charged with explaining their confinement within the particles they presumably make up.

1. The primary purpose of the passage is to

   (A) examine the research techniques of contemporary physicists, especially as they are apparent in the search for quarks
   (B) encourage physicists to spend more time in the laboratory testing their theories
   (C) advocate the development of more precise laboratory instruments that may lead to the verification of the quark theory
   (D) evaluate the wisdom of funding the kind of obscure and inconclusive research that is evident in the search for quarks
   (E) review the history of and the problems with the quark theory

2. The author mentions atoms and subatomic particles in lines 7-9 in order to

   (A) anticipate the objections of other physicists
   (B) explain quarks by an analogy
   (C) correct the bias in previous quark theories
   (D) illustrate the importance of the quark theory
   (E) enumerate previously discovered atomic particles

GO ON TO THE NEXT PAGE.

3. According to the passage, the most attractive feature of the quark theory as it was initially formulated was its

(A) relative simplicity
(B) universal application
(C) elimination of theoretical contradictions
(D) use of conventional mathematics
(E) explanation of nuclear reactions

4. It may be inferred from the passage that scientists studying quarks interpreted the close correspondence between theory and observation as an indication of the

(A) speciousness of a nontheoretical approach to physics
(B) ease with which quarks could be isolated
(C) likelihood of quarks' actual existence
(D) implausibility of similarities with other physical models
(E) probability of violent nuclear decomposition of atoms

5. The author indicates that a future version of the quark theory must

(A) explain why stable subatomic particles are composed of quarks
(B) indicate where to look for quarks
(C) permit calculation of the energy needed to release quarks from protons
(D) explain why quarks have not been observed
(E) propose a full set of properties for quarks

6. According to the passage, which of the following have been verified as constituent parts of atomic nuclei?

   I. Electrons
   II. Neutrons
   III. Protons
   IV. Quarks

(A) I only
(B) III only
(C) II and III only
(D) II, III, and IV only
(E) I, II, III, and IV

7. It can be inferred from the passage that the physicists who initially looked for quarks assumed that quarks

(A) are composed of small particles
(B) must leave some physical evidence of their presence
(C) bind themselves exclusively to other atomic particles
(D) are manifestations of energy rather than of matter
(E) had an amorphous, cloudlike structure

8. According to the passage, it can be inferred that which of the following is the chief deterrent to wider acceptance of the quark theory?

(A) The theory discourages future attempts to verify the existence of quarks through laboratory experimentation.
(B) The assumptions of the theory are inconsistent with each other as well as with observed phenomena.
(C) The theory imprisons physicists in a paradox that seems irresolvable.
(D) Efforts to obtain experimental verification of the theory have been fruitless.
(E) Quark research has diverted some physicists from more crucial work.

9. The author regards the development of further theoretical models of quarks as

(A) necessary
(B) misdirected
(C) hazardous
(D) contradictory
(E) difficult

GO ON TO THE NEXT PAGE.

The influence of Darwin's theory of evolution upon the poetic imagination has become a commonplace, documented by an assortment of studies. And yet, surveying the work of creative human imagination today, one is struck by the slightness of creative drive connected with an awareness of evolution, cosmic or organic. It is not that poets refuse to accept evolution. They render lip service to it. But it does not haunt their poetic imaginations.

One of the great evolutionary philosophers of our day, Father Pierre Teilhard de Chardin, has been accused of writing often as a poet. But we are hard put to find poets who make creative use of evolutionary insights comparable with Teilhard's. Teilhard faces forward, into the future, as, in its brighter moments, does the rest of our world, permeated as it is with evolutionary thinking. But poets tend to exalt the present moment when they are not facing the past. There is here certainly some kind of crisis concerning the relationship of the poet to time.

The situation is complicated by the fact that today's poets generally are acutely aware of the continuing development of art itself. The existence of a self-conscious avant-garde makes this plain enough. Poetry, together with art generally, has a sense of its own domestic time. But cosmic time, as this has been known since the discovery of evolution, is another matter. Most poets are not much interested in it, even when they are most intently concerned with human beings, who exist in this time. Writers who do deal with larger patterns of development in time tend to slip into thinly veiled sensationalism, as does George Bernard Shaw in Back to Methuselah, or sensationalism not so thinly veiled, as in George Orwell's 1984; or they handle cosmic time not very successfully, as does Hart Crane, or half-heartedly, as does T. S. Eliot. In the last analysis, the poet seems not very much at home in an evolutionary cosmos.

The basic issue between poetry and evolutionism is seemingly the need in poetry, as in all art, for repetition. The drives toward repetition show in poetry in countless ways—in rhythm, in rhyme, in other sound patterns, in thematic management and plotting (Joyce plots his novel Ulysses, which for all practical purposes is a poem in the full sense of this term, to match Homer's poem). Even the key to all plotting, recognition, is a kind of repetition, a return to something already known. In "Burnt Norton" T. S. Eliot writes:

And the end and the beginning were always there
Before the beginning and after the end.

Finnegans Wake is a serpent with its tail in its own mouth: the last words of the book run back into its first words.

10. The main point of the passage is that the use by poets of the theme of evolution is

(A) in the process of changing established views
(B) on the threshold of generating inspired poetry
(C) in conflict with the structural necessities of art
(D) at odds with the poets' use of sensationalism
(E) at a crisis point for future intellectual history

11. Which of the following most nearly approximates the sense of "poet," as the author uses the word?

(A) Writer of verse
(B) Practitioner of one of the fine arts
(C) Profound philosopher concerned with time
(D) Imaginative writer
(E) Creative innovator

12. The attitude of the author toward Teilhard de Chardin is best described as

(A) deprecatory
(B) loyal
(C) equivocal
(D) familiar
(E) admiring

13. It can be inferred that the author views the ideas of Darwin as

(A) socially useful
(B) generally accepted
(C) unduly redundant
(D) overly sensational
(E) fundamentally uninteresting

GO ON TO THE NEXT PAGE.

14. The author regards the attempts of contemporary writers of literature to use the theme of evolution as

(A) promising
(B) premature
(C) unjustified
(D) superficial
(E) underestimated

15. According to the passage, the clear awareness of poets that art develops over time can be described as all of the following EXCEPT

(A) relevant to the meaning of evolution for poets
(B) evidenced by the self-awareness of avant-garde artists
(C) similar to the awareness of other artists
(D) apparently important for the problem of the relationship of poets to time
(E) different from the sense of cosmic time

16. The author refers to Joyce's novel Finnegans Wake in order to illustrate the

(A) contrast between novels based on poems and novels with independent plots
(B) sinuousness of a contemporary, flexible approach to plotting
(C) role of reiteration in giving artistic closure to a work
(D) difference between the approaches to poetry of two contemporary writers
(E) place of Joyce's works in relation to those of T. S. Eliot

17. The author assumes that the potential impact of the idea of evolution on poetry has not been

(A) noticed by contemporary critics
(B) exhausted by earlier writers
(C) welcomed by modern intellectuals
(D) interesting to some philosophers of art
(E) antipathetic to some religious authorities

GO ON TO THE NEXT PAGE.

In order to show how black people throughout North America were culturally isolated from the start, it is important to recognize how strange and unnatural the initial contact with Western society
(5) was for the African. Once we realize what a shock this first encounter was, we can begin to understand the amazing, albeit agonizing transformation that produced the contemporary black American from the people who were first bound
(10) and brought to this country. Life in colonial America was completely different from what the African thought human existence should be. This was one of the most important aspects of the enslavement of the African: the radically different,
(15) even opposing cultural perspectives that the colonial American and the African brought to one another.

Early European-Americans could not appreciate the profundity of the African world view because it differed so greatly from the Western system of
(20) thought and ideas. Western culture, which views the "ultimate happiness of humanity" as the sole purpose of the universe, could not comprehend the goals or "canons of satisfaction" of a culture with elaborate concepts of predetermination and of the
(25) subservience of human beings to a complex of gods. The cruelty of this misunderstanding, when contained within the already terrifying circumstance of slavery, should be readily apparent.

Africans were unable to preserve many of the
(30) achievements of their civilization under a system of slavery which denied cultural autonomy to the oppressed. European-Americans immediately attempted to eradicate all manifestations of African political, social, and economic traditions.
(35) Moreover, the highly developed African system of jurisprudence could not function under the American form of slavery. Nevertheless, Africans were able to preserve some of their own cultural perspectives, and many of the
(40) attitudes, customs, and cultural characteristics of the black American can be traced directly back to Africa. Religion, music, and African aesthetic principles did survive. These nonmaterial aspects of African culture, which could not be suppressed,
(45) now form the most apparent legacies of the African past.

Because of the violent differences between what was indigenous to their culture and what was forced on them in slavery, Africans developed an eclectic
(50) view of the world, containing both those elements of African temperament that could not be suppressed and those elements of Western culture that were

essential to survival in North America. Afro-Americans (the first American-born black people,
(55) who retained many pure Africanisms) and, later, black Americans inherited these cultural complexities and added individual nuances of their own. So, after several generations in the United States, black Americans developed a separate culture which
(60) reflects both their African and their American experience. The African culture, the retention of some parts of this culture in America, and the weight of the stepculture produced a new people.

18. In line 6, the author uses the word "shock" to

(A) express his abhorrence of mistreatment of African slaves by European-Americans
(B) indicate the intensity with which European-Americans rejected African customs
(C) suggest why Africans were unable to preserve many elements of their culture
(D) show how fundamentally African ethical principles differed from Western ideals
(E) emphasize the traumatic nature of the initial contact between European-Americans and Africans

19. In lines 20-26, the author contrasts the European-American and the African value systems in order to

(A) demonstrate that the two cultures were in different stages of historical development
(B) illustrate one obstacle to establishing an understanding between peoples with such fundamental cultural differences
(C) excuse the European-Americans for misinterpreting a culture that was so different from their own
(D) point out the differences between the African and the European-American concepts of human nature
(E) show how European-Americans used their religious beliefs as a justification for slavery

GO ON TO THE NEXT PAGE.

20. The passage contains information that helps to explain which of the following?

   I. The fact that blacks have developed an eclectic culture
   II. The nature of contemporary black family structure
   III. The retention of some elements of African culture by the black American

   (A) I only   (B) III only   (C) I and III only
   (D) II and III only   (E) I, II, and III

21. With which of the following statements about cultural development would the author be most likely to agree?

   (A) The spirit of culture can be suppressed by the consistently ruthless use of force.
   (B) Culture is the direct product of the individual's immediate environment.
   (C) Culture is the by-product of an economic class struggle.
   (D) Cultures develop through accretion from one generation to the next.
   (E) Religion is the foundation on which all cultural development rests.

22. Which of the following topics would the author be most likely to discuss in a book based on this passage?

   (A) The role of freed slaves in settling the American West
   (B) The influence of African oral tradition on black literature in America
   (C) Black American contributions to the legal interpretation of the Fourteenth Amendment
   (D) The policy of racial segregation practiced in South Africa
   (E) European colonization of Africa in the late nineteenth century

23. Which of the following assertions, if true, would most seriously weaken the author's argument that "black people throughout North America were culturally isolated from the start" (lines 1-3) ?

   (A) Africans had been enslaved in Africa even before they were brought to America.
   (B) African slaves were taken from many different tribes, each with its own distinct culture.
   (C) American slave owners allowed African slaves to practice their own religion without interference.
   (D) Black Americans exhibit more Western cultural traits than they do African cultural traits.
   (E) The African world view was not ethnocentric and could readily comprehend foreign cultural systems.

24. The passage would be most likely to appear in

   (A) a historical reassessment of the black American experience
   (B) an anthropological examination of African legal systems
   (C) a civil rights pamphlet advocating voter registration
   (D) a history of European colonization of America
   (E) a newspaper evaluation of current race relations

25. According to the passage, the transformation of African culture into black American culture was the result of the

   (A) inevitable processes of assimilation
   (B) suppression of African political traditions
   (C) operation of "canons of satisfaction"
   (D) clash between Christianity and polytheism
   (E) synthesis of two apparently incompatible cultures

S T O P

IF YOU FINISH BEFORE TIME IS CALLED, YOU MAY CHECK YOUR WORK ON THIS SECTION ONLY.
DO NOT WORK ON ANY OTHER SECTION IN THE TEST.

2   2   2   2   2   2   2   2   2   2   2

SECTION II

Time—30 minutes

20 Questions

Directions: In this section solve each problem, using any available space on the page for scratchwork. Then indicate the best answer in the appropriate space on the answer sheet.

Note: Figures which accompany problems in this test are intended to provide information useful in solving the problems. They are drawn as accurately as possible EXCEPT when it is stated in a specific problem that its figure is not drawn to scale. All figures lie in a plane unless otherwise indicated.

All numbers used are real numbers.

1. $\left(\dfrac{\frac{5}{6}}{\frac{3}{4}}\right)\left(\dfrac{\frac{4}{3}}{\frac{4}{3}}\right) =$

   (A) 0   (B) $\dfrac{9}{10}$ (C) 1   (D) $\dfrac{10}{9}$ (E) $\dfrac{5}{3}$

2. Which of the following could be the measures of the angles of one triangle?

   I. $70°$, $60°$, $80°$
   II. $30°$, $60°$, $90°$
   III. $50°$, $80°$, $20°$

   (A) I only   (B) II only   (C) III only

   (D) I and II only   (E) I, II, and III

3. At a college football game, a boy can sell news-papers containing the lineup or he can sell official programs, but he cannot do both on the same day. He earns 40 per cent commission on the news-papers, selling at 25 cents each, and 10 per cent commission by selling programs at 75 cents each. One Saturday he sold 400 newspapers; on the following Saturday he sold 200 programs. How much more did he earn by selling newspapers than by selling programs?

   (A) $15   (B) $25   (C) $30   (D) $35   (E) $40

4. A box that has inside dimensions 20 centimeters by 40 centimeters by 60 centimeters is to be partially filled with sand. If a bag contains sand that occupies 6,000 cubic centimeters of space, how many of these bags will be needed to fill the box $\frac{3}{4}$ full of sand?

   (A) 3   (B) 4   (C) 6   (D) 8   (E) 11

GO ON TO THE NEXT PAGE.

5. If $8 - 3x = y$, then $6 - 3x =$

(A) $\frac{3}{4}y$ (B) $2y$ (C) $y + 2$

(D) $y - 1$ (E) $y - 2$

6. The charge for a telephone call between cities A and B is \$2.05 for the first 3 minutes and then \$0.22 for each additional minute. What is the maximum number of minutes that a call between those cities can last with a charge less than \$8.00 ?

(A) 27   (B) 28   (C) 29   (D) 30   (E) 31

7. If $\dfrac{1}{x+y} = \dfrac{3}{2}$ and $x - y = \dfrac{2}{3}$, then $\dfrac{x-y}{x+y} =$

(A) $\dfrac{2}{9}$ (B) $\dfrac{4}{9}$ (C) 1   (D) $\dfrac{4}{3}$ (E) 2

8. Mr. Smith deposits \$3,000 in an account that pays 4 per cent interest per year, compounded semi-annually. How much money will there be in the account at the end of one year?

(A) \$3,061.20   (B) \$3,120.00   (C) \$3,121.20
(D) \$3,240.00   (E) \$3,244.80

9. $\dfrac{6^6}{(6 \cdot 5 \cdot 4 \cdot 3 \cdot 2 \cdot 1)^3}$ is

(A) less than 1
(B) equal to 1
(C) greater than 1 but less than 6
(D) equal to 6
(E) greater than 6

GO ON TO THE NEXT PAGE.

10. Ms. Ropke had her orchard of 40 trees equally divided in rows. An irrigation trench needed to be dug, and therefore 1 tree had to be transplanted from each row, causing her to make 2 new rows. How many trees were in each row before the change?

    (A) 3   (B) 4   (C) 5   (D) 8   (E) 10

11. Matt swam at a constant rate of 100 meters per 3-minute period and rested for 1 minute after every 200 meters. Carl swam at a constant rate of 50 meters per minute and rested for 1 minute after every 500 meters. If Matt and Carl began swimming at the same time, how many meters did Carl swim during the time it took Matt to swim 500 meters?

    (A) 750   (B) 800   (C) 850
    (D) 900   (E) 1,000

12. The * of any whole number is defined as the result obtained by subtracting that number from the square of the number. What number is the * of the * of 10 ?

    (A) 90   (B) 790   (C) 8010
    (D) 8090   (E) 8100

13. A woman pays $97 per quarter for personal medical insurance. Of her eligible medical expenses, she must pay the first $250 and the policy pays 80 per cent of the balance. Assuming all of her medical expenses of $750 for one year are eligible, what is the difference between the amount she pays for medical expenses and insurance for that year and the amount she would have had to pay for medical expenses if she had no insurance?

    (A) $12
    (B) $38
    (C) $112
    (D) $206
    (E) $350

GO ON TO THE NEXT PAGE.

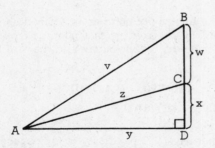

14. In the figure above, AC bisects ∠BAD of right triangle ABD. Which of the following is equal to $\dfrac{\text{area of } \triangle ABC}{\text{area of } \triangle ACD}$?

(A) $\dfrac{w+x}{x}$ (B) 1 (C) $\dfrac{z}{v}$ (D) $\dfrac{z}{y}$ (E) $\dfrac{w}{x}$

15. In the same amount of time, a new machine produces 7 times as many screws as does an old machine. If the new machine can produce n screws per minute, how many screws can both machines working together produce in 3 <u>hours</u>?

(A) $\dfrac{n+1}{7}$ (B) $\dfrac{8n}{7}$ (C) $\dfrac{24n}{7}$

(D) 480n (E) $\dfrac{1,440n}{7}$

16. If the numerator of a fraction is decreased by 50 per cent and the denominator is increased by 50 per cent, then the value of the resulting fraction reflects a decrease of what per cent of the original fraction?

(A) 25% (B) $33\frac{1}{3}$% (C) 50%

(D) $66\frac{2}{3}$% (E) 75%

GO ON TO THE NEXT PAGE.

17. Of 20 adults, 5 belong to club X, 7 belong to club Y, and 9 belong to club Z. If 2 belong to all three organizations and 3 belong to exactly two organizations, how many belong to none of these organizations?

(A) 2   (B) 3   (C) 4   (D) 5   (E) 6

18. In the Expo Corporation, 45 per cent of the employees are women. If 60 per cent of the employees are production workers and 30 per cent of these are women, what per cent of the nonproduction workers are women?

(A) 8.1%   (B) 27.0%   (C) 33.8%
(D) 67.5%   (E) 82.0%

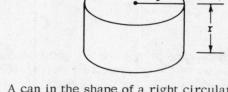

19. A can in the shape of a right circular cylinder has inside radius r and height r as indicated in the figure above. Two steel balls of radius $\frac{r}{2}$ are placed inside the can, and the can is then filled with liquid. In terms of r, what is the volume of the liquid in the can? $\left(\text{The volume of a sphere of radius x is } \frac{4}{3}\pi x^3.\right)$

(A) $\frac{\pi r^3}{3}$

(B) $\frac{2\pi r^3}{3}$

(C) $\frac{5\pi r^3}{6}$

(D) πr^3

(E) $\pi r^2 - \frac{8\pi r^3}{3}$

20. A history examination is made up of 3 sets of 5 questions each, and a student must select 3 questions from each set. How many different sets of 9 questions can the student select?

(A) 1,000   (B) 180   (C) 125   (D) 30   (E) 27

S T O P

IF YOU FINISH BEFORE TIME IS CALLED, YOU MAY CHECK YOUR WORK ON THIS TEST ONLY.
DO NOT WORK ON ANY OTHER TEST IN THIS BOOK.

SECTION III

Time—30 minutes

35 Questions

Directions: Each passage in this section is followed by questions that require you to classify certain of the facts presented in the passage on the basis of their importance, as illustrated in the following example:

SAMPLE PASSAGE

Fred North, a prospering hardware dealer in Hillidale, Connecticut, felt that he needed more store space to accommodate a new line of farm equipment and repair parts that he intended to carry. A number of New York City commuters had recently purchased tracts of land in the environs of Hillidale and there had taken up farming on a small scale. Mr. North, foreseeing a potential increase in farming in that area, wanted to expand his business to cater to this market. North felt that the most feasible and appealing recourse open to him would be to purchase the adjoining store property owned by Mike Johnson, who used the premises for his small grocery store. Johnson's business had been on the decline for over a year since the advent of a large supermarket in the town. North felt that Johnson would be willing to sell the property at reasonable terms, and this was important since North, after the purchase of the new merchandise, would have little capital available to invest in the expansion of his store.

The following questions consist of items related to the passage above. Consider each item separately in terms of the passage and on the answer sheet blacken space

A if the item is a Major Objective in making the decision; that is, one of the outcomes or results sought by the decision-maker;

B if the item is a Major Factor in making the decision; that is, a consideration, explicitly mentioned in the passage, that is basic in determining the decision;

C if the item is a Minor Factor in making the decision; that is, a secondary consideration that affects the criteria tangentially, relating to a Major Factor rather than to an Objective;

D if the item is a Major Assumption in making the decision; that is, a supposition or projection made by the decision-maker before weighing the variables;

E if the item is an Unimportant Issue in making the decision; that is, a factor that is insignificant or not immediately relevant to the situation.

SAMPLE QUESTIONS

1. Increase in farming in the Hillidale area   Ⓐ Ⓑ Ⓒ ● Ⓔ

2. Acquisition of property for expanding store   ● Ⓑ Ⓒ Ⓓ Ⓔ

3. Cost of Johnson's property   Ⓐ ● Ⓒ Ⓓ Ⓔ

4. State of Johnson's grocery business   Ⓐ Ⓑ ● Ⓓ Ⓔ

5. Quality of the farm equipment North intends to sell   Ⓐ Ⓑ Ⓒ Ⓓ ●

GO ON TO THE NEXT PAGE.

The correct designation for number 1 is (D), a <u>Major Assumption</u>, since North bases his whole expansion project on his supposition that the new commuter-farmers in the Hillidale area are indicative of a trend in that direction. Number 2 is (A), a <u>Major Objective</u>, inasmuch as North's immediate purpose is to obtain room for expansion. (B), a <u>Major Factor</u>, is the correct answer for number 3 because North's present lack of capital renders cost a vital consideration. The best classification of number 4 is (C), a <u>Minor Factor</u>, because the depreciating value of Johnson's business influences his willingness to sell and also the price he will demand for his property; thus, this factor pertains to 3, the cost of Johnson's property, and is an indirect consideration in the case. Number 5, finally, is (E), an <u>Unimportant Issue</u>, for the quality of North's goods has no relevance to the situation at hand; i.e., the desire for room to expand his business.

NOW READ THE PASSAGES AND ANSWER THE QUESTIONS FOLLOWING THEM.

GO ON TO THE NEXT PAGE.

High Top Cola Company is a large soft-drink manu-facturer. It has a twenty per cent share of the United States market, and its $2 billion revenues and eleven per cent net earnings on sales last year set the pace for the entire industry. The company's own demo-graphic studies, however, project a sharp decline in the potential consumer market within the next ten years, principally because of a decrease in the number of people in the United States between the ages of eighteen and thirty-four. To consider ways of con-tinuing to increase corporate profits and, at the same time, of becoming less dependent on their present product, the company's board of directors agreed to follow a proposal by chairman James Healy that the company diversify by selling wines. The board felt that High Top's lack of expertise in wine production ruled out any effort to construct and run an entirely new operation and so the company decided to purchase an established winery in central California. Healy believed that the company's sophisticated market research and advertising departments could make an almost immediate impact on the California wine industry, which has been traditionally more concerned with producing a quality product rather than with marketing it. Thus, the board met to consider which of several wineries being evaluated should be pur-chased. High Top's researchers studied three wineries, one that produced high-priced wines, one with a medium-priced product, and one known for its low-priced wines. The board hoped that one of these would provide a suitable base from which High Top could expand over the next ten years into various areas of the national wine market.

Before making a final decision, the board wanted to consider the prospective purchase price and the cost of expansion for each winery. Healy also had reports assembled about such crucial matters as the wineries' brand-name recognition, competition from other wines, potential markets, distributorship systems, management efficiency, and labor relations. The board believed that High Top could take over management of any winery smoothly with only a minimum of cooperation from the present owners. Finally, although costs of renovation would ordinarily be a point of concern, the three wineries under con-sideration were in remarkably good repair, so renovation was not an issue.

In the high-priced category, the board considered the Mazutti brothers' winery. Mazutti wines sold to a relatively small group of customers and faced no real competition. Instead of developing a large distributing system, the brothers preferred to produce only a small quantity of their wines and to market them within California. Even so, the Mazutti label always placed high in brand-name recognition surveys despite the product's general scarcity. In spite of its small size, the winery's sales and profits last year were quite high—$6 million profit before taxes on sales totaling $35 million. Plant management, unfortunately, was not accustomed to high-volume production schedules and was considered somewhat lackadaisical with respect to general corporate standards even though labor relations with the workers were excellent.

The purchase price for Mazutti would probably be $50 million, but to produce on the scale High Top had in mind, a $20-million expansion program would be re-quired immediately, with later expansion projects a virtual necessity. Most important, Healy feared that marketing cheaper wines under the Mazutti name might damage the company's reputation and eliminate its traditional customers without appealing sufficiently to other groups. Such fears are common in the California wine country.

Second to be considered was the Shield Winery, which produced a wide variety of medium-priced wines and marketed them under seven different labels. The winery's sales last year reached $100 million; this impressive statistic was attributable to a large dis-tributorship system extending throughout the United States and an efficient managerial staff capable of overseeing the production of so many varieties of wine. Shield's complex production arrangement required a large plant and extensive equipment that often went unused. The High Top Company hoped to put these features to better use and spend only $5 mil-lion on expansion.

In other respects the Shield Winery was unattrac-tive. Its different labels resulted in poor brand-name recognition; and the company was not among the nation's top 15 winemakers. Advertising in this competitive price range of the market was, therefore, expensive and frequently unsuccessful. Labor rela-tions were another source of concern. Although labor relations with the 500 plant employees were favorable, farm workers under contract to the company were dissatisfied with their contract and threatened to include Shield in a general boycott.

The final winery on the list was in many ways the most successful. The Triano Winery reported $300 million in sales last year and a $40-million profit before taxes. Triano wines placed second in name-recognition surveys and were produced under the supervision of an efficient managerial staff in a plant large enough to produce even the increased volume of wine that the High Top Company's plans would eventually call for. The winery had a superb distribution system. Competition in this low-price range came mostly from the Phoenix Wine Company, but Triano had a firm enough hold in the market to provide a secure base for future expansion and production of better wines. Thus the company's present reputation as a producer of low-grade wine would not be a liability in the long run. The price of the winery was likely to be $220 million.

After considering these companies carefully, Healy instructed the board to make initial offers to all three companies. After seeing how those offers were received, Healy and the board would know better how to proceed with their plans for diversi-fication.

GO ON TO THE NEXT PAGE.

Directions: The following questions consist of items related to the passage above. You may refer back to the passage and the directions. Consider each item separately in terms of the passage and on the answer sheet blacken space

    A if the item is a <u>Major Objective</u> in making the decision; that is, one of the outcomes or results sought by the decision-maker;

    B if the item is a <u>Major Factor</u> in making the decision; that is, a consideration, explicitly mentioned in the passage, <u>that is basic</u> in determining the decision;

    C if the item is a <u>Minor Factor</u> in making the decision; that is, a secondary consideration that affects the criteria tangentially, <u>relating to a Major Factor</u> rather than to an Objective;

    D if the item is a <u>Major Assumption</u> in making the decision; that is, a supposition or projection made by the <u>decision-maker before weighing</u> the variables;

    E if the item is an <u>Unimportant Issue</u> in making the decision; that is, a factor that is insignificant or not immediately <u>relevant to the situation</u>.

1. Amount of competition that can be expected in marketing wine made by a winery under consideration

2. Qualification of the High Top Cola Company to manage an established winery successfully

3. Expanding into the kinds of operations from which the High Top Cola Company can derive profits

4. High Top Cola Company's eleven per cent net earnings on sales last year

5. Ongoing demand for wine over the next ten years

6. State of labor relations at a winery under consideration for acquisition

7. Lack of competitors in the market served by the Mazutti winery

8. Brand-name recognition of wineries under consideration for acquisition

9. Predisposition of the present owners of each winery under consideration to sell to High Top

10. Greater profits for High Top Cola Company

11. Cost of renovating present winery facilities

12. Mazutti's small distributorship system

13. Acquisition of a California winery that can be modified to suit High Top Cola's future plans

14. Mazutti's widely recognized brand name

15. Potential of wineries for expansion over the next ten years

16. Efficiency of the management of the wineries under consideration

17. Efficiency of High Top Cola's distributing system for soft drinks

18. An adequate supply of crops for producing a profitable quantity of wine at any winery being evaluated

GO ON TO THE NEXT PAGE.

3   **3**   **3**   **3**   **3**   **3**   **3**   **3**   **3**   **3**

Myrna Uribe, a rock-and-roll singer of Haitian descent, became quite popular in the United States while recording albums for Polydisc, a major record company located on the East Coast. Polydisc had gone to great lengths to promote Uribe's career; the company had booked her on television specials, had financed concert tours, and had hired excellent musicians to perform with Uribe during her tours. When Uribe decided to stop touring, however, she and Polydisc began to have serious disagreements. Uribe wanted to stop touring completely; Polydisc insisted that she go on one major tour a year. Another source of Uribe's unhappiness with Polydisc was that the company would not allow her to record Haitian folk songs; although Uribe was now interested in folk songs produced "purely," that is accompanied only by traditional stringed instruments, Polydisc demanded that she continue to record commercially oriented rock-and-roll songs, songs produced with complicated remixing and overdubbing and involving a variety of different instruments. As Uribe's interest in Haitian folk songs increased, moreover, she had learned a great deal about Haitian history and art, and she wanted to appear more often in a series of programs about that subject produced by an educational television station. Polydisc did not want her to appear on television without its consent and it wanted to allow her to appear only on specific programs.

As the expiration date of her contract neared, Uribe began to consider leaving Polydisc in order to start her own record company, or "label" as it is called in the business. The idea of starting her own label appealed to Uribe because she believed that forming her own company would allow her control over her own material and the freedom to design her own album covers. Uribe wanted to design her own album covers because she had become interested in Haitian pictorial art, which she occasionally taught on the television program.

Uribe soon discovered, however, that starting her own company required a larger investment than she could afford. Although she had made money during her career and felt that she could live comfortably, Uribe had already invested most of that money in a farm on the East Coast and in the educational television program. Another rock-and-roll singer, David Power, also was interested in starting his own record company, and so he approached Uribe and suggested that the two singers form a new label together. Within the industry Power was known as a temperamental and emotional performer, but he readily agreed that Uribe should have complete control over the selection of her own material and the production of her albums. Because of the cost involved, however, Power did insist on contracting the distribution of their albums out to a larger, more established record company. Power's proposal interested Uribe, but she was not comfortable with the idea of giving some other company control over the distribution of her albums because that company would then have de facto control over both the cover design and the amount of money spent on promotion. Uribe believed that a record company could control the kind of material a singer recorded simply by refusing to promote any record that was not thought to have commercial appeal; Uribe also believed that no large record company would allow her to record Haitian folk songs in the manner she wanted.

The next person to contact Uribe was Robin Vance, an accountant for Haven Records and one of Uribe's closest friends. Haven Records was a small company that specialized in rhythm and blues music. Vance assured Uribe, however, that Haven now wanted to record artists who performed different kinds of material. Vance pointed out that Haven would not require Uribe to record a fixed number of albums each year, and this appealed to Uribe since one of her disagreements with Polydisc had been over the stipulation that she release at least one new album each year. Vance also said that she thought Uribe could gain complete control over her music only if she were initially willing to settle for a small percentage of the gross profit on each of the first five albums she recorded for Haven. If those albums made money, Uribe and Vance agreed, then the singer would be in a position to renegotiate for a better contract. Vance finally reminded Uribe that Haven was based on the West Coast, close to the newest and most sophisticated studios and production equipment in the country. Haven would also encourage Uribe's interest in Haitian art by allowing her to design her own albums, and by employing her as a creative consultant on the design of all of the company's album covers.

Reports of Uribe's dissatisfaction eventually found their way back to the management of Polydisc. Anxious not to lose one of their most popular artists, Polydisc offered Uribe absolute control over the design of her album covers, limited control over the selection of her material, and a larger percentage of the gross from each new album she recorded for them; they also agreed to forgo the stipulation that she record at least one new album per year. Polydisc, however, would not surrender any of its control over promotion and distribution.

Uribe did prefer Polydisc's location on the East Coast since it was close both to her new farm and to the station that filmed and showed the series of programs about the history and the art of Haiti. But there were still problems to be solved, such as Polydisc's requirement that she continue to tour and its attitude toward her appearances on television. Haven, while preferring that Uribe tour, would not demand that she do so. Time spent commuting to the West Coast, she feared, would be time taken away from the educational series. Uribe decided to go into seclusion for several weeks and reconsider each alternative.

GO ON TO THE NEXT PAGE.

3 3 3 3 3 3 3 3 3 3

Directions: The following questions consist of items related to the passage above. You may refer back to the passage and the directions. Consider each item separately in terms of the passage and on the answer sheet blacken space

A if the item is a Major Objective in making the decision; that is, one of the outcomes or results sought by the decision-maker;

B if the item is a Major Factor in making the decision; that is, a consideration, explicitly mentioned in the passage, that is basic in determining the decision;

C if the item is a Minor Factor in making the decision; that is, a secondary consideration that affects the criteria tangentially, relating to a Major Factor rather than to an Objective;

D if the item is a Major Assumption in making the decision; that is, a supposition or projection made by the decision-maker before weighing the variables;

E if the item is an Unimportant Issue in making the decision; that is, a factor that is insignificant or not immediately relevant to the situation.

19. Requirements for touring made by each of the companies

20. Freedom to design her own album covers

21. Aversion of large record companies to promoting Haitian folk songs

22. Power's personal preference for rock-and-roll music

23. Polydisc's willingness to hire the best musicians to back Uribe on her tours

24. Haven's unwillingness to pay Uribe a large share of the gross profit

25. The educational television station's continued willingness to produce the series about Haitian history and art

26. Ability to choose whether or not to record rock-and-roll songs

27. Degree to which the possible options would allow Uribe to participate in the design of her own album covers

28. Friendship between Uribe and Vance

29. Existence of an audience for Haitian folk songs

30. Small percentage of the gross profits that Haven would pay on the first five albums

31. Recording songs that do not necessarily have commercial appeal

32. Uribe's ability to continue a successful career without touring

33. Expense incurred if a new company started by Uribe distributes its own record albums

34. Adverse effect that singing Haitian music poses to Uribe's popularity

35. Control over the material Uribe will record

S T O P
IF YOU FINISH BEFORE TIME IS CALLED, YOU MAY CHECK YOUR WORK ON THIS SECTION ONLY.
DO NOT WORK ON ANY OTHER SECTION IN THE TEST.

SECTION IV

Time—30 minutes

25 Questions

<u>Directions:</u> Each of the data sufficiency problems below consists of a question and two statements, labeled (1) and (2), in which certain data are given. You have to decide whether the data given in the statements are <u>sufficient</u> for answering the question. Using the data given in the statements <u>plus</u> your knowledge of mathematics and everyday facts (such as the number of days in July or the meaning of <u>counterclockwise</u>), you are to blacken space

> A if statement (1) ALONE is sufficient, but statement (2) alone is not sufficient to answer the question asked;
> B if statement (2) ALONE is sufficient, but statement (1) alone is not sufficient to answer the question asked;
> C if BOTH statements (1) and (2) TOGETHER are sufficient to answer the question asked, but NEITHER statement ALONE is sufficient;
> D if EACH statement ALONE is sufficient to answer the question asked;
> E if statements (1) and (2) TOGETHER are NOT sufficient to answer the question asked, and additional data specific to the problem are needed.

<u>Note:</u> A figure in a data sufficiency problem will conform to the information given in the question, but will not necessarily conform to the additional information given in statements (1) and (2).

Example:

In $\triangle PQR$, what is the value of x ?

(1) PQ = PR

(2) y = 40

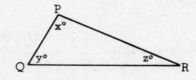

Explanation: According to statement (1), PQ = PR; therefore, $\triangle PQR$ is isosceles and y = z. Since $x + y + z = 180$, $x + 2y = 180$. Since statement (1) does not give a value for y, you cannot answer the question using statement (1) by itself. According to statement (2), y = 40; therefore, $x + z = 140$. Since statement (2) does not give a value for z, you cannot answer the question using statement (2) by itself. Using both statements together you can find y and z; therefore, you can find x, and the answer to the problem is C.

All numbers used are real numbers.

1. Which of two employees, Ms. Carter and Ms. Lewis, receives the greater amount of bonus money?

 (1) Ms. Carter receives a bonus of 10 per cent of her annual salary.

 (2) Ms. Lewis receives a bonus of 5 per cent of her annual salary.

2. How much does X cost?

 (1) X costs $\frac{1}{8}$ of one per cent of the selling price of Y, and the selling price of Y is $14\frac{2}{7}$ per cent of $565,600.

 (2) X costs $\frac{1}{800}$ of the selling price of Y.

3. What is the area of $\triangle ABC$?

 (1) AB = 3 and AC = 5.

 (2) $\angle ABC$ is a right angle.

GO ON TO THE NEXT PAGE.

A Statement (1) ALONE is sufficient, but statement (2) alone is not sufficient.
B Statement (2) ALONE is sufficient, but statement (1) alone is not sufficient.
C BOTH statements TOGETHER are sufficient, but NEITHER statement ALONE is sufficient.
D EACH statement ALONE is sufficient.
E Statements (1) and (2) TOGETHER are NOT sufficient.

4. At what price did a jeweler sell a certain bracelet?

   (1) The jeweler purchased 50 of the bracelets, at the same price, for a total of $800 and sold each of them with a 150 per cent markup.

   (2) The jeweler's net profit after expenses was $20 on each of the bracelets.

5. Is the product of two given numbers greater than 50 ?

   (1) The sum of the two numbers is greater than 25.

   (2) Each of the numbers is greater than 20.

6. In a certain factory, all production workers work independently. How many regular production workers working 8 hours each manufacture the same number of items that 24 apprentice production workers manufacture working 8 hours each?

   (1) It takes each apprentice production worker 50 per cent longer than it takes each regular production worker to manufacture the same number of items.

   (2) The 24 apprentice production workers manufacture a total of 96 items per hour.

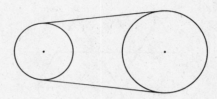

7. What is the diameter of the smaller pulley wheel shown in the figure above?

   (1) The pulley belt is $7\frac{1}{2}$ feet long.

   (2) The larger pulley wheel turns at a rate of 100 revolutions per minute.

8. Has Brand X been purchased by more than 50 per cent of the 5,000 people in Baytown?

   (1) Brand Y has been purchased by 75 per cent of the people in Baytown.

   (2) Brand X has been purchased by exactly 2,200 people in Baytown.

GO ON TO THE NEXT PAGE.

A Statement (1) ALONE is sufficient, but statement (2) alone is not sufficient.
B Statement (2) ALONE is sufficient, but statement (1) alone is not sufficient.
C BOTH statements TOGETHER are sufficient, but NEITHER statement ALONE is sufficient.
D EACH statement ALONE is sufficient.
E Statements (1) and (2) TOGETHER are NOT sufficient.

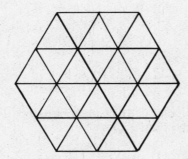

9. The window shown above consists of 24 equilateral triangular panes of glass, all of the same size, fitted together to make one solid glass window. What is the area of the window?

(1) The perimeter of each triangular pane is 6 feet.

(2) The perimeter of the window is 24 feet.

10. A traveler on a highway passes through towns R, S, T, and W, but not necessarily in that order. How long does it take to travel from R to W?

(1) S is 5 kilometers from R and 10 kilometers from T, but W is 20 kilometers from S.

(2) The traveler averages 2.5 kilometers per hour on the trip from R to W.

11. Is x greater than y?

(1) $xy - 7 = 3$

(2) $\frac{2}{x} = \frac{y}{5}$

12. Jim is going to a concert. Is George going to the concert?

(1) If George goes to a concert, then Jim will go to the concert.

(2) If George does not go to a concert, then Jim will not go to the concert.

13. A 20-meter cord is cut into three pieces, X, Y, and Z. How long is Z?

(1) X is 3 meters longer than Y.

(2) X is twice as long as Y.

14. Marvin put 51 cents worth of stamps on a package he mailed. How many 15-cent stamps did he use on the package?

(1) Marvin used only 15-cent and 6-cent stamps on the package.

(2) Marvin used more than one 15-cent stamp on the package.

15. What is the value of $x^4 - y^4$?

(1) $x^2 + y^2 = 100$
(2) $x^2 - y^2 = 0$

GO ON TO THE NEXT PAGE.

A Statement (1) ALONE is sufficient, but statement (2) alone is not sufficient.
B Statement (2) ALONE is sufficient, but statement (1) alone is not sufficient.
C BOTH statements TOGETHER are sufficient, but NEITHER statement ALONE is sufficient.
D EACH statement ALONE is sufficient.
E Statements (1) and (2) TOGETHER are NOT sufficient.

16. In 1978 the Walker family spent $600 to buy heating oil. How much did the family spend to buy heating oil in 1979 ?

  (1) In 1979 the average price per gallon of the heating oil bought by the Walkers increased 40 per cent over the price they paid in 1978.

  (2) In 1979 the amount of heating oil bought by the Walkers decreased 10 per cent below the amount they bought in 1978.

17. If $y > x > 0$, what per cent of x is y ?

  (1) The average of a, b, c, d, and e is x.

  (2) The sum of a, b, c, d, and e is y.

18. Is $\frac{p}{3}$ an integer?

  (1) $\frac{p}{363,636}$ is an integer.

  (2) $\frac{p}{256}$ is an integer.

19. What is the volume of a right circular cylinder with a diameter of 10 ?

  (1) The total surface area of the cylinder, including top and bottom, is 200π.

  (2) The surface area, excluding top and bottom, is 150π.

20. Is x a positive number?

  (1) $3x - 9 < 0$

  (2) $3x + 3 > 0$

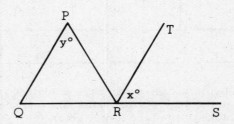

21. In the figure above, if RT ‖ QP and QRS is a straight line, is $x = y$?

  (1) RT bisects ∠PRS

  (2) PQ = PR

22. Ms. Clark invested $30,000 for one year. Part of the $30,000 was invested at 4 per cent simple interest and the remainder was invested at 6 per cent simple interest. How much was invested at 6 per cent?

  (1) The total interest earned on the $30,000 for the year was $1,600.

  (2) The amount Ms. Clark invested at 6 per cent was twice the amount she invested at 4 per cent.

GO ON TO THE NEXT PAGE.

A Statement (1) ALONE is sufficient, but statement (2) alone is not sufficient.
B Statement (2) ALONE is sufficient, but statement (1) alone is not sufficient.
C BOTH statements TOGETHER are sufficient, but NEITHER statement ALONE is sufficient.
D EACH statement ALONE is sufficient.
E Statements (1) and (2) TOGETHER are NOT sufficient.

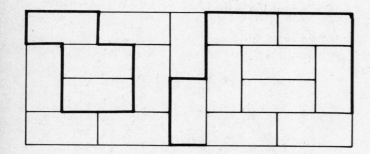

23. In the figure above, a rectangle is divided into smaller rectangles of the same size and shape. What is the area of the large rectangle?

   (1) The length of the darkened path on the left is 48.

   (2) The length of the darkened path on the right is 52.

24. Does $(x + y)^2 - (x - y)^2$ equal 120 ?

   (1) $xy = 30$

   (2) $x = 5$ and $y = 6$

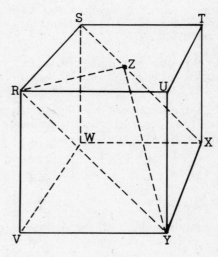

25. If the figure above is a cube, what is the area of $\triangle RYZ$?

   (1) $VY = 10$

   (2) Z is the midpoint of SX.

S T O P

IF YOU FINISH BEFORE TIME IS CALLED, YOU MAY CHECK YOUR WORK ON THIS SECTION ONLY.
DO NOT WORK ON ANY OTHER SECTION IN THE TEST.

SECTION V

Time—30 minutes

25 Questions

Directions: In each of the following sentences, some part of the sentence or the entire sentence is underlined. Beneath each sentence you will find five ways of phrasing the underlined part. The first of these repeats the original; the other four are different. If you think the original is better than any of the alternatives, choose answer A; otherwise choose one of the others. Select the best version and blacken the corresponding space on your answer sheet.

This is a test of correctness and effectiveness of expression. In choosing answers, follow the requirements of standard written English; that is, pay attention to grammar, choice of words, and sentence construction. Choose the answer that produces the most effective sentence—clear and exact, without awkwardness or ambiguity. Do not make a choice that changes the meaning of the original sentence.

1. The large population and impressive cultural achievements of the Aztecs, the Maya, and the Incas could not have come about without corn, which not only <u>is nutritious and also can be</u> dried, transported, and stored for long periods.

    (A) is nutritious and also can be
    (B) is nutritional and also could be
    (C) was nutritious but also could be
    (D) was nutritious but was
    (E) was nutritional and also can be

2. After the Civil War Harriet Tubman, herself an escaped slave, continued her efforts in behalf of former slaves, helping to educate freedmen, supporting children, and <u>she was assisting impoverished old people.</u>

    (A) she was assisting impoverished old people
    (B) impoverished old people were assisted
    (C) to assist impoverished old people
    (D) assisting impoverished old people
    (E) also in assisting impoverished old people

3. <u>Interest rates will likely increase if</u> the Federal Reserve Bank fails to reexamine its policies.

    (A) Interest rates will likely increase if
    (B) Interest rates are likely to increase if
    (C) Interest rates should be likely to increase if
    (D) The rate of interest will likely increase unless
    (E) Rates of interest will likely increase unless

4. Unlike the <u>Second World War, when long voyages home aboard troopships gave soldiers</u> a chance to talk out their experiences and begin to absorb them, Vietnam returnees often came home by jet, singly or in small groups.

    (A) Second World War, when long voyages home aboard troopships gave soldiers
    (B) soldier coming home after the Second World War on long voyages aboard troopships who had
    (C) soldiers of the Second World War, whose long voyage home aboard a troopship gave him
    (D) troopships on long voyages home after the Second World War which gave the soldier
    (E) soldiers of the Second World War, whose long voyages home aboard troopships gave them

5. In the nineteenth century, <u>five Presidents were refused a second nomination</u>—John Tyler, Millard Fillmore, Franklin Pierce, Andrew Johnson, and Chester A. Arthur.

    (A) In the nineteenth century, five Presidents were refused a second nomination
    (B) A second nomination was refused five Presidents in the nineteenth century
    (C) A second nomination had been refused to five Presidents in the nineteenth century
    (D) Five Presidents were, in the nineteenth century, refused a second nomination
    (E) Five Presidents had been, in the nineteenth century, refused a second nomination

GO ON TO THE NEXT PAGE.

6. In August 1883, Krakatoa erupted and sent clouds of dust, ash, and sulphate to a height of 50 miles, blotted out the sun for more than two days within a 50-mile radius and for nearly a day at an observation post 130 miles away.

   (A) blotted out the sun for more than two days within
   (B) blotting out the sun for more than two days within
   (C) the sun being blotted out for more than two days in
   (D) having blotted out the sun for more than two days in
   (E) for more than two days blotting out the sun within

7. Button believes that the reason the riots of the 1960's were politically successful was because they occurred at a time when public authorities, particularly the federal government, had the ability and resources to cope with grievances and because of widespread sympathy for the civil rights movement.

   (A) reason the riots of the 1960's were politically successful was because they occurred at a time when
   (B) reason why the riots of the 1960's were politically successful was because they occurred at a time that
   (C) reason for the political success of the riots of the 1960's was they occurred at a time that
   (D) riots of the 1960's were politically successful because they occurred at a time when
   (E) riots of the 1960's were politically successful because of occurring when

8. There may be more than a dozen boat parties in the Grand Canyon on a given day between May and October, each party positioned such that one seldom encounters the other.

   (A) such that one seldom encounters the other
   (B) such that there are few encounters one with another
   (C) in such ways as not to encounter others
   (D) so as not to encounter the other
   (E) so that one seldom encounters another

9. Government now supplies about a third to a half of the spending power in nearly all capitalist nations and supplies well over fifty per cent in some, like the Swedish.

   (A) like the Swedish
   (B) like that of Sweden
   (C) as in Sweden
   (D) such as Swedish
   (E) as is Sweden

10. Aging is a property of all animals that reach a fixed size at maturity, and the variations in life spans among different species are far greater as that among individuals from the same species: a fruit fly is ancient at 40 days, a mouse at 3 years, a horse at 30, a man at 100, and some tortoises at 150.

    (A) among different species are far greater as that among individuals from
    (B) among different species are far greater than that among individuals from
    (C) among different species are far greater than those among individuals of
    (D) between different species are far more than that between individuals of
    (E) between different species are greater by far than is that between individuals from

11. Broca demonstrated that whereas damage to a particular area of the left side of the brain leads to aphasia, similar damage to the right side leaves the faculty of speech intact.

    (A) similar damage to the right side leaves the faculty of speech intact
    (B) similarly, damage on the right side leaves intact the faculty of speech
    (C) the faculty of speech remains intact if there is similar damage on the right side
    (D) if the faculty of speech remains intact, there is similar damage to the right side
    (E) if there is similar damage on the right side, the faculty of speech is left intact

GO ON TO THE NEXT PAGE.

12. The strength of a chess master lies not in his ability to examine hundreds of possible moves <u>but rather in their ability to recognize patterns and to recall instantly similar positions they have played themselves or have</u> seen others play.

(A) but rather in their ability to recognize patterns and to recall instantly similar positions they have played themselves or have
(B) and rather in an ability to recognize patterns and recall instantly similar positions they have played themselves or
(C) but in an ability to recognize patterns and to recall instantly similar positions they have played themselves or have
(D) but in his ability to recognize patterns and to recall instantly similar positions he has himself played or has
(E) but rather his ability in recognizing patterns and recalling instantly similar positions he has himself played or has

13. <u>For all his professed disdain of such activities,</u> Auden was an inveterate literary gossip.

(A) For all his professed disdain of such activities,
(B) Having always professed disdain for such activities,
(C) All such activities were, he professed, disdained, and
(D) Professing that all such activities were disdained,
(E) In spite of professions of disdaining all such activities,

14. The fear of rabies is well founded; <u>few people are known to recover from the disease after the appearance of the clinical symptoms.</u>

(A) few people are known to recover from the disease after the appearance of the clinical symptoms
(B) few people are known to have recovered from the disease once the clinical symptoms have appeared
(C) there are few known people who have recovered from the disease once the clinical symptoms have appeared
(D) after the clinical symptoms appear, there are few known people who have recovered from the disease
(E) recovery from the disease is known for only a few people after the clinical symptoms appear

15. In order to conserve foreign exchange, the government requires <u>that a fee will be deposited by local importers with the central bank for six months ranging</u> from forty to fifty per cent of the value of an imported item.

(A) that a fee will be deposited by local importers with the central bank for six months ranging
(B) that local importers would deposit with the central bank for six months a fee ranging
(C) local importers to deposit with the central bank for six months a fee ranging
(D) from local importers a fee deposit for six months with the central bank of
(E) of local importers that they must deposit with the central bank for six months a fee which ranges

16. <u>In 1925 she won a scholarship to study anthropology under Franz Boas at Barnard, and</u> Zora Neale Hurston was the only black student in the entire college.

(A) In 1925 she won a scholarship to study anthropology under Franz Boas at Barnard, and
(B) For studying anthropology under Franz Boas at Barnard she won a scholarship in 1925, and
(C) Winning, in 1925, a scholarship for studying anthropology under Franz Boas at Barnard,
(D) When she had won a scholarship in 1925 for studying anthropology under Franz Boas at Barnard
(E) In 1925 when she won a scholarship to study anthropology under Franz Boas at Barnard,

17. There has been some speculation that the severed engine of the airplane might have struck the tail, but investigators <u>will withhold judgment until they examined further the engine's strike marks and its cause.</u>

(A) will withhold judgment until they examined further the engine's strike marks and its cause
(B) will withhold judgment until they have further examined the strike marks on the engine and their cause
(C) will withhold judgment until they have further examined the cause for the strike marks and the engine
(D) have withheld judgment while there was a further examination of the strike marks on the engine and its cause
(E) have withheld judgment until further examination of the engine, the strike marks, and the cause

GO ON TO THE NEXT PAGE.

18. Donaldson's study demonstrates that the presumed inability of children aged five for reasoning deductively result from the phrasing of the questions put to them being inadequate.

(A) for reasoning deductively result from the phrasing of the questions put to them being inadequate

(B) in deductive reasoning results from the phrasing of the questions put to them being inadequate

(C) to reason deductively results from the phrasing of the questions put to them being inadequate

(D) to reason deductively is a result of the questions put to them being phrased inadequately

(E) to reason deductively results from the inadequate phrasing of the questions put to them

19. High in the sky, soaring over the foothills that on hot, dry days look like brushed brown suede, the condor attains a majesty that is rare among birds in flight.

(A) High in the sky, soaring over the foothills that on hot, dry days look like brushed brown suede, the condor attains a majesty that is rare among birds in flight.

(B) The condor, being high in the sky and soaring over foothills that on hot, dry days look like brushed brown suede, attains a majesty that is rare among birds in flight.

(C) The condor, when it is high in the sky and soars over the foothills that on hot, dry days look like brushed brown suede, attains a majesty that is rare among birds in flight.

(D) On hot, dry days, when the foothills look like brushed brown suede and the condor, high in the sky, soars over them, it attains a majesty that is rare among birds in flight.

(E) Attaining a majesty that is rare among birds in flight, high in the sky, the condor soars over foothills that look like brushed brown suede on hot, dry days.

20. Child prodigies are marked not so much by their skills but instead by the fact that these skills are fully developed at a very early age.

(A) but instead
(B) rather than
(C) than
(D) as
(E) so much as

21. The department defines a private passenger vehicle as one registered to an individual with a gross weight of less than 8,000 pounds.

(A) as one registered to an individual with a gross weight of less than 8,000 pounds

(B) to be one that is registered to an individual with a gross weight of less than 8,000 pounds

(C) as one that is registered to an individual and that has a gross weight of less than 8,000 pounds

(D) to have a gross weight less than 8,000 pounds and being registered to an individual

(E) as having a gross weight of less than 8,000 pounds and registered to an individual

22. By definition, making a map is to select certain features as relevant and ignore others.

(A) By definition, making a map is
(B) To make a map is, by definition,
(C) Mapmaking is defined as
(D) The mapmaking process involves, by definition,
(E) In making a map, the definition is

GO ON TO THE NEXT PAGE.

23. A majority of the international journalists surveyed view nuclear power stations as unsafe at present but <u>that they will, or could,</u> be made sufficiently safe in the future.

    (A) that they will, or could,
    (B) that they would, or could,
    (C) they will be or could
    (D) think that they will be or could
    (E) think the power stations would or could

24. Acid rain and snow result from the chemical reactions between industrial emissions of sulfur dioxide and nitrogen oxides <u>with atmospheric water vapor to produce highly corrosive sulfuric and nitric acids.</u>

    (A) with atmospheric water vapor to produce highly corrosive sulfuric and nitric acids
    (B) with atmospheric water vapor producing highly corrosive sulfuric and nitric acids
    (C) and atmospheric water vapor which has produced highly corrosive sulfuric and nitric acids
    (D) and atmospheric water vapor which have produced sulfuric and nitric acids which are highly corrosive
    (E) and atmospheric water vapor to produce highly corrosive sulfuric and nitric acids

25. The herbicide Oryzalin was still being produced in 1979, three years after the wives of workers producing the chemical in Rensselaer, New York, were found <u>to have borne children with heart defects or miscarriages, and none of their pregnancies was normal.</u>

    (A) to have borne children with heart defects or miscarriages, and none of their pregnancies was
    (B) to have had children born with heart defects or miscarriages, and none of the pregnancies was
    (C) either to have had children with heart defects or miscarriages, without any of their pregnancies being
    (D) either to have had miscarriages or to have borne children with heart defects; none of the pregnancies was
    (E) either to have had miscarriages or children born with heart defects, without any of their pregnancies being

S T O P

IF YOU FINISH BEFORE TIME IS CALLED, YOU MAY CHECK YOUR WORK ON THIS SECTION ONLY.
DO NOT WORK ON ANY OTHER SECTION IN THE TEST.

SECTION VI

Time—30 minutes

20 Questions

Directions: In this section solve each problem, using any available space on the page for scratchwork. Then indicate the best answer in the appropriate space on the answer sheet.

Note: Figures which accompany problems in this test are intended to provide information useful in solving the problems. They are drawn as accurately as possible EXCEPT when it is stated in a specific problem that its figure is not drawn to scale. All figures lie in a plane unless otherwise indicated.

All numbers used are real numbers.

1. $0.6 \times 0.002 =$

(A) 0.00012   (B) 0.0012   (C) 0.012

(D) 0.12   (E) 1.2

2. While out of town, a salesperson regularly called the home office to check in. Each of these calls cost 50 cents plus 10 per cent tax. If during one month, 45 such calls were made, what was the total cost of these calls?

(A) $22.50   (B) $24.75   (C) $27.50

(D) $44.75   (E) $49.50

3. Of the following, which is closest to 1 ?

(A) $\dfrac{1}{1 + (0.05)^2}$

(B) $\dfrac{1}{(1 + 0.05)^2}$

(C) $\dfrac{1}{1 + (0.5)^2}$

(D) $\dfrac{1}{(1 + 0.5)^2}$

(E) $\left(\dfrac{1}{1 + 0.5} \right)^2$

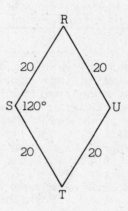

4. In the figure above, what is the distance between S and U ?

(A) 18   (B) 20   (C) 22   (D) 24   (E) 26

5. In a certain school, the ratio of teachers to clerical workers is 20 to 3 and the ratio of custodians to clerical workers is 1 to 2. The ratio of teachers to clerical workers to custodians is

(A) 20 : 1 : 2   (B) 20 : 1 : 3   (C) 20 : 3 : 1

(D) 40 : 3 : 6   (E) 40 : 6 : 3

GO ON TO THE NEXT PAGE.

6. The board of directors of a certain steel company is made up of 6 members elected by the labor union, 6 elected by the shareholders, and another member elected by the first twelve. If all 13 members voted on a proposal with $\frac{1}{2}$ of the union representatives voting for it and $\frac{1}{3}$ the shareholders' representatives voting against it, what fractional part of the membership voted for the proposal?

(A) $\frac{5}{13}$ (B) $\frac{5}{12}$ (C) $\frac{7}{13}$ (D) $\frac{7}{12}$

(E) It cannot be determined from the information given.

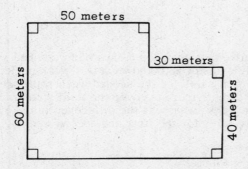

7. The figure above shows the dimensions of a swimming pool. What is the greatest distance, in meters, that one can possibly swim in a straight line on the surface of the water in this pool?

(A) $10\sqrt{41}$ (B) $10\sqrt{61}$ (C) 80

(D) $40\sqrt{5}$ (E) 100

8. Mary, Lee, and Sam are waiting in line for theater tickets. Four people are between Mary and Lee, and twelve people are between Lee and Sam. If Lee is next to last in line and Sam is second in line, how many people are ahead of Mary?

(A) 6   (B) 8   (C) 9   (D) 10   (E) 19

9. If x is an even integer, which of the following must be odd?

     I. $7x + 1$

     II. $3x^2 + 2$

     III. $(x - 1)^2$

(A) I only
(B) II only
(C) III only
(D) I and III only
(E) I, II, and III

10. $\sqrt[5]{5 \cdot 5^2 \cdot 5^3 \cdot 5^4} =$

(A) 125   (B) 25   (C) 10   (D) 5   (E) 1

11. A service worker is guaranteed a weekly salary of $70 plus 40 per cent commission on the value of services rendered in excess of $100 for the week. If the worker is to earn at least $160, the minimum value of services for that week must be

(A) $175   (B) $225   (C) $295

(D) $325   (E) $400

12. If $\dfrac{x^2 - y^2}{(x - y)^2} = 16$, then $\dfrac{x - y}{x + y} =$

(A) $\frac{1}{16}$ (B) $\frac{1}{8}$ (C) 1   (D) 8   (E) 16

GO ON TO THE NEXT PAGE.

13. What per cent is $\frac{1}{5^2}$ of 5^2 ?

(A) 160%   (B) 16%   (C) 1.6%

(D) 0.16%   (E) 0.016%

14. In the Porter Toy Company, the average time required for each of the n production workers to assemble a train set is t minutes. If all the workers work full time, how many hours of plant operation will be required to fill an order for 5,000 of these train sets?

(A) $\frac{5,000t}{60n}$ (B) $\frac{5,000(60)}{nt}$ (C) $\frac{5,000nt}{60}$

(D) $\frac{5,000(60n)}{t}$ (E) $\frac{60nt}{5,000}$

15. A number of recapped tires will be sold at $16 each, thus making a total markup of $\frac{1}{3}$ of the total whole-sale price. The numbers of tires bought at various prices were: 20 at $13 each, 10 at $14 each, and the remainder at $10 each. How many tires had a wholesale price of $10 each?

(A) 38   (B) 27   (C) 25   (D) 24   (E) 20

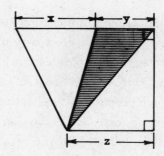

Note: **Figure not drawn to scale.**

16. In the figure above, if the area of the shaded region is one-half the area of the entire figure, which of the following must be true?

(A) y = x   (B) y = z − x   (C) y = x + z

(D) $y = \frac{z}{2}$ (E) $y = \frac{x+z}{2}$

17. A store that operates 6 days per week had average daily sales of $3,000 over a two-week period. If the total sales for the second week represented a 40 per cent increase over the total sales for the first week, what was the difference in the average daily sales for the first and second weeks?

(A) $250
(B) $500
(C) $750
(D) $1,000
(E) $1,250

GO ON TO THE NEXT PAGE.

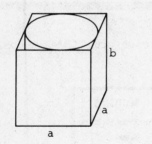 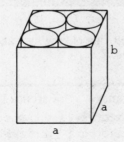

18. A product is always sold in cylindrical bottles of the same height but with either of two base areas. Regardless of size, the bottles are always shipped in rectangular cartons of the size shown in the figure above. If it is assumed that the thickness of the bottles is negligible, how much less space is wasted in the carton by packing 4 small bottles instead of one large bottle?

(A) 0   (B) $\dfrac{\pi a^2 b}{16}$ (C) $\dfrac{\pi a^2 b}{8}$

(D) $\dfrac{\pi a^2 b}{4}$ (E) $\dfrac{a^2 b(4 - \pi)}{4}$

19. Lee College insures its students for thefts up to \$1,000. The college makes no profit, but sets the premium to cover administrative costs of 10 per cent on an average claim of \$120. If the annual premium per student is \$24, what is the expected number of thefts per 100 students per year?

(A) 12   (B) 14   (C) 16   (D) 18   (E) 20

20. Compact cars accounted for 0.4 of the car sales of Company K last year. If 0.3 of the compact cars sold by Company K were imported and 0.6 of all the imported cars sold by Company K were compact, what fraction of the cars sold by Company K were imported?

(A) $\dfrac{3}{25}$ (B) $\dfrac{9}{50}$ (C) $\dfrac{1}{5}$ (D) $\dfrac{6}{25}$ (E) $\dfrac{12}{25}$

S T O P

IF YOU FINISH BEFORE TIME IS CALLED, YOU MAY CHECK YOUR WORK ON THIS SECTION ONLY.
DO NOT WORK ON ANY OTHER SECTION IN THE TEST.

Answer Key and Scoring Information

You can use the answer key below and the information that follows to score your test. Reading this section will give you a good idea of how your scores on an actual GMAT will be derived.

SECTION 1	SECTION 2	SECTION 3	SECTION 4	SECTION 5	SECTION 6

How to Calculate Your Scores

Your Verbal Raw Score

Step 1: Using the answer key, mark your answer sheet as follows: put a C next to each question that you answered correctly; put an I next to each question that you answered incorrectly. Cross out any questions that you did not answer or for which you marked more than one answer; these will not be counted in the scoring.

Step 2: Sections 1, 3, and 5 are used to determine your verbal score. In these sections only, count the number of correct answers (marked C) and enter this number here... _____

Step 3: In these same sections (1, 3, 5), count the number of questions that you answered incorrectly (marked I). Enter the number here .... _____

Step 4: Count the number of questions in sections 1, 3, and 5 that you crossed out because you didn't answer them or marked more than one answer. Enter this number here.................................. _____

Step 5: Add the numbers in Steps 2, 3, and 4. Enter the number here .... _____

(This number should be 85, the total number of verbal questions. If it is not, check your work for Steps 2, 3, and 4.)

Step 6: Enter the number from Step 2 here .... _____

Step 7: Enter the number from Step 3 here _____; divide it by 4. (This is the correction for guessing.) Write the resulting number here................................ $-$_____

$$\frac{}{4}$$

Step 8: Subtract the number in Step 7 from the number in Step 6; enter the result here .... _____

$+$ _____.5_____

Step 9: Add .5 to the number in Step 8. Enter the result here ... _____

Step 10: Drop all the digits to the right of the decimal point and write the result here .... _____

This is your verbal raw score corrected for guessing. Instructions for converting this score to a scaled score range follow the worksheets for obtaining your quantitative raw score and total raw score.

Your Quantitative Raw Score

Step 1:	Sections 2, 4, and 6 are used to determine your quantitative score. In these sections only, count the number of correct answers (marked C) and enter this number here....................................	_____
Step 2:	In these same sections (2, 4, and 6) count the number of questions that you answered incorrectly (marked I). Enter the number here	_____
Step 3:	Count the number of questions in sections 2, 4, and 6 that you crossed out because you didn't answer them or marked more than one answer. Enter this number here...	_____
Step 4:	Add the numbers in Steps 1, 2, and 3. Enter the total here	_____
	(This number should be 65, the total number of quantitative questions. If it is not, check your work for Steps 1, 2, and 3.)	
Step 5:	Enter the number from Step 1 here	_____
Step 6:	Enter the number from Step 2 here _____ ; divide it by 4. (This is the correction for guessing.) Write the resulting number here...............................	$-$ _____
Step 7:	Subtract the number in Step 6 from the number in Step 5; enter the result here	_____
Step 8:	Add .5 to the number in Step 7. Enter the result here ...	$+$ _____.5_____ _____
Step 9:	Drop all the digits to the right of the decimal point and write the result here	_____

This is your quantitative raw score corrected for guessing. Instructions for converting this score to a scaled score range follow the worksheet for obtaining your total raw score.

Your Total Raw Score

Step 1:	Using all the sections of the test, count the number of correct answers (marked C) and enter this number here	_____
Step 2:	Count the number of questions in all the sections that you answered incorrectly (marked I). Enter the number here	_____
Step 3:	Count the number of questions in all sections that you crossed out because you didn't answer them or marked more than one answer. Enter this number here	_____
Step 4:	Add the numbers in Steps 1, 2, and 3. Enter the total here . . . . (This number should be 150, the total number of questions in the test. If it is not, check your work for Steps 1, 2, and 3.)	_____
Step 5:	Enter the number from Step 1 here	_____
Step 6:	Enter the number from Step 2 here $\frac{\underline{}}{4}$; divide it by 4. (This is the correction for guessing.) Write the resulting number here	− _____
Step 7:	Subtract the number in Step 6 from the number in Step 5; enter the result here	_____
Step 8:	Add .5 to the number in Step 7. Enter the result here . . .	+ ____.5____ _____
Step 9:	Drop all the digits to the right of the decimal point and write the result here	_____

This is your total raw score corrected for guessing. It is possible that the sum of your verbal and quantitative raw scores may be one point higher or lower than the total raw score due to the rounding procedures for each score. Instructions for converting this score—along with your verbal and quantitative raw scores corrected for guessing—to scaled score ranges follow.

CONVERTING YOUR RAW SCORES TO SCALED SCORE RANGES

The raw scores corrected for guessing that you have obtained (last step in each worksheet) may be converted to scaled score ranges using the conversion tables below. Raw scores are converted to scaled scores to ensure that a score earned on any one form of the GMAT is directly comparable to the same scaled score earned (within a five-year period) on any other form of the test. Scaled scores are "standard scores" with understood and accepted meanings. The scores reported to schools when you take the actual GMAT will be scaled scores.

Using the conversion tables below, find the ranges of GMAT scaled scores that correspond to the ranges within which your three raw scores corrected for guessing fall. For example, a verbal raw score of 44 would fall within the scaled score range of 26 to 28; a quantitative raw score of 44 would be in the scaled score range of 39 to 42. A total raw score of 88 would be in the scaled score range of 560 to 580.

When you take the GMAT at an actual administration, one or more of your scores may fall outside the range(s) of scaled scores you obtained on this representative GMAT. Even the same student performs at different levels at different times—for a variety of reasons unrelated to the test itself. In addition, your test scores may differ because the conditions under which you took this test could not be exactly the same as those at an actual test administration.

After you have scored your test, analyze the results with a view to improving your performance when you take the actual GMAT.

■ Did the time you spent reading directions make serious inroads on the time you had available for answering questions? If you become thoroughly familiar with the directions given in this book (in Chapter I, Chapters III-VII, and the representative test), you may need to spend less time reading directions in the actual test.

■ Did you run out of time before you reached the end of a section? If so, could you pace yourself better in the actual test?

GMAT Conversion Tables for Sample Test

Verbal or Quantitative Corrected Raw Score Range	Verbal Scaled Score Range	Quantitative Scaled Score Range
81-85	50-53	
76-80	47-50	
71-75	44-47	
66-70	41-44	
61-65	38-41	54-57
56-60	35-37	50-53
51-55	32-34	47-49
46-50	29-31	43-46
41-45	26-28	39-42
36-40	22-25	36-39
31-35	19-22	32-35
26-30	16-19	28-31
21-25	13-16	25-28
16-20	10-12	21-24
11-15	7- 9	18-21
6-10	4- 6	14-17
0- 5	0- 3	10-13

Total Corrected Raw Score Range	Total Scaled Score Range
136-150	790-800
131-135	770-780
126-130	740-760
121-125	720-740
116-120	700-710
111-115	670-690
106-110	650-670
101-105	630-640
96-100	600-620
91-95	580-600
86-90	560-580
81-85	530-550
76-80	510-530
71-75	490-510
66-70	460-480
61-65	440-460
56-60	420-440
51-55	390-410
46-50	370-390
41-45	350-370
36-40	320-340
31-35	300-320
26-30	280-300
21-25	260-270
16-20	230-250
11-15	210-230
0-10	200

Remember, not everyone finishes all sections; accuracy is also important.

■ Look at the specific questions you missed. In which ones did you suffer from lack of knowledge? Faulty reasoning? Faulty reading of the questions? Being aware of the causes of your errors may enable you to avoid some errors when you actually take the GMAT.

WHAT YOUR SCALED SCORES MEAN

The following tables contain information that will be of help in understanding your scaled scores. Each table consists of a column marked "Scaled Score" and a column indicating the percentage of test takers in the time period specified who scored below the scores listed. For example, if you earned a total scaled score of about 600 on the representative test and you are able

to achieve the same score on an actual GMAT, the 89 opposite 600 tells you that 89 percent of the 621,667 people taking the test in the 1979 to 1982 period earned scores lower than that; the remainder earned the same or a higher score. Also given in each table is the average score of the group tested in the 1979–1982 time period.

Graduate school admissions officers understand the statistical meaning of GMAT scores, but each institution uses and interprets the scores according to the needs of its own programs. You should, therefore, consult the schools to which you are applying to learn how they will interpret and use your scores.

SOME CAUTIONS ABOUT SCORE INTERPRETATION

1. The GMAT is designed to yield only the reported verbal, quantitative, and total scaled scores. One should not cal-

Percentages of Examinees Tested from March 1979 through January 1982 (including Repeaters) Who Scored below Selected Total Test Scores	
Scaled Score	Percentage below
700	99
680	98
660	97
640	95
620	93
600	89
580	85
560	80
540	74
520	68
500	60
480	53
460	46
440	38
420	32
400	26
380	20
360	15
340	11
320	8
300	6
280	4
260	2
240	1
220	1 −
Number of Examinees	621,667
Average Score	465

Percentages of Examinees Tested from March 1979 through January 1982 (including Repeaters) Who Scored below Selected Verbal and Quantitative Scores			
Scaled Score	Percentage below	
	Verbal	Quantitative
46	99	98
44	98	97
42	96	95
40	93	92
38	89	88
36	83	84
34	77	78
32	69	72
30	61	64
28	53	55
26	44	45
24	36	36
22	29	27
20	23	19
18	17	12
16	13	8
14	9	4
12	6	2
10	4	1
Number of Candidates	621,667	621,667
Average Score	26	27

culate raw scores for individual test sections and infer specific strengths or weaknesses from a comparison of the raw score results by section. There are two reasons for this.

First, different sections have different numbers of questions and, even if the numbers were the same or if percentages were used to make the numbers comparable, the sections might not be equally difficult. For illustrative purposes only, suppose that one section had 20 items and another had 25. Furthermore, suppose you received a corrected raw score of 10 on the first and 10 on the second. It would be inappropriate to conclude that you had equal ability in the two sections because the corrected raw scores were equal, as you really obtained 50 percent on the first section and only 40 percent for the second. It could be equally inappropriate, however, to conclude from the percentages that you were better on the first section than on the second. Suppose the first section was relatively easy for most candidates (say, an average corrected raw score percentage across candidates of 55 percent) and the second was relatively difficult (an average corrected raw score percentage of 35 percent). Now you might conclude that you were worse than average on the first section and better than average on the second.

Differences in difficulty level between editions are accounted for in the procedure for converting the verbal, quantitative, and total corrected raw scores to scaled scores. Since the raw scores for individual sections are not converted to produce scaled scores by section, performance on individual sections of the test cannot be compared.

Second, corrected raw scores by section are not converted to scaled scores by section because the GMAT is not designed to reliably measure specific strengths and weaknesses beyond the general verbal and quantitative abilities for which separate scaled scores are reported. Reliability is dependent, in part, on the number of questions in the test—the more questions, the higher the reliability. The relatively few questions in each section, taken alone, are not sufficient to produce a reliable result for each section. Only the reported verbal, quantitative, and total scaled scores (which include questions across several sections) have sufficient reliability to permit their use in counseling and predicting graduate school performance.

2. It is possible, if you repeat the test, that your second raw scores corrected for guessing could be higher than on the first test, but your scaled scores could be lower and vice versa. This is a result of the slight differences in difficulty level between editions of the test, which are taken into account when corrected raw scores are converted to the GMAT scaled scores. That is, for a given scaled score, a more difficult edition requires a lower corrected raw score and an easier edition requires a higher corrected raw score.

TEST CONTENT

If you have questions about specific items in the representative test or in any of the sample tests included in Chapters III–VII, please write to GMAT, Educational Testing Service, Box 966-D, Princeton, NJ 08541, Attention: Test Development. Please include in your letter the page number on which the item appears and the number of the question, along with specifics of your inquiry or comment. If you have a question about a particular item or items in an actual GMAT, please write to the same address and include in your letter your name, address, sex, date of birth, the date on which you took the test, the test center name, the section number(s) and number(s) of the questions involved. This information is necessary for ETS to retrieve your answer sheet and determine the particular form of the GMAT you took.

Guidelines for Use of Graduate Management Admission Test Scores

INTRODUCTION

These guidelines have been prepared to provide information about appropriate score use for those who interpret scores and set criteria for admission and to protect students from unfair decisions based on inappropriate use of scores.

The guidelines are based on several policy and psychometric considerations.

■ The Graduate Management Admission Council has an obligation to inform users of the scores' strengths and limitations and the users have a concomitant obligation to use the scores in an appropriate, rather than the most convenient, manner.

■ The purpose of any testing instrument, including the Graduate Management Admission Test, is to provide information to *assist* in making decisions; the test alone should not be presumed to be a decision maker.

■ GMAT test scores are but one of a number of sources of information and should be used, whenever possible, in combination with other information and, in every case, with full recognition of what the test can and cannot do.

The primary asset of the GMAT is that it provides a common measure, administered under standard conditions, with known reliability, validity, and other psychometric qualities, for evaluating the academic skills of many individuals. The GMAT has two primary limitations: (1) it cannot and does not measure all the qualities important for graduate study in management and other pursuits, whether in education, career, or other areas of experience; (2) there are psychometric limitations to the test—for example, only score differences of certain magnitudes are reliable indicators of real differences in performance. Such limits should be taken into consideration as GMAT scores are used.

These guidelines consist of general standards and recommended appropriate uses of GMAT scores as well as a listing of inappropriate uses.

SPECIFIC GUIDELINES

1. **In recognition of the test's limitations, use multiple criteria.** Multiple sources of information should be used when evaluating an applicant for graduate management study. The GMAT itself does not measure every discipline-related skill necessary for academic work, nor does it measure subjective factors important to academic and career success, such as motivation, creativity, and interpersonal skills. Therefore, all available pertinent information about an applicant must be considered before a selection decision is made, with GMAT scores being *only* one of these several criteria. The test's limitations are discussed clearly in the GMAT *Bulletin of Information* and in the *GMAT Technical Report.*

2. **Establish the relationship between GMAT scores and performance in your graduate management school.** It is incumbent on any institution using GMAT scores in the admissions process that it demonstrate empirically the relationship between test scores and measures of performance in its academic program. Data should be collected and analyzed to provide information about the predictive validity of GMAT scores and their appropriateness for the particular use and in the particular circumstances at the score-using school. In addition, any formula used in the admissions process that combines test scores with other criteria should be validated to determine whether the weights attached to the particular measures are appropriate for optimizing the prediction of performance in the program. Once set, these weights should be reviewed regularly through the considered deliberation of qualified experts.

3. **Avoid the use of cutoff scores.** The use of arbitrary cutoff scores (below which no applicant will be considered for admission) is strongly discouraged, primarily for the reasons cited in the introduction to these guidelines. Distinctions based on score differences not substantial enough to be reliable should be avoided. (For information about reliability, see the GMAT *Bulletin of Information.*) Cutoff scores should be used only if there is clear empirical evidence that a large proportion of the applicants scoring below the cutoff scores have substantial difficulty doing satisfactory graduate work. In addition, it is incumbent on the school to demonstrate that the use of cutoff scores does not result in the systematic exclusion of members of either sex, of any age or ethnic groups, or of any other relevant groups in the face of other evidence that would indicate their competence or predict their success.

4. **Do not compare GMAT scores with those on other tests.** GMAT scores cannot be derived from scores on other tests. While minor differences among different editions of the GMAT that have been constructed to be parallel can be compensated for by the statistical process of score equating, the GMAT is not intended to be parallel to graduate admission tests offered by other testing programs.

5. **Handicapped persons.** The GMAT is offered with special arrangements to accommodate the needs of candidates with visual, physical, and learning disabilities. However, no studies have been performed to validate GMAT scores earned under nonstandard conditions. Therefore, test scores earned under nonstandard conditions are reported with a special notice that handicapped persons may be at a disadvantage when taking standardized tests such as the GMAT, even when the test is administered in a manner chosen by the candidate to minimize any adverse effect of his or her disability on test performance. In using these scores, admis-

sions officers should note the usual caution that GMAT scores be considered as only one part of an applicant's record.

NORMALLY APPROPRIATE USES OF GMAT SCORES

1. **For selection of applicants for graduate study in management.** A person's GMAT scores tell how the person performed on a test designed to measure general verbal and quantitative abilities that are associated with success in the first year of study at graduate schools of management and that have been developed over a long period of time. The scores can be used in conjunction with other information to help estimate performance in a graduate management program.

2. **For selection of applicants for financial aid based on academic potential.**

3. **For counseling and guidance.** Undergraduate counselors, if they maintain appropriate records, such as the test scores and undergraduate grade-point averages of their students accepted by various graduate management programs, may be able to help students estimate their chances of acceptance at given graduate management schools.

NORMALLY INAPPROPRIATE USES OF GMAT SCORES

1. **As a requisite for awarding a degree.** The GMAT is designed to measure broadly defined verbal and quantitative skills and is primarily useful for predicting success in graduate management schools. The use of the test for anything other than selection for graduate management study, financial aid awards, or counseling and guidance is to be avoided.

2. **As a requirement for employment, for licensing or certification to perform a job, or for job-related rewards (raises, promotions, etc.).** For the reasons listed in #1 above, the use of the GMAT for these purposes is inappropriate. Further, approved score-receiving institutions are not permitted to make score reports available for any of these purposes.

3. **As an achievement test.** The GMAT is not designed to assess an applicant's achievement or knowledge in specific subject areas.

4. **As a diagnostic test.** Beyond general statements about verbal and quantitative ability, the GMAT does not provide diagnostic information about relative strengths of a person's academic abilities.

Public Interest Principles for the Design and Use of Admissions Testing Programs

The Graduate Management Admission Council has formally adopted as policy these Public Interest Principles for the Design and Use of Admissions Testing Programs. The principles were originally proposed for public discussion on December 30, 1979, by the leaders of the GMAC, Educational Testing Service, and three other organizations responsible for major admissions testing programs. They address concerns that have been raised about the design and use of standardized tests in admission to higher education, e.g., public access to test questions and answers, verification of scoring procedures, and appropriate use of the information derived from the testing programs. The GMAC strongly supports the principles and is committed to implementing them within the Graduate Management Admission Test program.

PRINCIPLES

A number of the principles enumerated below have been cornerstones of most testing programs for some years. We believe it is important, however, to reaffirm them here to provide a fuller view of our beliefs and our expectations for the future.

1. We recognize the legitimate interest of the public in knowing what the tests contain and their efficacy in performing their intended functions. Therefore, we will implement the principle of publication of test content to a degree limited only by reasonable safeguards of efficiency, cost, quality, and the educational impact of the programs.

2. We fully support the principle of equity, and we will continue to maintain and strengthen credible procedures for detecting bias and eliminating it from the content of the tests, while making such procedures visible to the public.

3. We recognize the need for routine procedures that allow the test taker to arrange for verification of the accuracy of the procedures determining the score attributed to him or her.

4. We believe that tests should be readily available to all individuals, regardless of conditions such as physical handicap or religious beliefs that may prevent the taking of exams under circumstances that meet the convenience of the majority.

5. We recognize that tests, together with the procedures for scoring them and reporting the results, should be designed to provide test takers with as much useful information as may be feasible about the specifics of their performance on the tests.

6. We reaffirm the right of individuals and institutions to privacy with regard to information by and about them, which should be safeguarded from unauthorized disclosure.

7. We recognize the need to formulate, maintain, and publish widely principles of appropriate use of scores and other test information derived from testing programs and to be alert to and actively discourage misuse.

8. We recognize that both the institutions making use of test scores and the test takers themselves should have mechanisms through which to express their legitimate interests concerning the design and operation of testing programs and the use of the information derived from them.

OPERATIONAL ELEMENTS

The separately constituted and governed groups sponsoring testing programs may choose to implement these principles in different ways. This probable diversity stems from differences in the nature and purposes of the tests in the several programs and from the specifics of their structure and operation. Examples of possible approaches include the following:

1. Each prospective examinee should be able to receive a full-length sample of each test, similar to the one he or she will take, with the intended answers and with instructions for self-administration and self-scoring.

2. For tests given to a sufficient number of students annually to support the cost, at least one operational form of the test should be published periodically, in addition to the regular sample. A specific schedule of publication should be designated for each program.

3. Nontechnical information about the testing program should be furnished routinely to test takers, users, and the general public. It should include a description of what each test measures, the error of measurement, how the scores are intended to be used, and a summary of the validity of the scores for the intended uses.

4. A technical publication should provide information on the same topics in sufficient depth to permit professionals in the field to assess the evidence and the accuracy of the nontechnical summary.

5. Studies of the use of the test by professionals other than those in the sponsoring or administering agency should be actively encouraged and facilitated by provision of the necessary data with safeguards for individual privacy. The results of those studies should be published in regular journals and also incorporated in the technical and nontechnical publications.

6. The test sponsor should ensure that operational forms of the test are independently reviewed before they are given. The review should include the appropriateness of the content of the test and in particular should seek to detect and remove potential racial, cultural, or sex bias or other influences ex-

194

trinsic to the characteristics, skills, or knowledge to be measured. The review should also determine that the operational form is fairly represented by the sample test already distributed.

7. Test takers should have the right to question the accuracy of scoring, administrative procedures, specific questions in a test, or allegations of irregularities in test administrations. Current procedures to deal with this right should be reviewed and modified if necessary to ensure a fair and prompt response.

We hope communication of these principles and operational guidelines leads to greater understanding and constructive dialogue about the important issues surrounding testing. We stand ready to work with all interested groups in discussion of the policies and improvement of the procedures under which testing programs are conducted.

Order Forms for the Official Guides

Both the *Official Guide to GMAT* and the *Official Guide to MBA Programs, Admissions, & Careers* will be sold in many book stores, at list prices of $7.95 and $8.95, respectively. They may also be ordered directly from Educational Testing Service. Note that if you order *both* books from ETS at the same time, you will receive a discount. Fill out an order form/mailing label below and send it with the appropriate payment to ETS, in an envelope addressed to Publications, GMAC/ETS, Box 966, Princeton, NJ 08541.

Please note the various airmail delivery options. If you choose to have the book(s) sent by fourth-class/surface mail, you should allow a minimum of four weeks for delivery in North America and U.S. possessions and a minimum of seven weeks for delivery elsewhere. If you live in the United States, Guam, Puerto Rico, the U.S. Virgin Islands, a U.S. territory, or Canada and are willing to pay the airmail cost, delivery time will be cut by a week to ten days; airmail delivery to countries and areas other than those named above will be in three to four weeks rather than seven.

Be sure to check the appropriate box on the order form.

- - - - - - - - - - - - - - CUT HERE TO DETACH. - - - - - - - - - - - -

Complete the address label at the right and enclose both this order form and the address label with a check or money order made payable to Graduate Management Admission Council. **Do not send cash.** Orders received without payment cannot be processed.

ORDER FORM

Official Guide to GMAT, Official Guide to MBA Programs, Admissions, & Careers

Check ONE box below.

	Fourth-class, surface mail	Domestic airmail*	Foreign airmail†
☐ *Official Guide to GMAT*	☐ $7.95	☐ $9.95	☐ $17.95
☐ *Official Guide to MBA Programs, Admissions, & Careers*	☐ $8.95	☐ $11.95	☐ $18.95
☐ Both books ordered together	☐ $14.00	☐ $17.00	☐ $29.00

Enclosed is my payment of $_____

G21

*Airmail delivery to United States, Guam, Puerto Rico, U.S. Virgin Islands, U.S. territories, and Canada.
†Airmail delivery to countries and areas other than those named above.

Graduate Management Admission Council
Educational Testing Service
Box 966
Princeton, NJ 08541

692-49
692-50

(Please print.)

Name _____

Number and Street _____

City _____

State or Province _____

Country _____

Zip or Postal Code _____

DO NOT DETACH

- - - - - - - - - - - - - - CUT HERE TO DETACH. - - - - - - - - - - - -

Complete the address label at the right and enclose both this order form and the address label with a check or money order made payable to Graduate Management Admission Council. **Do not send cash.** Orders received without payment cannot be processed.

ORDER FORM

Official Guide to GMAT, Official Guide to MBA Programs, Admissions, & Careers

Check ONE box below.

	Fourth-class, surface mail	Domestic airmail*	Foreign airmail†
☐ *Official Guide to GMAT*	☐ $7.95	☐ $9.95	☐ $17.95
☐ *Official Guide to MBA Programs, Admissions, & Careers*	☐ $8.95	☐ $11.95	☐ $18.95
☐ Both books ordered together	☐ $14.00	☐ $17.00	☐ $29.00

Enclosed is my payment of $_____

G21

*Airmail delivery to United States, Guam, Puerto Rico, U.S. Virgin Islands, U.S. territories, and Canada.
†Airmail delivery to countries and areas other than those named above.

Graduate Management Admission Council
Educational Testing Service
Box 966
Princeton, NJ 08541

692-49
692-50

(Please print.)

Name _____

Number and Street _____

City _____

State or Province _____

Country _____

Zip or Postal Code _____

DO NOT DETACH